To

Pam

fond memories

walter

There is no way of writing well and also of writing easily. *Barchester Towers*

Biographical data, even those recorded in the public registers, are the most private things one has, and to declare them openly is rather like facing a psycho-analyst. *Italo Calvino*

An autobiography is an obituary with the last installment missing. *Quentin Crisp*

WMB '09

I walked the sloping hills

A Memoir by Walter Matthew Brown

Stovepipe Publishing

Durham, North Carolina

Design by Barbara E. Williams
Set in Galliard type by BW&A Books, Inc., Durham, N.C.
Printed in the United States of America
First edition, first printing

Photographs from North Carolina Central University have been reproduced courtesy of the James E. Shepard Memorial Library University Archives and Records. Photographs credited to Brown family papers are from the author's personal collection. For all other images, efforts have been made to locate the copyright owner; please send information about owners of images to the publisher, and corrected information will be included in future editions of this book.

All calligraphic lettering in this book was done by the author.

Library of Congress Control Number 2010902311
ISBN 978-0-615-34991-6

This book was written with a widely diverse audience in mind. With profound humility, therefore, I dedicate the book to them:

my family, foremost to my late wife and college sweetheart, Ozie Dowdell Foster Brown;

the various constituencies of historically Black colleges and universities—students, alumni, faculty, administrators, supporters;

individuals engaged in the study of higher education in America, the American South in particular;

members of faith communities;

individuals who contemplate writing an autobiography or memoir;

and *individuals for whom reading is a pleasurable pastime.*

Impressions
... a life time of Cultivating good friendships
... he lived a "principled" life — with intention, with purpose
... a generosity of spirit

Contents

Contents

Foreword

As DIRECTOR of the Osher Lifelong Learning Institute (OLLI) at Duke University, I am privileged to know Walter Brown and to have read his memoir with a special appreciation of the way it illustrates the many benefits of being a lifelong learner and a lifelong teacher. He makes his stories of childhood games come alive for us with vivid details of play kitchens and toady houses, and he puts those memories in the context of his professional understanding of the importance of unstructured play in the psychological development of children. He remembers painful experiences of growing up in the segregated South, but he also reminds us of the uplifting tenacity of dedicated parents, neighbors, teachers, and visionaries who made it possible for him not only to overcome obstacles but to analyze and relish his experiences and to pave the way for the success of others. He pays loving tribute to demanding and nurturing elders and wise and challenging friends, and he explains the value of his "positive addiction" to calligraphy. He creates a complete and complex picture of a life of questing, patience, laughter, and wisdom.

Much of Professor Brown's memoir was written while he participated in memoir-writing classes conducted at OLLI at Duke. For over thirty years this program has offered seasoned adults the opportunity to participate in a program of classes without tests or grades. Our students include high-school dropouts and former college presidents, all made equal by their shared passion for "learning for the love of it." We gather together to study everything from existentialism to collage making, from t'ai chi to Victorian literature. Some of our most loyal and engaged students are part of our memoir-writing classes. I have been leading one of these classes myself for a few years, and the time I spend with my memoirists is the highlight of my week. We come to know each other both through the stories of our past experiences and through our very current struggles with words. We cheer one another's successes and find encouraging words and suggestions to get us through our difficulties.

Many OLLI writers want to preserve their memories for their grandchildren, to give them a sense of what it was like "when I was growing up." Many want to make sense of what has happened to them; they are putting the pieces together, sorting out for themselves what gives their lives meaning, and writing down the philosophy they want to share to pave the way for others. Many of them find that by trying to remember honestly and vividly, by confronting the past and crafting their experience into language that will have meaning for others, they are embarking on a new journey that allows them to continue to grow and challenge themselves. There are plenty of scientific studies that explain why these challenges are good for our brains and why meeting weekly to struggle with putting words in their best order is a way to stay vital and active. Walter's fellow students and teachers have always tried to emulate his ability to tell his story completely and well. His success in completing his story will continue to serve as an inspiration to his fellow OLLI students and to anyone who considers his "walk on the sloping hills."

Catherine Frank, PH.D.
Director, Osher Lifelong Learning Institute
Duke University
Durham, North Carolina

Introduction

IN THIS DAY of instant messaging, e-mails, cell phones, Twitter, pod-casts, and twenty-four-hour news, it is difficult to know what the future holds for historians. Indeed, what has been offered today might well be lost in cyberspace sometime in the future. Missing from the barrage of electronic data are personal recollections and reminiscences.

That is only one of the reasons Walter Brown's personal memoir is so important. His journey was truly remarkable, as a student, teacher, coun-selor, consultant, administrator, author, and calligrapher. But his remi-niscence is also universal, illuminating many aspects of the American and African American experience during most of the twentieth century and the early part of the twenty-first.

Dr. Brown's journey tells us about the importance of education, the her-itage of African American institutions of learning—North Carolina Cen-tral University (NCCU) is "a place I had loved almost since the cradle," he writes—how to lead by example, and how to always venture toward new horizons. He was born and raised in Durham, North Carolina, in a family whose history stretched back generations in the state. At age eighteen, in the summer of 1945, he journeyed outside the state for the first time to the "Black capital of America, New York City's Harlem." Not only was this an incredible experience for this young man, it also revealed an adventure-some spirit that he carried with him throughout his life.

But perhaps most importantly, this memoir shows how energy, enthu-siasm, optimism, insight, and eloquence can defeat racial barriers; how a person can refuse to succumb to racial prejudice or let it shape his life. In this way he was not unlike his NCCU teacher and lifelong friend John Hope Franklin, as they both felt deeply the pain and anguish of the color line but remained buoyant, graceful, and generous. This memoir, then, is an antidote to the electronic revolution, revealing attitudes, lessons, and experiences that would otherwise be lost to posterity.

Loren Schweninger, PH.D.
Elizabeth Rosenthal Excellence Professor
Department of History
University of North Carolina at Greensboro

I walked the sloping hills

Not Long Dry Behind the Ears

JACKSON STREET *dead ends* (I couldn't resist the temptation) at Maplewood Cemetery, roughly two hundred yards from where it intersects with Maplewood Avenue. Mr. Rigsbee's barn was located in this section of Jackson Street.

Mr. Rigsbee's house was up on the hill, on a paved street that ran parallel to Jackson. Will and I played house with the daughters of our stepuncle in Mr. Rigsbee's barn. Sis was the mama when we played house. She was eleven. Although I was only five years old, I was Sis's play-husband.

Our playhouse was an imitation of our real house except our chairs didn't have legs. Our kitchen was our whole house. "Twett" picked the greens, tiny leaves from a nearby field. She also picked buttercups for our table centerpiece. Peter Rabbit caught grasshoppers—we called them hoppergrasses—and positioned them on a plate, where they secreted brown digestive juices. Sadie used this molasses to make ginger bread. During meal preparation, Bro played his imaginary piano. He used his vocal sounds for a keyboard—*Bom dee bom, bom dee dee bom bom,* and other vocal variations. It was Bro's thing. We half-listened. I provided imaginary essentials—tableware, condiments, water, and dessert. No napkins.

We pretended to eat the food, with one exception—the dirt—which we ate just enough to give an appearance of dietary delight. We were, after all, *playing* house.

Sis knew the location of an embankment where Miss Robena and some of our neighbors dug small quantities of clay (which they called "eatin' dirt") that they ate, supposedly for medicinal purposes. It was white and dull purple, and chewy. It had a chalky taste, not good, but good enough to make a meal with one spoonful and a little imagination. The practice of eating dirt is referred to in academic literature as "geophagy." The *American Heritage Dictionary of the English Language* defines geophagy as "the eating of earthly substances, such as clay or chalk, practiced among various peoples as a custom or for dietary or subsistence reasons." In some cultures, mainly in Central Africa and the southern United States, eating dirt and certain rocky crusts with nutritional value is a cultural activity that meets a physiological need during pregnancy, and it serves as a remedy for disease. It is also eaten during religious ceremonies. There have been reports of women in America who, in practicing geophagy, contracted intestinal problems and disease from eating unhealthy material in attempts to meet their physiological needs. However, I never heard, nor had reason to believe, that anyone I knew suffered ill effects from ingesting "eatin' dirt."

There is a far cry between the imagery that characterized our play kitchens in Mr. Rigsbee's barn in 1932 and the modern play kitchens designed ostensibly to develop imagery skills in contemporary life. Some holiday advertisements of play kitchens in 2009 feature sinks, dishwashers, refrigerators, and chalkboards for grocery lists and notes to family members. Additional built-in features include ovens, stoves, microwaves, paper-towel holders, and water-cup holders on refrigerator doors. One might well point me in the direction of a psychiatric center if I were to rail against such modern toys in favor of mere space for imaginary toys, whether that space be kitchens, dining rooms, or bedrooms. Yet in retrospection, I am persuaded that the developmental benefits of my childhood play activities were just as remarkable as those that are considered essential by most modern consumers.

Let's Hear It for the NAEYC

THE NATIONAL Association for the Education of Young Children (NAEYC) has taken a stand against the trend toward eliminating recess in elementary school. The Association's rationale is straightforward: "Our society has become increasingly complex, but there remains a need for every child to feel the sun and wind on his cheek and engage in self-paced play. Ignoring the developmental functions of unstructured outdoor play denies the opportunity to expand their imaginations beyond the constraints of the classroom."

I concur with this position, not merely because I was an educator for more than fifty years, but because of benefits I gained from childhood experiences in outdoor play in school and in my neighborhood.

Between ages five and ten, we expanded our imagination by making "toady frog" houses. I never knew until long after my boyhood that a beach was the natural place to make sand houses. This was not so on Jackson and Dover (now Estes) Streets in Durham's West End. Sand accumulated in trenches parallel to dirt streets. When it was not damp from rain or heavy dew, we dampened it with water from the house.

In summer, we boys *and* girls often went barefoot. For making toady frog houses, we used feet as molds. We piled sand onto a foot and patted it down to the right firmness. Then, ever so cautiously, we withdrew the foot from the house and delighted in the design. Houses varied in size according to the sizes of feet. A village of houses varying in size was especially pleasing.

Editor's note: This vignette won first place in the Literary Arts division of the 2006 Senior Games Competition in Durham, North Carolina.

We never saw toads in our toady frog houses. We didn't expect to. Satisfaction came mainly from the design and construction. Beyond that, our imagination took over as we talked about what the occupants were doing in and around our houses.

Between ages five and nine, we played "Rise Sally." We would form a circle, holding hands. The number of players depended almost entirely on the number of children available. A girl—always a girl—was ushered to the center. We moved in a circle around our featured playmate, who was sometimes shy but always accommodating, as we sang:

> Little Sally Walker, sitting in a saucer,
> Rise, Sally, rise,
> Wipe your weeping eyes,
> Turn to the east,
> Turn to the west,
> Turn to the very one that you love the best.
> Put your hands on your hips,
> And let your backbone slip.
> Aw, shake it to the east,
> Shake it to the west,
> Shake it to the very one that you love the best.

Sally's stop would evoke laughter, whether she turned to a playmate the rest of us suspected was "the very one" or surprised us by identifying a different one. Play ended when there were no more Sally Walkers or when a playmate suggested that we do something different—usually another game.

Boys between ages four and nine rolled an automobile tire. I have no idea how widespread this practice was, mainly because I have been unable to find it in the literature on children's play. The tire was our make-believe automobile as we rolled it from one play site to another. When we reached our destination, we simply laid the tire on the ground or leaned it against a stationary object while we played the game of the hour.

Most of the time, we obtained a tire from a junk heap or from an owner who discarded it when at least one hole was visible from overuse. Playmates who were more affluent in their collection shared their tires with others. Tire rolling was strictly a neighborhood practice, not one done at school.

Between ages five and eleven, boys and girls played "Honey in the Bee

Ball," which I later learned was also called "Hide-and-Seek." A leader began the first round of this game by standing at a tree, post, or some another identifiable point and chanting a verse loud enough to be heard while the rest scampered to their hiding places:

> Honey in the bee ball,
> I can't see y'all.
> All hid?
> Time I count to a hundred by ten,
> All ain't hid will just be out.
> Ten, twenty, thirty, forty, fifty,
> Sixty, seventy, eighty, ninety, a hundred.
> All hid?
> Ready or not, here I come.

The leader would leave his or her post and go where playmates might be hiding—behind shrubbery, in recessed areas of buildings, behind cars or trucks, under steps—places that provided cover. When the leader spotted one in hiding, he or she called the playmate's name and raced with the discovered one to the leader's post. If the leader beat the discovered one to the starting post, the leader would call, "*out*." If the discovered one won the race, he or she would call, "*safe*." The last one who called "safe" became the leader for the next round. A variation of the leader's chant went something like this:

> Last night, night before,
> Twenty-four robbers at my door,
> I got up, let them in,
> Hit them in the head with a rolling pin.
> All hid?
> Ready or not, here I come.

The game was much more fun when played by both sexes. Twilight was the best time to play Honey in the Bee Ball. A boy and girl who liked one another could hide together.

Boys between ages seven and fifteen shot marbles. To begin the game, a line would be drawn, and each player would toe the line and toss a marble to another line approximately ten feet away. The player whose marble ended nearest the line would be the first to shoot.

Ten or twelve marbles were bunched in the center of a ring between the drawn lines. The first player would place his shooter marble between his thumb and two fingers of his right or left hand, and he would shoot from the edge of the ring into the bunched marbles, trying to hit the bunch with such force as to knock one or more marbles outside the ring. If successful in this attempt, he would use the shooter marble to knock other marbles out of the ring, one by one, until he missed in an attempt. The game ended when the last marble was knocked out of the ring, each player having shot in proper turn.

We played marbles in the school yard and at home. Jars of marbles won in play could be displayed like trophies. I was pretty good at playing marbles, but I didn't keep the marbles that I won. Winning games even without keeping the other players' marbles was satisfying enough.

Between ages seven and fourteen, boys and girls played stickball. We used a tennis ball to play stickball without even knowing that there was a sport called tennis. The game was played in the street with two bases roughly thirty yards apart. For bats, boys used broomsticks. Girls generally used paddles for bats, the wider surface making it easier to hit a ball in flight.

Unwritten courtesy rules allowed one of the better players to hit for a younger child who would run the bases as soon as the pinch hitter hit a fair ball. Actual play was like miniature baseball games, with friendly variations such as no called strikes or stolen bases, no bases on balls, and no predetermined number of innings. When a player made an out, he went to the outfield and worked his way back in the order of positions for another turn at bat. Invariably, we tolerated intruding automobile traffic and gingerly retrieved balls from neighbors' yards that beckoned foul balls. Faced with these problems, we learned how to hit balls amazingly straight, a skill that put some of us in good stead when later we played on teams in softball leagues.

A variation was stickball played between teams, using home plate and an additional base or two. Distances between bases varied, depending on available space. It wasn't unusual for each team to score twenty or more runs.

"Mumbly Peg" was played by boys generally between ages nine and fifteen. The game was a series of feats in which players took turns in trying to toss or flip an ice pick from twelve to fourteen different angles and positions with the skill and dexterity needed to make it stick in the ground. If the pick did not stick in the ground in trying either feat, the player lost his turn and had to try from the beginning of the series when his turn came again.

The first player to complete the series without losing a turn was privileged to drive a peg about two inches long into the ground, using the pick handle as a hammer. The last player to complete the series without a blunder paid the price for losing: the loser pulled the peg from the ground with his teeth—Mumbly Peg.

I later learned that in some places, players used jackknives instead of ice picks for playing Mumbly Peg. Ice picks were household items for us because we used them for breaking blocks of ice in the kitchen icebox.

We played horseshoes with shoes that had been worn by real horses. Recreational horseshoes of regulation size and weight were unheard of.

We played football—tag and tackle—in an open field at the corner of Jackson Street and Maplewood Avenue. The number of players on each team depended almost entirely on the number available at any given time.

Basketball was not a popular sport on Durham's West End. There was no gymnasium at Lyon Park School, and there were no basketball courts in the community.

Swimming and water sports were out. There was no swimming pool in or near my neighborhood. The first public pool for Negroes (that was the preferred designation for African Americans in those days) in Durham was constructed at Hillside Park in 1937, and that was three miles from the West End. There were four pools for Whites.

My brothers and I didn't play games that mimicked gunplay, like cops and robbers or cowboys and Indians. This was never a source of contention with our parents, not because we feared punishment or reprisals. It was simply the nature of our family ethos. We engaged in outdoor play activities that evoked laughter, helping, sharing, and problem-solving. Except at school recess periods, we played without adult supervision or interference. My experience showed that bonds formed among children in unstructured outdoor play were as meaningful and as enduring as bonds formed in any other children's activities.

[3]

Overcoming Mama's Objections
to Long Pants

P AUL JOHNSON, Frank Burnett, John Dark, Lorenzo Cozart, Dan Johnson, and Floyd Watson—all wore long pants as fifth- and sixth-graders when we were students at Lyon Park School. I wanted to wear long pants, too, but my mother wanted me to wear short pants or knickerbockers until I graduated from high school. She said that boys who wore long pants became mannish, felt their oats, and tended to become impudent when they didn't get their way.

Fifth- and sixth-graders with a grade average of B or above at Lyon Park School qualified for membership in the school safety patrol. I was proud to qualify and proud to become a member of the patrol. We wore white shirts and navy blue sweaters, and we had the option of wearing navy blue knickerbockers or long pants. I wore knickerbockers. The uniform included a white canvas belt that went around the waist and across the right shoulder. It fastened slightly left of center at the waist. A navy blue garrison cap with the initials LPS and a metal badge lettered with *Lyon Park School Safety Patrol* completed the uniform.

Students who finished the sixth grade at Lyon Park School went directly to the seventh grade at Hillside High School. Hillside had a school safety patrol with the same academic requirement and the same uniform, except that the letters on the cap were HHS. When my friends Bill Malone and Carter Smith were seniors, they held the office of major in the patrol. Majors wore a military officer's cap, riding pants, and knee-high boots. Patrol membership was open to boys *and* girls. Gloria Garrett was the major during her senior year.

I told my mother that I had the required grade average and wanted to be on the school patrol. She was pleased. I also told her that all boys on the patrol wore long pants. I didn't know if it was mandatory, and I didn't ask Miss Rachel Pratt, the faculty adviser.

Mama bought a pair of black long pants for me. They cost less than either of my gabardine knickerbockers. In spring, long white pants were fashionable attire for boys on the patrol. I continued to wear knickerbockers sometimes, but not as often as I wore long pants, black or white. Mama bought a pair of white long pants for me when I was in the ninth grade. I wore long pants to the junior-senior prom—both years.

I felt that one of the good things about going to college was that I would wear long pants all the time. But I would wear short pants later, when Bermuda shorts came into style. By that time, I was a man.

[4]

Looking at the Family Tree

MAMA'S FULL unmarried name was Mary Thomas Tate. Her mother, Ora Atkins, was one of eleven children born to my great-grandparents, Charles and Mary Trice Atkins, in rural Orange County, North Carolina. Grandmother Ora was married to Walter Tate. My brothers and I called him Daddy Tate. Ora Atkins Tate died in childbirth; the baby, a boy who would have been Mama's only sibling, died with her.

I don't know how long Grandmother Ora had been dead when Daddy Tate married Nannie Gunn. We called her Mother Nannie. She was born August 7, 1892, to Peter and Etta Gunn of Elon, North Carolina. To the extent that it was possible, Mother Nannie patterned her own homemaking style on that of the rich white family for whom she worked as a nanny. Her house was impeccable in appearance, and meals were served in patrician style, with expensive silverware, fine china, lace tablecloths, linen napkins, attractively presented dishes, and polite conversation. In the times when my wife, Ozie, and I had meals with them, Daddy Tate did not show that he was attuned to his wife's preferred style, much to her chagrin. On those occasions, I was perhaps a bit effusive in my comments about the accoutrements of refined living, in an attempt to offset her husband's cavalier attitude toward the whole thing. She appeared to appreciate the compliments. Nannie Gunn Tate died July 22, 1958.

People in West Durham Baptist Church and throughout Brookstown seemed especially deferential to "Mr. Tate." He bought expensive Sunday clothes and wore them as casually as he did his work clothes—brown suit and black shoes, maroon tie and white socks, whatever. He didn't own a car but paid people to take him where he wanted to go. He was also the owner of Durham's first Black professional baseball team, the Durham Black Sox.

Daddy Tate solicited membership dues for the National Association for the Advancement of Colored People (NAACP) and once received a plaque for soliciting the highest number of NAACP memberships in Durham.

Mama took care of Daddy Tate at her home until he died in 1960 after a long illness. When Mama learned that her papa had willed that his home be divided equally among three—a niece in Elon, herself, and me—she was visibly disappointed. She had expected to inherit the entire property, or most assuredly the greater part of it. I have never made a quicker decision than when I gave my share of the property to Mama. I hadn't anticipated such an inheritance, and it was well worth giving it up to be free from the emotional fallout that I might have experienced otherwise. To my knowledge, the niece made no overture one way or another.

Grandmother Ora had a sister named Sarah—Aunt Sarah to us. After Grandmother Ora died, Frank and Aunt Sarah Atkins Couch raised my mother along with their own children: Harold, James, Thomas, Junious, Richard, Sophronia, William, Mary, and Charles. Occasionally, I walk through the Mount Sinai Church cemetery and look at tombstones of the Couches, Barbees, and others I knew as a boy. It is an experience in solemnity and fond recollections.

When my mother was living with the Couches, she attended Cool Spring School, a one-room schoolhouse for Black children. She left that school when Daddy Tate sent her to Saint Augustine's College in Raleigh, North Carolina. The college had a high school division in addition to its college division. I never knew the level at which my mother entered the school. I do know that she left after three years and, in 1926, married Matthew Jackson Brown. I was born a year later.

Everybody was fond of "Mack Brown." Well, almost everybody. I don't think Daddy Tate was very keen on the man who married his only child and made her pregnant when she was a student in college.

My paternal great-grandfather was Jesse Barbee. We called him Grandpap. He lived alone in a one-room hut with a cast-iron heater on a small farm in northern Orange County, North Carolina. Some of our Barbee relatives lived in a house roughly fifty yards from Grandpap's hut. I surmise that the reason for his isolation was either estrangement or his strong sense of independence. The hut was also less than a mile from the church of my ancestors, Mount Sinai Baptist Church.

Grandpap smoked a corncob pipe. He made chair bottoms by weaving cane strips into precise geometric patterns. He had known slavery as a boy

Siblings of the Couch family, who adopted Mama when she was a little girl. *Front row left to right:* Richard, Sophronia, Will, Mary, and Charlie. *Back row left to right:* Harold, James, Thomas, and Junious. *(Courtesy of Mrs. Edna Couch)*

but was more interested in asking about my family than in talking about his background. He was ninety-nine when he died in his hut, on the night that it burned to the ground. If there were questions about the cause of the fire, I never heard them.

Matthew Brown, father of my brother Will and me, was one of three children born to Arthur and Ella Barbee Brown. I remember Daddy's grandfather, but not his father. I knew Daddy's mother, Ella Barbee Brown, and loved her as much as any grandchild loves a grandmother. My brother Will and I called our father Daddy some of the time, and Daddy Mack at other times. We would later do something similar with Mama's second husband, William Horton. We called him Daddy Horton.

We first lived in Brookstown, a pocket in West Durham, situated between the east and west campuses of Duke University. Our neighborhood was flanked on one side by warehouses for the Liggett and Myers tobacco factory, and on the other side by a two-block strip of low-income housing for White residents. The tobacco warehouses would later be converted into what in 2009 is called Brightleaf Square, a small but trendy shopping mall of restaurants, boutiques, antique shops, and art galleries in downtown Durham.

West Durham Baptist Church stood at the center of the neighborhood. Thomas Carr Graham served as its pastor from 1921 to 1964. Our house at 1006 Thaxton Avenue was next door to the church, across the street from Daddy Tate and Mother Nannie.

Daddy Mack attended elementary school in rural Orange County before his family moved to Durham. I do not know if he attended school in Durham. He was employed in his teen years as a sweeper at Liggett and Myers and had worked his way up to front-office courier (a porter-messenger, in other words) when he retired in 1973. He wore his porter's uniform as if in competition for best-dressed serviceman in a military unit. He smoked Chesterfield cigarettes and chewed Red Man tobacco, both Liggett and Myers products. If he drank alcoholic drinks, I never knew it, but he never tried to give counsel or advice on temperance.

My birth certificate—headed "Department of Health, Durham City and County"—reads in part, "Walter Matthew Brown, Jr., child of Matthew Jackson Brown and Mary Tate Brown was born on April 9, 1927 at 1006 Thaxton Ave., Durham, N.C." My first name is for my maternal grandfather, Walter Tate. My middle name is my father's first name, Matthew.

How "Junior" became a part of my name is open to conjecture. A number of relatives and neighborhood folk called me Walter Matthew. A beloved cousin—Mildred, who died around 1990—was the last to do so.

My birth certificate from the North Carolina State Board of Health, Bureau of Vital Statistics, shows my place and time of birth as Lincoln Hospital at 6:30 a.m. It indicates that my mother's attending physician was Stanford L. Warren, M.D. Dr. Warren was a Black physician for whom the public library branch in the city's south-central community is named. My father's age is recorded as twenty-one, my mother's age as nineteen. My father's occupation is recorded as "Common

My maternal grandfather, Walter Tate. *(Brown family papers)*

Matthew Brown, aka Daddy Mack. *(Courtesy of Mrs. Maccene Brown-Lyerly)*

Laborer." Mama's is recorded as "House-wife." The certificate is one in a bound volume of records segregated by race—Whites in front, "Colored" in back—filed in the Durham County Health Department, Vital Records division. I do not have an explanation for discrepancies between the two certificates, which give different places for my birth.

I was well into adulthood when Mama told me that Daddy Tate wanted her to put me up for adoption when I was born. I never had a moment of contentiousness with my mother, so it is unlikely that she made the comment as an act of retribution. Nor can I say that I made a sagacious reply to this startling revelation. I simply filed the observation in my memory bank, probably never to be repeated had I not been moved to disclose it as an autobiographical note.

My brother William was born on February 21, 1929. He became an educator of considerable renown in North Carolina, particularly in Cumberland County. (More about him in vignette 47, "You Will Love My Brother Will.")

In the years of our boyhood, Daddy Mack's sister, Minnie Mae, lived with Grandma Ella on one side of a duplex on Powe Street in Brookstown. Grandma worked as a domestic at the Bishop's House on the east campus of Duke University. The Bishop's House was completed in the spring of 1911, and is the same house where I have taken classes since 1993 in the Osher Lifelong Learning Institute, formerly Duke Institute for Learning In Retirement.

Brookstown was demolished in the 1970s, a chapter in Durham's urban renewal project. Most of its residents relocated in the southern part of the city. I do not know where the neighboring White residents of Brookstown relocated.

I will probably never know whether a particularly fond experience at Grandma's is one that I remember from the time it happened or whether I heard my aunt Minnie Mae tell it so many times that I think I remember it. I couldn't have been more than five years old, and Will three years old, on a day of the season's first snowfall. Grandma was at work when Minnie Mae decided to make snow cream. She had misgivings about making snow cream that day because she had heard more than a few times that it should not be made from the first snow because it had impurities that later snowfalls would not have.

Minnie Mae exacted a promise from Will and me that we would not tell Grandma about the snow cream. But lo, when Grandma came home and gave us warm hugs, Will asked, "Grandma, do you like snow cream?" When Grandma replied that she did indeed like snow cream, she also asked why he wanted to know. With arms around her legs and a disarming smile, Will looked up and said, "We had some." I topped it off with childish consternation saying, "Will, didn't Minnie Mae tell us not to tell Grandma?" The whole episode evoked laughter at the time, and each time Minnie Mae told it through the years. Meanwhile, I learned that the basic ingredients for snow cream couldn't be simpler—vanilla flavoring, sugar, milk, and, of course, snow.

Will and I felt great affection toward Grandma Ella's second husband, Van Roberson. I don't know why we called him "Mr. Van." Maybe it was because that is what Mama called him.

Daddy Mack was a sports enthusiast, especially about baseball, fishing, and hunting. He followed baseball on radio and later on television with a passion, and sometimes he came to see games when Will and I played on community-league softball teams. He hunted small game, mainly rabbits and squirrels. His fishing cronies considered him the best freshwater fisherman in the area. I would later see that this reputation was well-deserved.

Daddy Mack had a pleasant demeanor and a contagious laugh. He had expensive tastes, especially in clothes, and was characteristically dapper. In an attempt to keep the crease in his trousers razor-sharp, he waited to put on his trousers until just before leaving the house. Mama said he once forgot to put on his trousers and was about to leave fully dressed except for the trousers. She said she laughed heartily when she called the oversight to his attention. I know she laughed when she told the story years later, long after she and Daddy Mack had divorced.

When Daddy Mack and my mother separated, I was four years old and Will was two. Mama moved with us to a duplex on Kent Street, less than a block from where Kent and Morehead intersect on the city's West End. I can't recall how long we stayed on Kent Street, but it was long enough for

Mama and Daddy Horton. *(Brown family papers)*

my mother to meet and marry the man who, in 1932, became stepfather to Will and me, William L. "Jack" Horton.

After this marriage, our family moved in with the family of Charles and Robena Nunn on Maplewood Avenue. Charles Nunn was the brother of Lizzie Nunn Horton, Daddy Horton's mother. Will and I called him Uncle Charlie. We called Uncle Charlie and Miss Robena's children our cousins. The children of Mama's second marriage—my half brothers, Leonders and Charles Horton—were the true cousins of the Nunn family. Rarely have I called them half brothers, despite the different surnames.

It may be a logical assumption that Maplewood Avenue was so named because it is the divider between sections of Maplewood Cemetery. And that very well may be the case, for there isn't a maple tree on the two-block long "avenue."

Leonders's nickname during his early childhood was "Snub." I remember the name as one of endearment, but the name didn't follow him in later years. I don't know why, and I never heard him mention it after he had grown up. He was born on May 13, 1932. He graduated from Durham's Hillside High School in 1952, and for a year attended what was then named North Carolina College at Durham, where he was a member of the marching band. He served in the U.S. Marine Corps for three years and played the trumpet in the Corps band at Camp Lejeune, North Carolina.

Leonders was married to Curley Bankston. They had five children. "Lee," as he was also known, was employed with Durham Regional Hospital as a manager of the materials support and equipment unit. After an extended illness with a bad heart and related complications, he died in 1995 at the Northwood Manor Nursing Home in Durham. His funeral was at Greater St. Paul Missionary Baptist Church, where he had membership for more than fifteen years.

Charles was born on June 25, 1933. He took classes in masonry in high school and worked one summer with Daddy Tate, who then had a subcontract for bricklaying. Whether it was love of money, low academic achievement, or a combination of the two, he dropped out of school in the eleventh grade. He has been married twice and is the father of seven. He retired from the City of Durham as an equipment operator. In 2009 he owns and operates a small-engine repair service in Durham.

Mama first worked as a maid for wealthy White families, and in later years as a seasonal worker in the tobacco factories. Her times of employment were short because she chose to be at home long enough between jobs to give my brothers and me periods of uninterrupted nurturing.

I do not know how Daddy Tate learned his skills as a bricklayer. He never told me, and it never occurred to me to ask. On reflection, I can't recall ever having a conversation with Mama's daddy. Somehow, he loomed as a different kind of relative, which may have been in part because he was well-off financially. Bricklayers of his skill level were rare among Blacks in the 1930s and early '40s. One example of his largess that I recall is that he bought a ton of coal for our family every fall, and I believe Mama's awareness that he was in position to help her with material needs kept her in a state of solicitousness toward him.

Will and I never stayed under the same roof with Daddy Mack after he and Mama divorced, but we saw him at church and sometimes stopped by after church to see him at his place on Thaxton Avenue. When Daddy Mack married the second time, in 1945, Will and I were teenagers, old enough to call his wife, Eleanor Mumford Brown, by her first name.

Eleanor was a teacher in the Orange County public schools. She and Daddy Mack were parents of two daughters and a son—Maccene (pronounced "Maxine"), Delphine, and Thelbert Jackson, whose nickname was Jackie.

In the 1960s and '70s, Daddy Mack and Eleanor raised their children in Durham at the same time that Ozie and I were raising our children in Maryland and the Washington, D.C., area. In Durham, the other Brown children attended Pearsontown Elementary School. Thelbert Jackson and Delphine graduated from Hillside High School. (But as I've mentioned before, I have never used the technical genealogical terms *half* or *step* to refer to any of my siblings.)

In 1964, when Maccene was in the eighth grade at Pearsontown, her school counselor, Mrs. V. E. Pindle, arranged for her to apply for an educational opportunity with an organization known as A Better Chance. The organization was founded in 1963 with a mission "to increase the number of well-educated minority youth capable of assuming positions of responsibility and leadership in American society."

When Maccene received notice of schools with which A Better Chance matched her qualifications, she applied to and was accepted at Miss Hall's School, a private high school for girls in Pittsfield, Massachusetts. She recalls that she took this step with the encouragement of her parents. She recalls further that two Black students were admitted to the school in 1967 and that she was the only Black student in the 1966 freshman class at Miss Hall's.

Maccene was then interested in a teaching career. She won a scholarship as part of a grants-in-aid package at Wheelock College in Boston, Massachusetts, and majored in early childhood education. She entered Wheelock in 1969 and graduated in 1973.

We were on the same page when Maccene and I compared recollections of our daddy. We agreed that he was reticent in the presence of people who were better-educated than he but assertive when he felt that the rights of his family were at stake. Maccene remembers, for example, that Daddy Mack participated in negotiations that led to the organization of labor unions for Liggett and Myers employees. She also remembers the time in the 1960s when a rumor circulated that the Ku Klux Klan intended to march through the city's African American community. "Daddy sat up all night with his shotgun just in case the Klan approached our house," she told me. Maccene also described him as outgoing and fun-loving.

Maccene was a classroom teacher at Hillandale Elementary School in Durham County for five years, from 1973 to 1978, after which she entered the School of Law at North Carolina Central University. She received the Juris Doctor degree in May 1982 and was admitted to the North Carolina Bar in April 1983. Her practice has included civil law matters in state courts, legal representation of farmers and landowners in administrative proceedings, and federal and state court proceedings. In 2009, she is an attorney for Legal Aid of North Carolina, representing victims of domestic violence.

Thelbert and Delphine attended North Carolina Central University for two years, and both were members of the university's marching band. Thelbert, better known as Jackie, was a minister and small-business owner when he had a fatal motorcycle accident in 1989. In 2009, his widow and two children still live in Durham. Delphine lives in Durham and has two adult children. She was a bright student in high school and college, but she was physically incapacitated when this memoir was written.

Little more than a year after Ozie, our daughters, and I moved back to Durham from Maryland in 1980, Daddy Mack suffered a massive stroke. He was engaged in one of his favorite hobbies at the time: gardening. He died at Duke Hospital on September 26, 1981. He was seventy-three years old. His funeral was at West Durham Baptist Church, where he served on the Board of Trustees and as an usher.

Under the pastorate of Rev. Frederick Terry, West Durham Baptist Church was relocated to Athens Street in *south* Durham, but it retained the name *West* Durham Baptist. I never heard of such until I learned that Nineteenth Street Baptist Church in Washington, D.C., which currently is located at 4606 *Sixteenth* Street, was originally located on *Nineteenth* Street!

I have a gold star in mind when I mention the man who was my and Will's stepfather and father to our brothers, Leonders and Charles. I have never known what promises, if any, Daddy Horton made to our mother about how he would treat Will and me, as opposed to his biological sons. What I do know is that he loved each of us genuinely and without an iota of partiality. No one—lay or professional—in any of the human services could cite a better example.

The superintendent of parks and cemeteries for the City of Durham, George Montgomery, appointed Daddy Horton as foreman of work crews for the city cemeteries. This was a landmark appointment for a Black man in Durham, North Carolina—lettered or unlettered—in the 1930s. I believe it would have been just as significant even if the appointment had been made a decade later. In our early teens, Will and I had the job of closing the gates of Durham's Maplewood Cemetery each evening.

(above left) William Brown, the first of my brothers, *(above right)* Leonders "Lee" Horton, the second of my brothers, and *(facing)* Charles Horton, the third of my brothers. *(Brown family papers)*

Some patterns in our household were predictable and constant. Daddy Horton and Mama were early risers. He made the fire in the kitchen stove throughout the year, and in the bedroom laundry heater in cold weather. Mama cooked breakfast and also cooked or started dinner. Daddy Horton checked the newspaper for obituaries and recorded the burials to be made in the city cemeteries. I used to overhear the early-morning chatter, sometimes about cemetery workmen and their families, other times about neighbors, and often about what my brothers and I were doing.

Mama was religious. Daddy Horton was not. Mama read the Bible and prayed audibly. Daddy Horton neither read the Bible nor prayed audibly, if he prayed at all. Mama attended church, sang in the choir, and participated in a variety of missionary activities. Daddy Horton neither attended church nor engaged in conversation about religion. It wasn't his shot, and he didn't pretend that it was.

He kept our yard beautifully landscaped and at times gently chided Mama for planting what he regarded as too many varieties in the same flower bed. He took Sunday afternoon walks with my brothers and me in wooded areas adjoining the cemeteries. He attended Durham Black Sox

baseball games with the family and openly rooted for opposing teams, just to tease Mama.

I was a college freshman when Daddy Horton was inducted into military service. Will was in the eleventh grade at Hillside High School. Leonders and Charles were in the fifth and fourth grades at Lyon Park Elementary School.

Daddy Horton was inducted into the U.S. Army at Fort Bragg, North Carolina, on December 31, 1943. His Enlisted Record and Report of Honorable Discharge has his height as 5'6". A civilian medical record listed him as 5'8" and 175 pounds. He served as a corporal in the European theater from September 1944 to August 1945, when World War II ended. He earned a good conduct medal and the campaign medal with three bronze stars. He was discharged at the Fort Bragg Separation Center on September 20, 1945.

I was inducted into the army at Fort Bragg on September 5, 1945, and was in basic training at Fort Leonard Wood in Missouri when I learned of Daddy Horton's separation from military service. Although I was certain that he would reclaim his old job with the City of Durham, I applied for a monthly subsistence payment for my mother. I indicated that my stepfather was an unemployed military veteran and that as a private in the U.S. Army, I was the only employed member of my family of six. It was true.

My application was approved, and my mother received the subsidy during the time of my military service. Daddy Horton had a one-week hiatus between the date of his army discharge and the resumption of his civilian job.

Daddy Horton had a drinking problem, a problem I remember as more serious after his military service than before. I do not know whether the problem was service-related.

In late 1946, my brother, William, was a student at North Carolina Agricultural and Technical College in Greensboro (now North Carolina A&T State University), and I resumed studies at North Carolina College after my stint with the U.S. Army. Mama's interests then included service as president of the Durham Missionary Society. Although my brothers, Leonders and Charles, were pupils at Lyon Park Elementary School, I don't believe Mama was as active with the school's parent-teacher association as she had been when Will and I attended the same school.

For roughly ten years, Mama was an operator of a single elevator for two Black-owned businesses, North Carolina Mutual Life Insurance Company and Mechanics and Farmers' Bank in downtown Durham. Although her job as elevator operator would hardly be more than a rung or two up on an occupational prestige ladder, she was Mrs. Horton to employees and customers alike. She subsequently became an ardent supporter of the all-Black Durham Business and Professional Chain, and she worked diligently in its membership recruitment and outreach activities.

Daddy Horton was in another world. It seemed the more Mama did her thing, the more Daddy Horton did his—in quiet rebellion. He drank hard liquor. He frequented the two neighborhood speakeasies, one of which was at his mother's house on Gerard Street. I remember going with Daddy Horton to his mother's speakeasy. The drinks I saw customers order were the fifteen-cent shooters—one and one-quarter ounces of straight corn whiskey in glasses about two and one-half inches tall. I am not sure about the pattern of drinking—one gulp, two, chasers or no chasers. My memory has been shaped largely by what I have seen in licensed bars and in the movies.

I don't remember ever seeing Daddy Horton intoxicated, violent, vulgar, or silly. He was never out of control. Yet alcohol took its toll on his life, and ours. Sclerosis of the liver was a partial diagnosis when he died at the Durham Veterans Administration Hospital on September 15, 1962, the twelfth wedding anniversary of my brother Will and his wife, Jennie. He was buried in Durham's Beechwood Cemetery on September 18, my and Ozie's thirteenth wedding anniversary. He was fifty-three years old.

I have a view based on personal observation of my family, as well as generally, that until around the early 1970s, Black women tended to marry men with considerably less formal education than they had. My reviews of scholarly research studies have not yielded answers to the question, although the late Charles E. King, emeritus professor of sociology at North Carolina Central University, agreed that my view is "very plausible." King and I also agree that this trend reflects a residual effect of slavery in the United States. It is well-documented that educating slaves, Black males in particular, was not only socially taboo but a crime in many areas of the American South. The gap is closing but still much in evidence.

Once in the early 1970s, John Glennie, a White colleague at Fry Consultants in Washington, D.C., asked me how I could explain "the phenomenon of becoming a complete person in the American social order." This was not a question in connection with a conversation with Glennie, but a question he asked right out of the blue. Although I believed he intended to be complimentary instead of patronizing, I feel that I did not have a satisfactory answer. To this day, I still don't, except that it recalls for me the adage popularly attributed to African wisdom, and widely quoted and paraphrased: "It takes a village to raise a child." The neighborhood of my childhood was an insulated pocket of Black residents well acquainted with each other, appreciably supportive of each other, and heavily influenced by churches with strong and influential Black ministers. I knew the love of family and felt the love and support of nearly every adult with whom I interacted. Over time, I acquired a self-concept that enabled me to choose wisely between individuals and circumstances that were good for my well-being and those that would be detrimental. This view is reinforced when I look at my family tree.

5

Lyon Park Elementary School

FUNNY, I was never aware that I was being evaluated for performance in "physical culture" in grades one through four at Lyon Park Elementary School, where I was a pupil from 1933 through 1938. Funny, in writing my memoir I took note of this many years later while reviewing my school records. Funnier still: according to Wikipedia, *physical culture* emanated from the Industrial Revolution, as "a perception that members of the middle classes were suffering from various 'diseases of affluence' that were partially attributed to their increasingly sedentary lifestyles." Can you imagine: "diseases of affluence" on Durham's West End in the 1930s, with every indicator of low-socioeconomic-status neighborhoods.

Lyon Park School was—or had been—a Rosenwald school, one of several thousand Black schools in the American South, public or private, subsidized with charity grants from the Rosenwald Fund. What greater blessing could a concerned African American mother on Jackson Street in Durham, North Carolina, want for her children! The Fund recalls the contributions of Julius Rosenwald, a Jewish philanthropist who was a friend of the educator Booker T. Washington and an adherent of Washington's views on education and self-sufficiency for Black Americans.

Mama was successful in persuading school principal G. A. Edwards to enroll me in school earlier than I was legally entitled (or required) to. For one thing, she believed it was a way of insulating me from malevolent influences of the street. But perhaps of greater significance was her conviction that educated people had every advantage over people who were uneducated, and she therefore wanted me to step on the first rung of formal education as soon as possible.

We had a school pep song that went in part, "Lyon Park, we love you

Walter, second-grade scholar. *(Brown family papers)*

best of all. Lyon Park, we'll never let you fall . . ." And for the most part, I loved my elementary school "best of all." Three Lyon Park School teachers stand out as having the greatest influence in my early education: Misses Nettie Brown, Mary L. Stephens, and Pauline F. Dame.

Nettie Brown wore pretty clothes; she was attractive, kind, and a good teacher. I cannot recall how it came about, but I rode to school daily with her when I was in the second grade, and I walked home from school in the afternoon. I loved Miss Nettie Brown as much as a six-year-old could love a woman four times his age. When I learned in 1934 that she had married a man named Robert "Bob" Clay, I was wounded.

About twenty years later, I was saddened to learn that Mrs. Brown-Clay had developed a severe mental illness. The symptoms were not unlike what I would later come to know as advanced dementia. She was unkempt and obese, and she had an insensate expression as she walked the city streets. Perhaps the thing that kept me from losing my equilibrium whenever I saw her was that she always greeted me with a smile and said something that I construed to be pleasant, though mostly incomprehensible. I loved her still, a love based on my memory of my second-grade teacher who had made a lasting impression on a six-year-old boy.

If there was any laughter in Miss Mary Louise Stephens's third-grade classroom, I don't remember it. It isn't that Miss Stephens was mean or intimidating. She just went about the business of teaching, and she was all business. In Miss Stephens's third grade, "writing" meant penmanship. The only subject for which I received grades below B were the Cs I earned in her Writing class. I simply didn't fare very well at replicating the hallowed Palmer hand. Could this have been a subconscious incentive when I began to study calligraphic writing thirty years later?

Miss Stephens was a talented pianist, and she used her talent playing for school assemblies and directing dramatic productions that featured her students. One such production was our class's appearance on the campus of North Carolina College for Negroes. Although I don't recall what the occasion was, I have a mental picture of being one in a line of maybe ten or twelve students, each of whom held a placard with a single letter. Together the letters spelled a word, something noble, no doubt. Mine was the letter C, and when it came my turn, I took a step forward and said, "C is for cleanliness. Cleanliness is next to godliness," and stepped back in line. That is all I remember, but nothing has changed: cleanliness is *still* next to godliness.

A performance I do remember was a Saint Patrick's Day playlet in 1936. In this all-Black school and teachers, and principal—all-Black everything— we sang "Did Your Mother Come From Ireland?" With hoisted card-board shamrocks, boys were telling classmate lassies that something in them Irish stole their hearts away. I don't remember that there was a commentary or discussion about diversity in art forms or cross-cultural emphases when we learned the song. Our teacher introduced it to us. We liked the lyrics and the melody. In other words, it was no big deal.

Miss Stephens was also director of the senior choir at my family church, West Durham Baptist Church. Whenever I compare the choral music at West Durham Baptist Church with that of most other churches, Baptist churches in particular, I am pleased. It was a precursor to the music I would later sing in high school, in college, and in churches where my wife, our daughters, and I have had memberships.

I knew Miss Stephens's father, George Washington Stephens, mainly by reputation. He owned a grocery store on Powe Street in Durham, a street in Brookstown. I knew her sisters, Ruth and Margaret, quite well. Each was talented in music. Mary Louise Stephens died January 5, 1985. She was seventy-nine years old.

"AND SEEING the multitudes, he went up into a mountain; and when he was set, his disciples came unto him. And he opened his mouth and taught them, saying . . ." Thus begin the Beatitudes from the Sermon on the Mount (Matthew 5:1–15), in which Miss Pauline Fitzgerald Dame, my fourth-grade teacher, led the class in recitation at the beginning of each school day.

The recitation preceded lessons in any of the ten subjects in our fourth-grade curriculum: Reading, Language, Spelling, Geography, History, Arithmetic, Writing, Drawing, Music, and Hygiene. I don't recall that Miss Dame referred to the Sermon at any time other than during the devotional period. Nor do I recall any sermons about the Sermon. It was a ritual, presumably one intended to make us better children, and better adults as well. It must have worked, at least in the school year 1935–1936. I don't remember that Miss Dame had to contend with any major disciplinary problems.

I was delighted when I learned some fifteen years after I was Miss Dame's pupil that her niece was Pauli Murray, celebrated writer, lawyer, and civil-rights activist, and the first African American woman Episcopal priest. Miss Murray may be best known for her book *Proud Shoes: The Story of an American Family. A New York Herald Tribune* reviewer wrote that the book is "of such variety of incidents and such depths and changes of tone as to astonish one who mistakes it simply for a family chronicle." Pauli Murray dedicated *Proud Shoes* "To Caroline, Edmund, Marie, and the memory of Pauline Fitzgerald Dame." In Durham, the Dames lived in a two-story house at 906 Carroll Street. In 2009, the house is still standing.

Miss Dame was in her late forties by the time I reached the fourth grade. She was gentle, of very fair complexion, and had white hair. Parents were fond of her, perhaps because of her matronly demeanor and her demonstrably keen interest in their children. I believe she prepared me well for the fifth grade and quite likely beyond.

M Y FIRST-GRADE teacher, Miss Constance Young, began teaching at the old West End School and moved to Lyon Park School when it opened. That school was roughly two miles from Lyon Park and, you gotta believe it, was the elementary school that my mother attended. Miss Young seemed matronly to me, although I believe she couldn't have been more than thirty at the time.

M Y FIFTH-GRADE teacher, Miss Mildred Martin, was well-liked and the subject of considerable conversation by pupils in the upper grades. We knew or suspected that she and the school's other fifth-grade teacher, Mr. Henry Albert Hill, were romantically connected. A native of Winston-Salem, North Carolina, Miss Martin was pretty, of light complexion and slightly freckled. She was taller than most women and rarely seemed rattled when pupils were noisy or boisterous.

For reasons that have never been clear to me, my grades in the fifth

Lyon Park Safety Patrol. *Front row, left to right:* Paul Johnson, John Dark, Daniel Johnson, the author, Wilbur Nunn, and William Marsh. *Back row, left to right:* Frank Jacobs, Floyd Watson, not identified, Lorenzo Cozart, Frank Burnett, Brodie McCrae, and Henry A. Hill, advisor. *(Courtesy of William A. Marsh Jr.)*

grade were on the average lower than in any other year at Lyon Park. That was especially true for Effort and Attitude, for which my mother felt there was no justifiable grade lower than A. In fairness to her, however, grades at any level or on any subject were never a source of contentiousness with my parents. Perhaps this explains, at least in part, why I have only a murky recollection of Miss Martin as a classroom teacher, even though I liked her all right as a person.

Although I was not in Mr. Henry Albert Hill's homeroom, I got to know him when he played softball with the boys at recess periods. In that role, he was my first male teacher. He was slightly over six feet tall, a good looking man, with dark-brown complexion and jovial demeanor.

Henry Albert Hill and Mildred Martin were married on October 12, 1937, in Durham County before the Justice of the Peace. It was the first semester of my sixth-grade year. The likelihood is that Mr. and Mrs. Hill moved from Durham soon after the 1937–1938 school year. Unlike the case insofar as my other elementary school teachers are concerned, I have neither seen nor heard about them again. But I have always wished them well.

THE HIGHEST grade at Lyon Park Elementary School was the sixth grade. Miss Ruby Grissom was my sixth-grade teacher. When I talked with former students of Miss Grissom during my time, the one thing they all mentioned—more often than not, the only thing—was how she administered corporal punishment.

She whipped students in her cloakroom with a folded leather belt roughly twenty inches long. Some classmates have playfully mocked me about never getting a whipping from Miss Grissom, a reputation I never relished because I never believed in corporal punishment by school personnel. I confess that I got no grade less than A in Attitude under Miss Grissom. One might say that I was just plain scared, but it didn't take the threat of a whipping for me to stay under control in school.

Miss Grissom was a teacher who, whenever she saw me after I graduated from high school, smiled, embraced me, and said something to the effect that she was "so proud" of me. I believe what she had in mind was pride that I benefited from her teaching. I always thanked her, but I could not quantify what I learned from her any more than I could quantify what I learned from my other elementary school teachers. I was just hoping that there had been some intervention after I left Lyon Park that made her realize that corporal punishment as a form of discipline for elementary school children was more harmful than beneficial.

The last year that Lyon Park School was open as an elementary school was 1971–1972.

FOR OVER a decade, my efforts to learn how Lyon Park School got its name were unsuccessful. But in late 2009, when I was well on the way toward closure on this manuscript, I received a call from Lynn Richardson, head of the North Carolina Room of the Durham County Library. She had discovered an article by one Wyatt T. Dixon, who reported that in May 1902 officials and patrons of a local baseball team were thwarted in their wish to play a game at Trinity College (now Duke University), which "had the only baseball diamond of any consequence." A "suitable place" was found, however, and "the team heads and citizens got together and the George L. Lyon Ball Park resulted."

Young George Lyon was secretary-treasurer for the Durham Baseball Club. The park was named as a memorial to him following his untimely death. And as if to erase any doubt about where the team played its games, Dixon also reported: "The Lyon Ball Park was located on the Chapel Hill Road across from the old section of Maplewood Cemetery and around the sharp curve leading to the Lakewood community." In other words, the park was located in Durham's West End.

6

Hillside High School

F OR MORE than fifty years, I had a romanticized image of how Hillside High School in Durham, North Carolina, got its name. I imagined the name was inspired by a natural elevation, perhaps with wild flowers amid visible stones. I was disabused of this image when I learned the school was named in honor of John Sprunt Hill, a local White business magnate. In 1921, Hill donated land for construction of the school where Pine and Umstead Streets intersected. Pine Street was later renamed South Roxboro Street.

Whenever I hear the abandoned school building on Durham's Concord Street referred to as "the old Hillside School," it occurs to me that it could more accurately be referred to as old Hillside School number five. The first Hillside School, then named the James A. Whitted High School, dates back to 1887. It was located on the corner of Blackwell and Pettigrew Streets. It burned down in 1888 and was rebuilt on Tatum and Matthew Streets. When it burned down in 1899, the school was rebuilt on Ramsey Street. This building was burned, although not completely, in 1921. I have not found sources that suggest the cause of these fires.

M Y FIRST year at Hillside School during my years as a student there (1938–1943) was the seventh grade. One of the commendable things about the school was that most of the teachers were a credit to the profession from the standpoint of their personal attributes as well as their academic qualifications. One exemplary teacher was Mr. James M. Schooler. I liked him from the beginning. I knew nothing about his background when I was enrolled in his ninth-grade general science class. But almost intui-

James M. Schooler Sr., age 104.
(Courtesy of James M. Schooler Jr.)

tively I perceived that there was reason to be favorably impressed with him as a man.

He exhibited a fondness for teaching and helped by relating content from the textbook to our circumscribed world of day-to-day experiences. "If you want to remember the colors of the rainbow, remember the name Roy G. Biv," he told us. "Red, Orange, Yellow, Green, Blue, Indigo, and Violet." He made students feel good about themselves, as when he commended me in class because I knew what days of the week—two at that time—the sanitation crew picked up garbage in my neighborhood. I felt good being openly complimented by a teacher I admired.

I interviewed Mr. Schooler in the summer of 2002. He was then ninety-six years old and a resident of the Carolina House on Ben Franklin Boulevard in Durham. I asked if he had considered career options other than teaching when he was a boy. "Frankly," he said, "when I was a boy, I never knew that there were career options in the professions other than teaching and preaching. I saw teachers at their work and decided I would like to do someday what they were doing."

He told me that he was one of eight children; he had five sisters and two brothers. He attended an all-Black elementary school in Richmond, Kentucky. The family moved to Lockland, Ohio, and later to Springfield, Ohio, where he attended the predominantly White Bryan High School. He graduated from high school in 1923. He and a White girl tied for the highest academic average in his class. The speaker at his commencement exercise was the president of Wittenberg College (now University) in Springfield. The president invited young Schooler to apply for admission at Wittenberg. Later, he learned that the high school principal was fired for "allowing" him to tie a White girl for academic honors. "I remind you, this was not North Carolina, but *Ohio*," he said, as if to forestall disbelief on my part. He did not know whatever happened to the girl or the principal.

James Schooler was the first member of his family to attend college. He majored in English at Wittenberg, and he drove a truck and sold ice to earn money for his college expenses. He graduated from Wittenberg in

Hillside High School Safety Patrol, 1941. *Row 1:* William Marsh, Doris Edwards, Johnny Hall, Vera Ragland, Major Carter Smith, Gloria Garrett, Syble Brewer, Verena Thompson, Walter Brown. *Row 2:* Dorothy McDaniels, Margaret Noel, Pearl Page, Octavia Barbee, Fannie O'Bannon, Cleopatra Scott, Charles Redding. *Row 3:* Miss R.B. Pratt, Margaret Page, Ella Parham, Majorie Harris, Ernestine Bynum. *Row 4:* Mattie Faucette, James Allen, Mary Williams, Fannie Caine, Inez Suitt. *(Courtesy of Carter Smith)*

1927. "My father wasn't interested in college, but he didn't discourage me from going," he said.

After he graduated from college, Schooler met William Gaston Pearson, then principal of Hillside School, who was on a teacher recruitment visit in Wilberforce, Ohio. "Professor Pearson," as he was referred to with admiration and respect, offered Schooler a teaching position in the Durham City Schools, with an appointment to Hillside. "I didn't hesitate to accept the offer," Mr. Schooler said. The school was located in the southern part of the city.

Durham, North Carolina, in my school days was a typical city of racial apartheid in the American South. Caste systems in both races were a stark reality. In my years as a student at Hillside High School, I got to know well many of my fellow students from every section of Durham. I observed that students who lived in the southern section of Durham were presumed by some teachers to be academically talented until they proved otherwise. To the contrary, students from other sections of the city were generally presumed by those same teachers to have little academic talent or potential unless *they* proved otherwise.

At that time, the preponderance of Black-owned enterprises and the families connected with them lived in the southern part of the city. There were middle-class Blacks in other sections of the city, but even they looked to southern Durham for opportunities in business, education, and some cultural features that were not available to them in their own communities, and certainly not in White Durham. Black-owned businesses in the West End during the same time were a small grocery store, barbershops and beauty salons, a photography studio, and an ice cream store. There was also a pool hall where I saw only Black faces, although I am not sure of the hall's ownership.

According to R. Kelly Bryant, longtime official with the Durham Business and Professional Chain (the Black counterpart to the city's Chamber of Commerce), the categories of Black enterprises in southern Durham during the 1940s included:

- Hillside High School
- the Stanford L. Warren branch of the Durham Public Library
- Lincoln Hospital
- the *Carolina Times*, a weekly newspaper
- North Carolina College for Negroes
- the Regal Theatre
- the Biltmore Hotel
- Garrett's Drug Store
- the United Service Organization (USO)
- the city's largest Black churches: White Rock Baptist Church, St. Joseph's AME Church, and St. Mark AME Zion Church (there were, of course, other churches in southern Durham but the only criterion I use here is size of membership)

- North Carolina Mutual Life Insurance Company and Mechanics and Farmers Bank, on Parrish Street in downtown Durham (some offices of lawyers and physicians were also on Parrish Street)
- the offices of the Durham Committee on Negro Affairs (later renamed the Committee On Black Affairs)

AT TIMES, since the passing of laws requiring the desegregation of public schools in America, I have heard generalizations by some Black brothers and sisters—mostly sisters for some reason—that Black teachers of generations past were good and compassionate. More often than not, there was either an explicit statement or an implication that Black teachers were inherently more compassionate than White teachers.

I never had a White teacher in elementary school or high school. So I could not say from direct personal experience whether White teachers during my era were characteristically good, bad, or somewhere in between. I can say that my teachers at Lyon Park Elementary School were mostly good. But I have always believed that a few of my high school teachers were so mean-spirited that they were the prime reason that some students dropped out of school.

I HAVE been haunted with memories of instances in which some Hillside teachers verbally abused students among those from the not-so-fortunate sections of the city. A case in point was Mr. K. J. P.

Pearlena B. attended the East End Elementary School before she entered the seventh grade at Hillside. We were classmates in Mr. K. J. P.'s eighth-grade civics class. Pearlena was attractive, well-groomed, and soft-spoken, and she was as good a student as most of us. Once when Pearlena did not know the textbook answer to a question asked by Mr. K. J. P., he described her to the class as "beautiful but dumb."

Pearlena survived Mr. K. J. P. We were in the same graduating class. But she has never attended a high school class reunion, although our class celebrated its first reunion in 1963, and had a reunion at least every ten years since until 2008. I would not have singled out this case except that others who graduated from Hillside during the same era have shared with me equally reprehensible stories about the same teacher.

Author's graduation from high school, age sixteen. *(Brown family papers)*

The most disquieting note is that Pearlena was not only the victim of racial apartheid; she also was the victim of class apartheid enforced by a Black teacher in the only high school she could attend because of her race. In the June 3, 2002, issue of the *New Yorker,* Stephen L. Carter is quoted by interviewer David Owen: "There are plenty of Black kids who look out at the world and see a place that has no room for them." (Stephen L. Carter was Cromwell Professor of Law at Yale University. He is the author of the 1991 book *Reflections of an Affirmative Action Baby*.) I maintain that tragedy is heaped upon tragedy when Black children do not see a respectable place for them in either the White *or* Black world. Who knows how many Pearlenas have been victimized by K. J. P.s who themselves were misfits in a profession that purports to help children develop to their full potential.

TEACHING AS a profession had far fewer admissions barriers to African Americans, especially in the southern states, than other professions, including the whole range of human services. It was one of the peculiar byproducts of racial segregation and discrimination. Another byproduct, however, was that an untold number of African Americans pursued teaching as a career when they were far better suited for professions that denied admission to them because of the color of their skin. This problem was gravest when such teachers were hostile, oppressive, or bitter as a consequence of injustices over which their students had absolutely no control. Fortunately for some students, the James Schoolers enabled them to overcome some barriers of legal segregation and discrimination based on social class, or on *perceived* social class. But alas, too many were unable to overcome these odds.

JAMES SCHOOLER'S girlfriend, Frances Williams, was a 1929 graduate of Springfield High School. She received the Bachelor of Arts degree from Wilberforce University, Wilberforce, Ohio, in 1933. Founded in 1856 by members of the African Methodist Episcopal Church, Wilberforce is the oldest historically Black private college in the United States.

Schooler and Frances Williams married in 1935, and they settled in Durham. Mrs. Schooler received a Master of Arts degree from North Carolina College at Durham (now North Carolina Central University—NCCU) in 1958. When her children were small, she was employed as a substitute teacher in the Durham City Schools, later as a teacher, and finally as Dean of Girls at Hillside. She retired in 1973. Mrs. Schooler died on January 6, 2000. James M. Schooler died on January 1, 2009. He was 104 years old.

His son, James M. Schooler, Jr., was a faculty colleague at NCCU and a fellow member in Beta Theta Lambda chapter of Alpha Phi Alpha fraternity in Durham. Another son, Ronald Schooler, was a fellow choir member of Trinity United Methodist Church, also in Durham.

IN 2009, the most recent embodiment of the Phoenix-like Hillside High School is located at 3727 Fayetteville Street in Durham. According to literature from The Freelon Group, the school's designing architectural firm, this school was designed as a model high school for 1,200 students initially, with the expectation that it will eventually house 1,600 students.

[7]

Theresa H. Claggett: In a League of Her Own

ALTHOUGH I have known or heard of teachers described as demanding, tough, soft, dynamic, temperamental, and so on, I have not ascribed a category to Miss Theresa Claggett, except to say she was the kind of teacher that I needed when I was in her classes at Hillside High School. She was born in Geneva, New York, and educated in the Geneva public schools, Cornell University, the Ithaca Conservatory of Music, Atlanta University, Columbia University, and the University of North Carolina.

In addition to the city schools, Miss Claggett taught at Johnson C. Smith University (Charlotte, North Carolina) and Fayetteville State University (Fayetteville, North Carolina). She founded the North Carolina State Music Teachers Association, which later sponsored state and regional festivals.

When I registered for classes each semester from 1939 to 1943, I started with choral music before adding the required college preparatory courses. Miss Claggett was the school's only teacher of choral music, and she introduced us to a broad and diverse repertoire.

Not only did she teach us how to sing; she also increased our knowledge of and appreciation for history, literature, spirituality, and humor. We analyzed the lyrics of each song, many of which had religious themes. At the time there were few restrictions, if any, on interweaving religious and secular content in public schools.

I have been heartened over the years in recalling themes in choral music that Miss Claggett taught us, including:

- "The Volga Boatmen," written by an anonymous Russian composer and orchestrated by Igor Stravinsky;

- "To Celia," also known as "Drink to Me Only with Thine Eyes," words by Ben Jonson;
- "Adoramus te Christe," by Giovanni Pierluigi da Palestrina;
- "As Torrents in Summer," text by Henry Wadsworth Longfellow, music by Sir Edward Elgar;
- "Sylvia," words by Clinton Scollard, music by Oley Speaks;
- "Listen to the Lambs" and "I Will Never Turn Back," words and music by R. Nathaniel Dett;
- "The Cossack's Song," a tribute to the Russian reapers from the repertoire of Slavic songs by the Don Cossack Chorus;
- and "Lift Every Voice and Sing," a hymn by James Weldon Johnson, referred to in contemporary literature as the Black National Anthem.

Each year we participated in a Christmas concert at Durham's White Rock Baptist Church, ending the concerts with the "Hallelujah Chorus" from George Frederic Handel's *Messiah*. Miss Claggett helped to prepare us for the concert by telling us about Handel's dramatic emotional experience ranging from depression to exhilaration while writing what she described as a majestic work.

The words of a ditty that we sang in one of Miss Claggett's classes were in sharp contrast to religious anthems by Handel and other classical composers that we were introduced to, but we found it humorous:

> He met her in the meadow
> as the sun was sinking low.
> They walked along together
> in the twilight afterglow.
> She waited until patiently he lowered all the bars.
> Her soft eyes beamed upon him
> as brightly as the stars.
> She neither smiled nor thanked him
> for yet she knew not how.
> For he was but a farmer's lad
> and she a Jersey cow.

I have not heard this little ditty (composed by Harry T. Burleigh [1866–1949]) since the days in Miss Claggett's music class when it amused me and my fellow chorus members so much.

Miss Claggett did not double as a civic worker, politician, real-estate broker, or salesperson. She was simply a good teacher. This no doubt helps to explain why, in 1967, a group of her former students organized the T. H. Claggett Awards Club to raise money for scholarships for Hillside graduates who studied music in college.

My wife, our daughters, and I were living in Maryland when the club was organized. Had I known, I would have been among the first to join. Two founders of the organization were Leon Goldston and Martha Vivian Branch Thorpe, both of whom achieved prominence as public-school teachers and local musicians. Mrs. Thorpe recalled that Miss Claggett arranged for composer-arranger R. Nathaniel Dett to hear her perform Dett's "Juba Dance" in Durham, when Dett was on the faculty of Bennett College. Not surprisingly, young Martha Branch subsequently attended Bennett on a music scholarship.

Theresa H. Claggett died on May 8, 1970, at Watts Hospital in Durham, North Carolina. She was seventy years old. Her funeral was held at Durham's Covenant Presbyterian Church. Members of the T. H. Claggett Club served as pallbearers and floral bearers.

[8]

Carlin Paul Graham: Mentor in My Adolescent Years

CARLIN GRAHAM was my mentor in my early teens. No such request was made of him and no such agreement reached. It was something that happened without my knowing it was happening. His soft-spoken wife, known to everyone as Libbie, had an infectious smile and a glow that always made me feel comfortable in their home regardless of the time or occasion.

Unless you are familiar with the history of Black Durham, North Carolina, you probably wouldn't know that West Durham Baptist Church, long located in the western part of the city, is now located in southern Durham. Before urban renewal in the 1970s the church was in the section of West Durham known as Brookstown. That section no longer exists except in the minds of some old-guard members who, in 2009, are still around. West Durham Baptist Church was the church of my family and the church of my membership until early adulthood.

Carlin Paul Graham organized the church's Boy Scout troop. At age twelve, I was one of the troop's first members. Carlin was my Sunday school teacher before he was my scoutmaster. His teaching was different from that of other church school teachers I had known. Their method was to have us read scriptures, one boy and one verse at a time. Haywood Tucker and Otis Filmore (not their real names) struggled with severely limited reading skills. When their time to read came, their attempts were frequently followed by name-calling and horseplay from boys who also were underachievers. Classes typically ended with teachers' abstractions about how good Jesus was to us.

But when boys acted up in Carlin's class, he made them agree to hold off until they could compete in activities such as arm wrestling or boxing

Carlin Paul Graham and family. *(Courtesy of Mrs. Ellen B. Amey)*

after the next scout meeting. Then he told us about people who were real to us, challenges they faced and how they overcame them—like Dr. James E. Shepard, who borrowed money to found a college, the North Carolina College for Negroes (now North Carolina Central University) right in our hometown.

Carlin was the only son of our church's minister, Rev. T. C. Graham, and his wife, whom we called *Miss* Graham. (Boys and girls in our community addressed all women as "Miss," whether married or single.) An extrovert with the body of a football guard, he seemed to thrive on engaging others in conversation and characteristically stopped whatever he was doing to talk. He spoke with authority on subjects such as the qualifications for small-aircraft pilot licensure and the sale of U.S. surplus materials to Britain. But sometime around the age of fourteen, I came to realize that much of my mentor's knowledge base was parroted information from discussions he overheard among the professional staff at Duke Hospital, where he was employed. His reading interests were shallow. He skimmed the daily newspaper, but he didn't read books or journals, not even novels. My reflections on this discovery resulted in one of the most fundamental guiding principles of my life: I would never regard others as role models, but I would place value on attributes I deemed worthy of emulation.

Once, in a scout meeting, Carlin said he was proud of his mahogany complexion and pitied people who were displeased with the color given them by God. That was two decades before H. Rap Brown and Stokley Carmichael coined the phrase "Black is Beautiful." He played the piano, not well, but enough to entertain himself and others, especially at house parties. Next to Mr. Buck Howard, Carlin Graham had the best voice in the bass section of the senior choir. Nobody was more gifted than Carlin at telling jokes. In some circles, his jokes would probably have been considered corny, but to a fourteen-year-old, they were hilarious.

When I was fifteen, I wrote a play that I titled *This Man Called Carlin*. It was presented in the church's education annex as a surprise birthday tribute to the man who was mentor to me as well as to six or eight other boys. I was producer and director of the play. I also performed the title role. Other members of Boy Scout Troop 110 and several girls in our peer group played roles of church leaders, parents, and community spokespersons.

Early in the script, I pointed out that Carlin had attended public schools in Durham and later Hampton Institute in Virginia, the school once attended by Booker T. Washington. In addition to saluting Carlin on behalf of the troop, my intent was to heighten the appreciation of church members and others for his sacrifices of time and money and his determination that every boy in Brookstown who wanted to be a scout could be one.

The first rung on Carlin Graham's career ladder was as a janitor, where he received unofficial on-the-job training in photographic medical illustration. In time, some members of the Duke medical school faculty and research personnel preferred to have Carlin do the photography for their illustrations rather than the school's formally trained medical personnel. He provided internship mentoring to other men, all of them White, who subsequently were employed as medical illustrators in the same division. The best of my recollection is that the hospital had no female medical illustrators at the time.

Eventually, Carlin's sense of readiness, the encouragement of a senior illustrator in the division, and Libbie's gentle persuasion led him to apply for employment as a photographic medical illustrator at the hospital. His application was denied. The designation as janitor at Duke Hospital was etched in stone. Neither the hospital nor the university hired Black professionals or conferred professional titles on workers of African descent, notwithstanding their competencies or levels of performance. I have often reasoned that people who so adamantly oppose affirmative action are of the same mentality as the people who developed and enforced the discriminatory employment policies in America, especially in the South.

In the early 1940s, while still a hospital employee, Carlin did freelance photography at his home on Morehead Avenue in Durham's West End. He did portrait photography, covered weddings, and did photography for other special occasions, including the yearbooks of Black high schools and colleges. I worked with him as a part-time assistant until the spring of 1945, when I went to New York City to look for a summer job, only to be drafted for military service before the summer ended.

In 1946, Carlin resigned as janitor at Duke Hospital. He borrowed a substantial sum of money and embarked upon a career as a full-time entrepreneur and proprietor of Graham's Studio. As a businessman, Carlin Graham was a superb photographer! In 1948 he landed a job as a medical illustrator at the predominantly Black Veterans Administration Hospital in Tuskegee, Alabama, and closed his studio in Durham. With Libbie and their sons, Paul, Thomas, and James, Carlin moved to Alabama. Carlin Graham rose to chief of the Division of Medical Illustration at the VA Hospital in Tuskegee, a position he held until he died of cancer in 1961, at the age of 52.

Paul became a physician, James became a partner in an automobile dealership, and Thomas became a veterinarian. Carlin's boy scouts, his adopted sons as it were, have been successful in a variety of careers in business, education, and the Christian ministry—but perhaps most of all as citizens.

When I served as chief of the Division of Training and Technical Assistance with the U.S. Department of Labor in Washington, D.C., one of the programs under the division's oversight responsibilities was the Manpower Administration's New Careers Program. In 1969, when Congressman James Scheur (D-NY), author of the New Careers legislation, learned that I was about to leave the department, he wrote to express regrets and thanked me "for maintaining the integrity of the New Careers Program." The Honorable Mr. Scheur knew that I had been vigilant in insisting that program participants, irrespective of race or gender, receive the full measure of career opportunities provided for in the program legislation. What he could not have known was that my stint with the Department of Labor might have been considerably less successful had not Carlin Paul Graham been one of my village elders.

[9]

North Carolina Central University
by Any Name

S O FAR in writing my memoir, I have referred to the same institution with the three names it has had since I entered it as a freshman in 1943:

North Carolina College for Negroes (1925–1947);
North Carolina College at Durham (1947–1969);
North Carolina Central University (NCCU) (1969–present).

Even before 1925, the school underwent several name changes. The school's first name—given in its certificate of incorporation, dated June 30, 1909—was the National Religious Training School and Chautauqua for the Colored Race. Not until I saw a copy of the certificate in 2009 did I know that "for the Colored Race" was part of the name given to it by its founder and first president, Dr. James E. Shepard.

James Edward Shepard was the son of Rev. Augustus Shepard and Harriett Whitted Shepard. He was born November 3, 1875, in Raleigh, North Carolina, and received his undergraduate and professional training at Shaw University. When he graduated from Shaw's School of Pharmacy in 1894, he became one of the state's first African American pharmacists. He went on to found the National Religious Training School and Chautauqua for the Colored Race in 1909.

The school's subsequent name changes had nothing to do with romanticism or petitions by constituents; rather, they were representative of new eras in Dr. Shepard's determination to keep the school open despite financial difficulties and other problems, including the loss of buildings caused by arson three different times.

When the school was sold and reorganized in 1915, it received its second

Dr. James E. Shepard. *(Courtesy of James E. Shepard Memorial Library University Archives and Records, North Carolina Central University, Durham, North Carolina)*

name, the National Training School. The school became a publicly supported institution in 1923, when the General Assembly of North Carolina appropriated funds to purchase and maintain it as Durham State Normal College. In 1925, the state legislature changed the name to North Carolina College for Negroes and stated the school's purpose: offering a liberal-arts education and preparing teachers and principals for secondary schools.

I have always been intrigued by the inclusion of the phrase "and Chautauqua" in the school's first name. Historian John Hope Franklin, who knew Dr. Shepard personally as well as professionally, speculated that Dr. Shepard might have been inspired to add the phrase by a visit that Dr. Shepard may have made to the Chautauqua Institution, an educational center in western New York. The Chautauqua Institution was founded in 1874 as a center for training Sunday School teachers and church workers, and Dr. Shepard may have visited Chautauqua when he was the southern field superintendent of "work among Negroes" for the International Sunday School in Chicago, Illinois. Franklin agreed with me that this chapter in Shepard's career no doubt heavily influenced him in developing the institutional mission and goals for the school he would later start in Durham, North Carolina.

Dr. Shepard had an intense preoccupation with the need to raise the literacy skills of African American church leaders, and in my judgment, he chose a name for the school that highlighted a major facet of its historic mission: providing a liberal-arts education for Black students. It might well have factored as a prime reason that the Durham institution became the first state-supported college for Negroes—the politically correct term in 1910 and for a long time thereafter—in America.

Alpha Phi Alpha fraternity, North Carolina College for Negroes, 1947. *Front row, left to right:* Samuel Shepard, Richard Barfield, John V. Turner, Harold Epps, William Aiken, Clarence Coles, Curtis Quick, and the author. *Back row, left to right:* Thomas Malone, not identified, Henry Kirksey, James Greenlee, not identified, William Waller, Henry Edwards, James Hayes, Leo Townsend, Jethro Hooper, and William Malone. *(Brown family papers)*

Just weeks after my eighth birthday, in the spring of 1936, I participated in a playlet with Miss Mary Louise Stephens's third-grade class on the campus of North Carolina College for Negroes. It was the first time I saw the college's founder and first president; he welcomed my fellow pupils and me to the campus. After my inaugural performance on the campus as a third-grader, the next time I saw Dr. Shepard was when I attended a regularly scheduled, mandatory Monday-morning assembly in the school's B. N. Duke Auditorium.

As a small boy in Durham's West End, I overheard people refer to North Carolina College for Negroes as "N.C. State," and at times simply as "State." Some referred to it in those terms when they encouraged me to stay in school "and go on to State" after high school. I had absolutely no idea then that a White land-grant college had been founded in 1887 as North Carolina State College (now North Carolina State University) and was referred to by the general populace as "N.C. State" and "State."

I was hardly a youthful visionary, if preparation for attending college is an indicator. I loved school from the first grade on. Not until my senior year in high school, however, did I begin to think seriously about what I would do after graduation. North Carolina College for Negroes (NCC) in my hometown appeared to be the logical next step for me. By that time, I knew I would *not* be going to N.C. State College in Raleigh.

Private Walter M. Brown, U.S. Army. *(Brown family papers)*

Two years after I entered NCC, my brother William enrolled in the state's land-grant college for Negroes, North Carolina Agricultural and Technical College in Greensboro (later to become North Carolina A&T State University). It was founded in 1899, twelve years after its White counterpart in Raleigh. (See vignette 47, "You Will Love My Brother Will.")

WHEN I entered NCC in September 1943, the institution had a single governing body, its Board of Trustees. The lone African American on the Board was C. C. Spaulding, then president of North Carolina Mutual Life Insurance Company in Durham. Boards of trustees for all state-supported colleges in North Carolina became subordinate to the University of North Carolina Board of Governors when it was established in 1972.

In 1943, the academic year at NCC was divided into quarters instead of semesters. Tuition was $25 per quarter. (The Consumer Price Equivalent [CPE] of this amount in 2009 was $308.09). With additional fees for the first or entrance quarter only—registration, athletic, library and concert, and medical—the "total amount due at entrance" for nonboarding students was $46 (2009 CPE = $566.89). Otherwise, for the second and third quarters, tuition costs were the only costs. For boarding students, the entrance-quarter fee was $121.75 (2009 CPE = $1,500.41). I was a non-boarding student.

I was probably overly sensitive about being in college at age sixteen. For one thing, roughly 25 percent of the student body attended elementary and secondary schools in the north, where they enrolled in the first grade at age six and attended school for twelve years. I entered the first grade at five and attended school for eleven years. (I was among the students who skipped a grade in my high school when the twelfth grade was added. It was an administrative adjustment that I never fully understood.)

INDIVIDUALS who are uninformed or have distorted information about southern American history might wonder how one could be awed by a little college in Durham, North Carolina, in the same town as nationally renowned Duke University. It is not so difficult for me to understand. I grew up in the shadow of Duke University, but in my boyhood and adolescent years, there were two different worlds, separate and unequal. These "worlds" retained separate identities even as their constituencies sometimes interacted in sundry ways, generally between the privileged and underprivileged, and too often between the powerful and the powerless. I attended public elementary and high schools in this city and, like my peers, viewed my new school, which happened to be named North Carolina College for Negroes, as an opportunity that was the best that could be provided in my separate and unequal world.

Is there any wonder, therefore, that I was favorably impressed with NCC's Administration Building, which included Dr. Shepard's office; offices of the Registrar, Bursar, and various personnel deans; an assembly hall and a post office; and classrooms for art, music, the humanities, education, and the social sciences? How could I not be in wonder when I attended student assemblies including Sunday vespers services, concerts, recital and theatrical productions in the B. N. Duke Auditorium, with its nine hundred seats, a concert grand piano, and Hammond electric organ? Added to these facilities were a gymnasium for women, a men's gymnasium with a swimming pool, a "Practice Cottage" for senior women in home economics, five residence halls, a new Science Building, a refectory, a College and Law School Library, faculty houses, the president's house, tennis courts, and an athletic stadium.

Even in 2009, historians in higher education laud the fact that in the

1940s and 1950s, North Carolina College for Negroes had a coterie of gifted scholars who would have been a credit to any college in the land.

Aside from the age factor, my self-portrait as a freshman at North Carolina College for Negroes looked something like this:

– My career interest was medical illustration, reflecting my fascination with the work of medical illustrators at Duke Hospital. I acquired this interest when I worked part time with Carlin P. Graham, a father surrogate who doubled as a hospital maintenance worker and self-employed professional photographer. (See vignette 8, "Carlin Paul Graham: Mentor in My Adolescent Years.")

– I majored in biology, minored in art, and took the required core-curriculum courses in English, algebra, social science, and physical education. (History was categorized as a social science.) I envisioned a career in which I would combine my interests in biology and art. I had never seen an African American medical illustrator. Nor had I seen one of any ethnic minority. My world was so circumscribed that I came to believe that there would be no place for an African American medical illustrator at any time or in any place. In time, I abandoned this career interest altogether.

– I declined fraternity pledge club invitations in my freshman year because I knew too little about them to make an informed decision about which one to join, if I joined one at all.

– My stepfather was inducted into the U.S. Army in December 1943. Mama, my brothers, and I were closely knit. We kept our needs and wants in sensible perspective. We owned a black, ten-year-old Buick, which Mama drove.

– For transportation to school, I rode buses contracted by the City of Durham with Duke Power Company. I hated the racially segregated rides and got a peculiar sense of relief each time I transferred from a bus marked Lakewood Park and boarded a bus marked Fayetteville Street. The fare, one way, was five cents.

– I loved campus life, perhaps too much. I soon came to the realization that I could earn passing grades without sustained, disciplined study, a skill I would not acquire until later, when I was in the U.S. Army.

I enjoyed participating in the college choir, especially at Sunday vespers services. Miss Ruth Gillum was the choral director. During the choir's first rehearsal of the year, Miss Gillum came to the tenor section and gave ear to seatmate Ernest McAdams and me. "Isn't this wonderful?" she exclaimed, evidently pleased to have our new, uninhibited voices. Ernest and I have recalled this experience with considerable delight through the years.

Although Miss Gillum referred to Ernest and me as "wonderful" new-comers to the choir, neither of us was good enough to be given solo parts. That distinction in the tenor section went to Arthur Gibson, an upper-classman from Gary, Indiana. Gibson's voice was smooth and melodious, a voice that made me glad to be in the choir so I could hear him sing, even in rehearsals.

I have been unable to recall selections in which Gibson was the soloist. But I do have a clear recollection of an African American spiritual in which Clarence Newsome, then a junior from Ahoskie, North Carolina, was the soloist. My recollection was unbelievably strong, but I called Newsome in the spring of 2002 for confirmation.

Yes, he was the soloist when the choir sang the spiritual at vespers ser-vices. "That was a long time ago, Walt, a very long time," he said. "I am amazed that you remember it." Newsome mentioned maladies he'd had in recent years. We said how good it was to be connected again after fifty-nine years and wished each other well. Even though it was Clarence Newsome who sang the solo part, it is unlikely that he has hummed or sung the spiri-tual to himself over the years as often as I have.

The refrain:

> I'm going down to the river of Jordan.
> I'm going down to the river of Jordan some of these days.
> I'm going down to the river of Jordan,
> I'm going down to the river of Jordan some of these days.
> I'm going to run and never get weary . . .
> I'm going to sit at the welcome table . . .
> I'm going to see my loving mother . . .
> I'm going to see my loving father . . .
> I'm going to see my loving Jesus . . .

The college was chartered as a religious institution and remained so until its name change in 1925. However, it was true to its religious heri-tage during my freshman year, and indeed throughout my undergraduate years. The statement on "Religious Activities" in the college catalog for 1942–1943 is indicative:

> *The college, although non-sectarian, feels that no institution, which fails*
> *to emphasize religion, is fulfilling its mission to humanity. Education has*

for its ideal the fitting of the individual for life. Unless one has spiritual discernment and moral appreciation, one is not prepared for social responsibility. Education, therefore, must address itself to the problem of training and directing the emotions as well as the intellect.

To this ideal, this institution is pledged. It endeavors to provide a wholesome religious atmosphere for its students, free from all sectarian bias.

Even though I was only sixteen, my classmates and I found pleasure in the custom of instructors addressing us as "Mr." and "Miss." We felt that these salutations helped to fortify us from the insults of White people who refused to address African American adults courteously, especially in the South.

I rejoiced that all students at North Carolina College for Negroes were presumed by their instructors to be initially able to achieve success in their academic pursuits no matter the artificial distinctions of social class or residency, and I was enthralled with the unending opportunities to develop friendships and acquaintances with students from different towns and cities in North Carolina—and, perhaps more exciting from my perspective, from other states and regions.

Gow M. Bush, B.S., M.S., PH.D., taught biology and was one of the most talented persons across disciplines I have ever known. I was amazed by his freehand illustrations of biological specimens and functions when working at the blackboard. He once did a superb charcoal portrait of Dr. Shepard, and I am told that he played the piano at some faculty parties. He was also the architect for the construction of his own house near the college campus.

I first knew Eulalee Marion Cordice, A.M., M.A., as Miss "Vickie" Cordice. She taught art, which was an area of academic concentration for me when I was aspiring to become a medical illustrator. I never knew if she preferred one art form over another because she was a one-person art department and seemed quite proficient in a variety of mediums.

Helen Gray Edmonds, A.B., A.M., PH.D., taught history and dramatic arts. Her undergraduate school was St. Paul's College, but it is inconceivable that she had greater loyalty to any school than she had to NCCU. As was the case with a number of faculty members, Helen was also a colleague when I was a member of the college faculty. She gave a sterling tribute to me at the retirement dinner given in my honor by the School of Education faculty. The Edmonds Classroom Building is named in her honor.

William Edward Farrison, A.B., A.M., PH.D., taught English. His reputation as a scholar and demanding teacher made him a legendary figure among students and peers alike. He was also a colleague who at times was a burr under the saddle of administrators. A favorite quote of his was, "In a den of lions, he who speaks the truth is a stranger." The Farrison-Newton Building was named in his honor, and for Pauline Newton, B.S., A.M., with whom I took my required sophomore course in Speech.

John Hope Franklin, A.B., A.M., taught history. (See vignette 52, "John Hope Franklin: Historian, Teacher, Friend.")

Joseph S. Himes, A.B., A.M., PH.D., taught sociology. (See vignette 16, "Joe Himes: God Sent Me His Way.")

J. Neal Hughley, A.B., B.D., PH.D., taught economics and for a time served as college minister during college vespers services. He was one of the least-heralded faculty members by students, probably because comparatively few took economics as a course in the social sciences options. Even though I was among those who never took a course under Dr. Hughley, I heralded him as one of the first preachers I knew who was a lettered theologian. He was author of *Rethinking Our Christianity*, published in 1942 by Dorrance Press.

James Lee, A.B., M.S., PH.D., always impressed me with his use of "what we find"—referring to fellow scientists—when teaching classes in biology. He was my wife's supervisor when she was secretary to his department. Ozie greatly admired him and was not the least bit surprised when the college named a building in his honor.

John B. McLendon, B.S., A.M., taught physical education for men and was the college's head basketball coach. He was a superman, scholar, and gentleman who did it all as a model in the intramural sports in which I participated under his instruction: boxing, wrestling, gymnastics, swimming, football, field hockey, baseball, and, to be sure, basketball. The NCCU basketball gymnasium is named in honor of business entrepreneur R. L. McDougald and Coach McLendon.

Ernst Moritz Manassee, PH.D., taught German and Latin. He was an immigrant scholar who developed an abiding appreciation for Dr. Shepard and love for the college. I studied German with him the year preceding my assignment with the U.S. Army occupation forces in Germany. (Dr. Ma-

C. E. Boulware. *(NCCU Archives)*

nassee is also referred to in vignette 21, "Woody and Howard to the Rescue.")

Charles A. Ray., B.A., M.A., PH.D., taught English. (See vignette 14, "A Ray in the Forties: Charles A. Ray.")

William H. Robinson, B.S., A.M., PH.D., taught mathematics and physics. I include his name as an indicator of teachers whose careers at NCC attested in part to the college's reputation as a leading institution among historically Black colleges and universities (HBCUs). Physics was not a required course in my major although I lament not having tried it is as an elective. I knew Dr. Robinson as a mentor during my probationary period as a candidate for membership in the college chapter of Alpha Phi Alpha fraternity. His daughter, Fannie O'Bannon, was my classmate at Hillside High School in Durham.

James T. Taylor, B.S., M.A., taught psychology and education. Some students referred to him affectionately as "Psych Taylor." I feel certain that his persistent fight for the equalization of salaries for teachers regardless of race factored in naming the Taylor Education Building in his honor. Taylor was a loyal NCCU alumnus, a friend of Dr. Shepard and his successor, Dr. Elder, and in years to come, one of my fishing buddies.

Percy Young, A.B., M.A., ED.D., taught courses in Secondary Education. (NCCU did not offer undergraduate courses in elementary education until sometime in the 1970s.) A quiet, seemingly unassuming gentleman, he was imbued with an appreciation of the seven "Cardinal Principles of Secondary Education," issued in 1918 after three years of deliberations by the Commission on the Reorganization of Secondary Education. I have probably said them in my sleep for nearly sixty years because I believe that, except possibly for a mere play on words, these should be the guiding "Principles" in public education; but, the key to their effectiveness is whether the nation is serious about providing adequate and equal educational opportunities for all American youth. The seven principles are: 1. Health, 2. Command of the Fundamental Processes, 3. Worthy Home

Membership, 4. Vocation, 5. Civic Education, 6. Worthy Use of Leisure Time, and 7. Ethical Character.

C. Elwood Boulware, B.S., M.A., ED.D., taught mathematics. Perhaps Dr. Boulware's influence figured as prominently after I graduated from North Carolina College for Negroes as when he taught me college algebra in the 1943–1944 academic year. In the spring of 1950, I already had a contract to begin teaching at Bennett College, but I needed income to help bridge the gap until the following September. Dr. Boulware had learned that there would be opportunities for house-to-house census takers in the nation's seventeenth decennial census. He insisted that the opportunity should be extended to qualified individuals irrespective of race. I do not know how many others Dr. Boulware asked to apply, but I was one of five who took the test and were hired. For me the experience was much appreciated and unquestionably valuable.

Three years later, in 1953, when I was enrolled in the doctoral program at North Carolina College in Durham, Dr. Boulware pressed for graduate students at NCC to be given temporary employment at the U.S. Post Office preceding and during the Christmas holidays. Here again, I applied for a new and different opportunity and was hired. I am aware that for Dr. Boulware, these were characteristic kindnesses to others as well as to me, but I want my record to acknowledge his exemplary life as teacher, city councilman (1967–1970), and civil-rights activist.

DR. SHEPARD's wife, Mrs. Annie Day Shepard, wrote the lyrics to NCCU's Alma Mater, a song that my wife Ozie and I sang through the years as students and as proud alumni. The music was written by the brilliant composer Harry T. Burleigh. I am singing it even as I am writing:

> The sloping hills, the verdant green,
> The lovely blossoms' beauteous sheen,
> Surround our college proud and gay,
> Where wave our colors, Maroon and Gray.
> What matters it how far we roam,
> Our thoughts will all return to home
> And hearts will oft return to thee
> Our Alma Mater, N.C.C.

Refrain:
Then Rah! Rah! Rah! For our colors so gay
Dear old N.C.C.'s Maroon and Gray.
Thy Sons and Daughters will honor thee,
Dear old N.C.C.
We've gathered here to fit our lives,
As from the darkness light revives,
So let us hail, both night and day
Our glorious colors, Maroon and Gray.
We'll ever love and honor thee
For thou hast taught us loyalty.
Then let our watchword "Service" be
To Alma Mater, N.C.C.

You send us forth with hearts of love
So, like a blessing from above,
And from the path we'll never stray,
Our dear Alma Mater, Maroon and Gray.
We'll work and fight, we'll win our way
When duty calls we shall obey
And may we e'er return to thee
Our Alma Mater, N.C.C.

James Edward Shepard died on October 6, 1947, while still in office as NCC's president. I was honored to write his obituary, which was the lead front-page article of the school's paper, the *Campus Echo*.

IN 2009 North Carolina Central University was the nation's highest-ranked public HBCU on measures of the quality of undergraduate education. According to results of a survey by *U.S. News and World Report*, "The ranking was based on retention rates, class size, faculty preparedness and compensation, and the opinions of administrators among the 81 HBCUs in the nation."

These findings are not very different from measures or perceptions among peer institutions in 1943. I have observed through the years that there is high correlation between socioeconomic levels and income, and high correlation between socioeconomic levels and academic achievement.

The tuition at private colleges—historically White and Black—tends to be considerably higher than at public colleges. Thus, students from families in upper socioeconomic levels tend to be higher achievers and are more likely to satisfactorily meet retention and graduation requirements at their respective institutions. I do not envisage a change in this sociological phenomenon in the foreseeable future.

[10]

The Summer of '44

Had I known about the circumstance in which Miss Adelaide A. Pollard wrote the hymn "Have Thine Own Way, Lord," I probably wouldn't have harbored such a bitter feeling toward singing it as I did for sixty-five-plus years. The hymn was published in 1902, forty-two years before I sang it at a prayer meeting every Monday morning at E. C. Mack Paint and Wallpaper Company (not the company's real name) in downtown Durham, North Carolina.

Miss Pollard wrote the words to this hymn after attending a prayer meeting where an older woman pleaded, "It really doesn't matter what you do with us, Lord. Just have your way with our lives." Both Miss Pollard and Mr. Mack were White Christians, as was Mr. George C. Stebbins, who put the hymn to music in 1907.

E. C. Mack Paint and Wallpaper Company had a reputation as the best of its kind in the city and one of the best in the state. Townsfolk referred to the company by shorthand, simply calling it E. C. Mack. I started working for the company soon after it got a contract to decorate the interior of Durham's Malbourne Hotel. In addition to me, two other Black men—Clayton Allen and Major Colcough—were among the company's nineteen employees. (On the job, I called Clayton "Mister Allen" and Major "Mister Colcough." In my neighborhood, addressing adults by the social titles Mister or Miss was a way of showing respect. I don't know why we never said *Mrs.* Somebody, always *Miss*—married or single.)

I asked Major if he could get me on at E. C. Mack for the summer. A week later Major stopped by with the good news that I could report for work the following Monday. I didn't have to fill out a job application, just a W-2 form for Social Security deductions.

I guess Mr. Mack trusted Major's judgment that I would be a good worker. He probably put the risk squarely on Major's shoulders by assigning me to work with him on the Malbourne Hotel job. Major did the prep work for the painters and paperhangers. My best recollection is that he'd been with E. C. Mack for about ten years.

Clayton had been with the company twenty-six years, doing everything from sweeping floors and mixing paint to keeping the inventory of supplies. He could have been a clone for baseball Hall of Famer Henry Aaron, except that Clayton's body was bent at about a forty-five degree angle. He had sustained injuries while scraping flaked paint from a ceiling at one of the company's work sites when a scaffold gave way. Mr. Mack assigned Clayton to do light housekeeping when he was still on crutches. As Clayton got better he made himself indispensable as a handyman. "He's fixed for the rest of his life," Major told me. Clayton earned a high school diploma by attending an evening school—then commonly called night school. He knew more about the company's inventory than any of the other employees.

If Clayton Allen was Hank Aaron's clone, Major Colcough could have passed for Evander Holyfield, who became the undisputed heavyweight boxing champion of the world in 1990 by defeating James "Buster" Douglas. Major and his family lived down the street from us on Durham's West End.

Major Colcough came into my life when he was umpiring a boyhood softball game. The game was on a Saturday afternoon and a foul ball was hit toward him while he was watching us play. Major snared the ball like a purple martin taking a mosquito on the fly.

Until then, we were playing without an umpire, and one of the guys asked Major if he'd umpire the game for us. "Looks like y'all need somebody to do it," Major replied, and added something like, "I never seen nobody trying to play ball with so much bickering and carrying on in all my life." I have always believed that Major knew intuitively at that moment that he was adopting the entire neighborhood softball team as his sons. For roughly the next three years, he was our umpire, father surrogate, and sage—a true village elder.

In the thirty-odd years since it opened, the Malbourne Hotel had been redecorated five times. Each time, new wallpaper was put on top of the old. This time, the hotel owner—I never knew his name—wanted the walls stripped and new paper put on to ensure that the Malbourne was exactly what its billings noted: one of the handsomest hotels in the South.

You might say that Major and I were the advance team at the Malbourne work site. We had the job of removing the old paper from the Malbourne's walls and cleaning up the mess afterwards. Evander Holyfield couldn't have done it. He only had to fight in a boxing ring for not more than fifteen rounds, most of the time less than fifteen. Outside the hotel, the average temperature was 96 degrees. Inside, with the gasoline-fueled steamer and steam-fogged rooms, the mercury hovered at 130 degrees. With a ten-by-sixteen-inch steam pan, Major and I steamed every square inch of paper in six layers and peeled it while it was blisteringly hot. Major showed me how to hold the steam pan at angles to prevent steam droplets from torturing my body when I was scraping paper from the ceilings.

Take my word: if you ever have a choice between using steam to soak five layers of paper on plastered walls and doing anything else, choose the anything else! And if you're still uncertain about which option to take, it may help to know that paper on the bathroom walls is usually water-repellent.

When we had removed the paper and sanded and sized the walls, the painters painted the doors and moldings, and the hangers hung the paper—in cooler rooms. I was enchanted with the transformation of faded and dull rooms to rooms bright and colorful. I decided to tell Mr. E. C. Mack that I wanted to learn to be a painter or a wallpaper hanger, maybe both.

I was eager to disclose my career decision to Mr. Mack. For one reason, one of his apprentice painters (a White boy) and I were the same age, seventeen. But the main reason was that Mr. E. C. Mack was a Christian man who required his employees to take part in a prayer meeting at the shop each Monday morning before going to their assigned work sites. The prayer meetings were held in the showroom and led by Mr. Mack himself. I thought: there are a lot of White people who would deny me this opportunity, but not a White Christian like Mr. E. C. Mack. His favorite song was "Have Thine Own Way, Lord," which he sang lustily in a raspy monotone, all four verses.

In midsummer, following a prayer meeting and before Major and I left for the Malbourne, I told Mr. Mack that I would like to become a painter and paperhanger, and I asked if there was a way I could learn the trade while working there. Mr. E. C. Mack, the tall, silver-haired man in his sixties whose complexion was a fine grain of sandpaper, gave me a look of ill-tempered annoyance and spoke like Richard Widmark in a B movie: "Just do what I hired you to do. No need to even talk about it because I don't hire colored to do nothing but what you're doing now." Case closed. Major had asked his boss to hire me. Don't get him in trouble by being an uppity Negro—the preferred characterization at the time, the summer of 1944.

By the time I attended my last prayer meeting at E. C. Mack, I had fully decided to join the body of students enrolled at the North Carolina College for Negroes in Durham. There I would resume the change from barnyard fowl to flying eagle. And along the way, I would be singing "Have Thine Own Way, Lord"—all four verses.

[11]

The Summer of '45

THE MEMORY of my 1944 summer job lingered hauntingly. I was determined that my next summer experience would be dramatically different, a different kind of job in a different location.

As required by law, I registered with the U.S. Selective Service on my eighteenth birthday, April 9, 1945, making me eligible to be drafted for military service *immediately*. The corresponding classification was 1-A. I schemed that a change of address for the summer would delay for at least three months any notice to report for enlistment. By this time a student deferment might be possible, beginning in September.

A college classmate, Curtis Quick, had spent two summers in New York City and was going again that summer. Curtis, a native of High Point, North Carolina, took but a few minutes to convince me to accompany him to the place that tour guides called the Black capital of America, New York City's Harlem. Curtis was three years older than I, and it was reassuring to have him as my cohort.

The train ride from Raleigh, North Carolina, to New York's Pennsylvania Station was hardly one I would describe for a travel magazine, certainly not in comparison to views by rail of the British Isles countryside. However, the subway ride from Penn Station to Harlem usually comes to mind whenever I hear the all-time jazz hit by Duke Ellington and Billy Strayhorn, "Take the A Train."

In Harlem, we went to the apartment where Curtis had stayed the previous summer, on 146th Street between Seventh Avenue and Eighth Avenue. I could tell from his former landlady's demeanor that she was glad to see him. She had an unusual name, something like Rozella. After introductions were over, they talked about goings-on during the past year, school, the war, cost of living, the weather. In the course of conversation, Curtis said, "Walt here and I need a place to stay for the summer."

Rozella asked Curtis why he hadn't written to say he was coming. He mumbled something intentionally unintelligible, and he said playfully that she was too good-hearted to deny two schoolboys from down home a roof over their heads so they could make a little money for the summer. She reproached him mildly, saying he hadn't changed one bit, and offered both of us the same room he had in the summer of '44. The price was to our liking: seven dollars per man per week. The room had one small standing bed and a folding bed. I deferred to Curt's undeclared seniority and took the folding bed.

This was my first travel outside North Carolina, and I was as excited in Harlem as a six-year-old at his first state fair. I observed that tourists paid handsomely to see the place, and most of the residents tolerated their gaping. For me, Harlem meant fruit and vegetables and candy on vendors' carts, apartment buildings jammed together, and a sage preaching on every corner. It meant men carrying blocks of ice on their shoulders and delivering them on order to apartments or rooms; children playing hopscotch on crayoned sidewalks; children laughing and crying; babies in arms and babies toddling with other babies; and young mothers and old adults. It meant boys playing stickball; boys on skateboards, mostly homemade; boys and men playing basketball; pigeons strutting and pecking in defiance of all that was going on around them. It meant people walking; people racing; people sitting on stoops and steps; people walking their dogs; weathered-looking men on horse-drawn wagons with loads of old newspapers in bundles, bottles, and God only knows what else. People dressed as fashion plates; people in rags; people washing and waxing cars; people reading; people playing music alone and in small groups; people talking and shouting and cussing and singing in different languages and accents; people laughing; people staring. It meant satellite centers for religious personages, Father Divine and Daddy Grace.

My nostrils took in pungent scents of perfumes, onions and garlic, smoke from charcoaling pork and beef and chicken with the aroma of frying fish. Add to these the odors of alcoholic drinks, tobacco in sundry forms, the contents of garbage receptacles. The whiffs were almost indistinguishable.

I saw places I'd heard people from up north talking about: Seventh, Eighth, and Lenox avenues, and Sugar Hill. One Hundred Twenty-fifth

Street was the hub of Harlem's commercial activity, with general merchandise and specialty stores, African American clerks, with restaurants, banks, and bars. And for the first time to my southern eyes: African American policemen, firemen, drivers of buses and subway trains. Men and women of all ethnicities in military uniforms. And there was the best mental-health outlet I could have imagined: the Apollo Theater.

The Theater Foundation is justified in calling the Theater a monument to the contributions of Black Americans to the entertainment industry. Built in 1913, it was largely White until the 1930s social protests and riots brought about its racial integration. The entertainment media describe the place as the Apollo Theater, but the people of Harlem simply call it "the Apollo."

The format for shows at the Apollo in the 1940s was threefold: A C-grade movie, a performance by celebrated jazz musicians as the main feature, and an act by a comedy team. I endured the movies just to see the jazz artists and comedy teams, and I was enthralled by the musicians' performances, with orchestras that sometimes featured popular vocalists. The comedy teams put me in hysterics. I always left the theater thrilled and eagerly looking forward to the next show of entertainers, most of whom were household names: Duke Ellington, Count Basie, the Nat "King" Cole Trio, Lionel Hampton, Ella Fitzgerald, Sarah Vaughn, Charlie Barnett, Cab Callaway, and Louis Jordan.

The youth of 2009—indeed, many adults—would no doubt find the Apollo's comedy teams of the '40s bland, if not corny. I still prefer comedy without obscenities and insults to people of any persuasion—as in this dialogue of two comics, each of whom called the other "dumbest."

"You so dumb, you don't even know the color of fire trucks."

"Sure, I know the color of fire trucks. They're red."

"Can you prove it?"

"Sure, I can prove it."

"Well, let me hear you prove fire trucks are red."

"Newspapers are read. Magazines are read. Newspapers cost three cents. Magazines cost three cents. Three and three are six. Six and six are twelve. Twelve inches in a ruler. Queen Mary is a ruler. Queen Mary is a ship. Ships sail on water. Fish swim in water. Fish have fins. Finns fought the Russians. Russians are Reds. Fire trucks always rushin' so they gotta be red."

I laughed until tears rolled.

My introduction to Harlem included the unforgettable experience of attending a Sunday morning worship hour at the Abyssinian Baptist Church. I remember the sanctuary with jammed pews, white marble pulpit floor, Black and mulatto faces in a thirty-five-voice choir in white robes with black collars, and Rev. Adam Clayton Powell Jr.'s revolutionary sermon about institutional racism. I remember the choir's rendition of "Precious Lord," and Powell exclaiming, "Sing it, Dottie!" at the point where the soloist pleaded, "Hear my cry, hear my call, guide my feet, lest I fall . . ."

I would not have disputed Harlem residents or tourists who described Adam Clayton Powell Jr.'s presence as "enchanting." Congressman Powell had won a seat in the U.S. House of Representatives the year before I went to New York. I deemed it a privilege to be at Abyssinian on Sundays when he was in the city. A transplanted North Carolinian once told me, "People in Harlem think Adam Clayton Powell is a god, and God had better be careful."

Twenty years later, Powell chaired the House Committee on Education and Labor. By that time, I was employed with the Office of Economic Opportunity in Washington, D.C., administrative hub of the Kennedy-Johnson War on Poverty. In 1970, Powell was voted out of Congress for alleged abuses of power. He died of prostate cancer in April 1972, at the age of 63. Writer Tony Chapelle wrote an expressive tribute to Powell:

> *Today, he isn't as ubiquitous a symbol of African American determination as Malcolm X; you seldom find his likeness on T-shirts, or see film clips of his speeches within music video. Nor is his picture reverently displayed in magazine ads during Black History Month like Martin Luther King Jr.'s. But African Americans with a knowledge of their history remember Powell as the risk taker who made it possible for later generations of African American politicians such as Jesse Jackson, Rep. Ron Dellums, and Willie Brown of the California Assembly to stand unbowed in the arena of political horse-trading.*

After my arrival, I attended a Sunday afternoon reception hosted by the New York City chapter of the North Carolina College Alumni Association for students and recent graduates of the college. The reception was held at the St. Mark AME Zion Church on St. Nicholas Avenue. I recall that a panel of established New Yorkers enlightened newcomers on how the city had been enriched by such writers as Langston Hughes, Zora Neale Hurston, Countee Cullen, and Claude McKay; by artists Jacob Lawrence, Romare Bearden, and William H. Johnson, by singer-actor-activist Paul

Robeson, and by activists A. Philip Randolph, W. E. B. DuBois, and Marcus Garvey. The informal sessions that followed the panel presentations provided opportunities to get recommendations on places to eat, shop, worship, and apply for jobs. The gods couldn't have been kinder!

Curtis's selective Service status was 4-F, which meant that for one reason or another he was not acceptable for military service. Within a week after our arrival in New York he got a job as a laborer in the Brooklyn Navy Yard.

I fast-forward here to say that Curtis Quick's untimely death sometime in the 1970s recalled for me reports that hundreds, maybe thousands, who worked in the Brooklyn Navy Yard died from exposure to asbestos used in manufacturing and repairing ships during the twentieth century. To this day, I do not know if there were cause-and-effect relationships at the Brooklyn Navy Yard in my friend's death.

I had two impediments: my 1-A draft classification and a work history that did not indicate long-term employment anywhere. These barriers were virtually impossible to overcome until I met the right job-referral clerk in the New York office of the U.S. Department of Labor, who turned out to be a handsome, distinguished-looking woman with salt-and-pepper hair pulled into a ball at the back.

She looked part Native American, part West Indian, and part African American. Said she was "sorry" she couldn't help me. A silver track shoe on the lapel of her tweed jacket caught my eye. It was striking, and I told her so. She said the shoe had been awarded to her son, who was on the track team at a university in one of the midwestern states—Iowa State University, I seem to recall. I said she must be proud of him. She was. She looked at me as if to say her son and I would probably be friends if we knew each other. That was just before she said she was going to bend the rules for me and refer me to a company that was "willing to take risks with possible draftees but not with students who would leave for school at the end of the summer."

She told me the job was with a defense plant in Carteret, New Jersey, the United States Metal Refining Company, roughly eighteen miles from downtown Manhattan. The factory had a contract with a bus company to provide transportation for workers who needed it—for a fee, naturally. She gave me the referral papers and suggested I go for an interview as soon as possible. I thanked her and gave assurance that her point was well-taken.

At the U.S. Metal Refining Company, a personnel clerk reviewed my application before calling me from the waiting room for my interview. It struck me that I'd seen her look-alike—brunette, blue eyes, and thinly curved lips—on the cover of *Seventeen.*

This interview has been replayed in my memory hundreds of times.

"All the way from North Carolina?" she asked.

"Yes, Durham, North Carolina."

"And where is North Carolina College located?"

I told her the college was also in Durham. What I didn't tell her or write on the application form was that the actual name of the college was North Carolina College for Negroes. I wasn't up to trying to explain the absurdity of it.

"So you've never had a permanent job?" she asked. Her tone made the queries seem perfunctory, and not the least intimidating. "Did they tell you at the Employment Office that we don't hire student workers?"

"They did, but I'm not a student now."

"Then you don't intend to return to college this fall?"

I replied that I had left North Carolina to start a new life, that I liked New York and wanted to make it my home.

She said she imagined I was a good student. My response was that I made out well in school and enjoyed it. She asked if I knew that workers at the plant rotated every two weeks on three shifts: 7:30 in the morning to 3:30 in the afternoon, 3:30 in the afternoon to 11:30 at night, and 11:30 at night to 7:30 in the morning. I wondered if she was trying to get me to change my mind about working at the company. I said it wouldn't make any difference which shifts I worked on.

I would be assigned to work in a building where copper ore was smelted in a reverberatory oven. My job would be to put the ore in fourteen-by-eighteen-inch pans and place them on a track that moved at snail's pace through the oven. The heat rid the ore of its impurities.

She showed me a picture of the oven, which was the length of a basket-ball court. "Waiting for the pans to move through can get awfully boring unless you have something to occupy your mind in the meantime," she added.

"Like what?"

Reading. Ore would be brought to my station in large boxes. I would put a layer of newspaper in each pan before putting the ore in it. The company got shipments of old newspapers by the ton—all kinds of papers: *New York Times*, *New York Post*, *Wall Street Journal*, *Daily News and Mirror*, and so on. She smiled and said reading was not in my job description but I would be able to read newspapers while trays were moving so slowly through the oven.

For transportation to and from the factory, I was to get the bus at the city's 42nd Street station. She gave me a copy of the bus schedule with the weekly fare: nine dollars. I would start the following Monday on the afternoon shift. At the same time, I would also be issued an employee personnel packet and my identification badge. She promised to call the foreman on my behalf.

She stood. Our hands were joined in personnel protocol when she asked if I would do her "a big favor."

"Sure."

In just above a whisper, she said, "Go back to college in September."

My eyes were smiling as I echoed her whisper, saying, "Thanks, I intend to."

Postwar Vision

"OVER THERE, said one of the receptionists, who was White.

"Thanks, but this will be fine," I said as I took a seat in the room six times more spacious and far better furnished than the colored waiting room.

I had gone to McPherson Eye and Ear Hospital in Durham during my boyhood, first with an earache and later for an eye examination. Each time, I sat in the colored waiting room. During eye examinations, all patients went to three or four small waiting rooms. Upon leaving each room, patients were directed to still another room before being called to see the next specialist. The wait between stations seemed interminable.

The U.S. Army made certain that I would not see life as I had seen it before my induction. I had four pairs of glasses at the same time, all with the same prescription: my civilian glasses with no frames around the lenses, two pairs of G.I. glasses with dull gray frames, and glasses fitted in my gas mask. Still, I needed a new prescription the year after I was discharged.

By the time I went to McPherson in 1947, I was looking at the world through different lenses. I went straight to the White waiting room, situated directly across from the receptionists' counter.

I picked up a newspaper, ostensibly to read, but actually to have a screen between the receptionists and me.

One of the receptionists told me that "they" wanted me to go to the other room.

I asked who "they" were, aware that she had in mind the same kind of "they" who had designated segregated accommodations for Blacks at bus and train stations, airports, public buildings, and elsewhere.

"The management," she replied.

I thanked her and said I was all right. She left the receptionists' area. Three or four minutes passed. A side door cracked open. An African American face peeked through. Two more looked around the corner. The word had gotten around. None of the White patients said anything. None left the room. Apparently they were content to see how the scene played out, or later to serve as witnesses, if needed. It occurred to me that some of the White patients might be sympathetic, maybe even supportive. I was nervous and caught myself reading the newspaper upside down.

"Walter Brown." I was being called before White patients who had been there even before I entered the room.

From that point on, there wasn't a single reference to my sitting in McPherson's White waiting room. The examining physicians did their jobs as professionals. But it was also evident that they were following some-one's orders to move me on to each specialist without asking me to return to a wait station. I have always wondered if, under the circumstances, my examination was as thorough as it should have been. But being discrimi-nated against because of his color keeps a man wondering for a long time and about a lot of things.

The "management" at McPherson could have had me arrested for something—perhaps trespassing—in 1947, but they did not. They could have refused to serve me. They did not. I reasoned that someone in the hospital power structure decided that I was either too dumb to know my place or not worth a scene.

[13]

A Way Station at the Malone Residence

I HATED THE army, but I liked being a military veteran because I felt it signaled that I was a man. I lost no time getting back in school, this time as a junior at North Carolina College (NCC). I had begun to think about the future beyond college, and it made a difference in my lifestyle.

Before my stint with the military, Cecil Holt and Bill Alexander gave me extensive use of their dormitory room at NCC when I needed a place to freshen up or take a breather between classes or extracurricular activities. Now they were no longer roommates, and I needed another place to hang my hat. Enter the Malone family household, three blocks from campus and three miles from my home on Gerard Street in Durham's West End.

I salute the Malone children, but I give special salutations to their parents, Mr. and Mrs. William P. Malone Sr. They and their children made their home a pleasant "way station" for me during my junior and senior years in college. Through the years, I have marveled at how the Malone parents raised such an exemplary set of five children. The parents were unpretentious, gentle, and reserved in manner. Mr. Malone was a maintenance worker at a Durham hotel. Mrs. Malone, the former Ruth Glen, was a domestic in a downtown office building. The children were supportive of each other in school and later in their respective careers.

·William "Bill" Malone Jr. was the first of the Malone children to attend NCC. He was several years ahead of me as a student at Durham's Hillside High School. Bill was a public health educator for the Guilford County Health Department in Greensboro, North Carolina, when Ozie and I were at Bennett College from 1950 to 1952. He succeeded me as director of the career counseling and placement bureau at North Carolina College, and he retired from NCC in 1986 as special assistant to Chancellor Albert

N. Whiting. Bill's wife, Madeline, was an Alzheimer's patient for several years before my wife Ozie fell victim to the dreaded disease. Although they were not related, Madeline and Ozie could hardly have been more alike in temperament, love of family, and physical attractiveness. Madeline died in 2000.

Edith Malone Johnson became a high school physical educator. She and I took comparative anatomy together under Dr. Gow Bush, whose talents included portrait drawing, architecture, and playing the piano.

Ralph Malone was an administrator in guidance and counseling at Fort Valley State College in Georgia for thirty years. He died of colon cancer in the late 1980s.

Ann Malone Kelly, youngest of the Malone children, became an elementary school teacher in Durham. As is typical of the entire Malone family, it would be virtually impossible to find anyone who did not speak fondly of Ann.

In addition to their studious qualities, the Malone children had other attributes in common: they were all well-mannered, kind, and always well-groomed.

Thomas Ellis Malone was one of my high school classmates. To the general populace as well as schoolmates, Thomas became better known as "T." Before he was inducted into the army in 1945, T was a student at Morehouse College. He enrolled at NCC after his discharge from military service. In 1947, we were students together again, this time at NCC. I was living in New York in 1949 when I learned that some Black leaders in Durham were trying to get T to apply for admission to the University of North Carolina. (The school would later be named UNC–Chapel Hill.)

The jeers and catcalls were more than he could put up with when he visited the UNC campus. Many African American students have faced such cowardly acts, particularly in the American South. Some survived, though frequently at the cost of severe emotional and psychological stress. Some dropped out of school. Others had better alternatives. In 1949, T Malone applied to Harvard's Graduate School of Arts and Sciences and was accepted. He earned the PH.D. at Harvard and in 1952 was awarded the degree with a concentration in cell biology.

T taught biology for six years at NCC, and he held a postdoctoral research fellowship at the Argonne National Laboratory for two years. For twenty years, he served in a variety of positions, including eight years as deputy director of the National Institutes of Health (NIH). His employment at the NIH was interrupted by a term from 1969 to 1972 as professor of biology and chair of the department at the American University of Beirut, Lebanon.

One of T's efforts at NIH resulted in a landmark blueprint for addressing problems related to the health status of Blacks, Hispanics, Asian/Pacific Islanders, and Native Americans in the United States. In 1985, he declined an offer to be appointed director of NIH because it would have been a political appointment.

In 1986, shortly after he retired from NIH, T was appointed vice chancellor for research at the University of Maryland's medical complex in Baltimore. Two years later, he became vice president for biomedical research for the Association of American Medical Colleges. After five years, he retired from that position to give attention to his daughter, who was in rehabilitation after a tragic automobile accident, and to her two children.

T is the central figure in some of my fondest reminiscences. He was a brilliant student, but he also had a good balance between scholarship and social activities. We were members of a post-adolescent club of boys called Gaylords. Our concurrent group of girls was the Gayladies. (This was long before the term *gay* became identified with homosexuality.) I still tease T about the time that the Gaylords decided to have a softball team and had its first practice. When T reported, he asked for a glove, put it on his right hand, and went to play third base from the coach's box. He didn't make the team, but he had as much fun as the rest of us.

I believe it was in spring of 1947 that T saw an ad in the Durham *Morning Herald* for an automobile being sold for $200. He called the owner, made an appointment to see the car, and "fell in love with the car at first sight," he said.

I went with T to the Morris Plan Bank in downtown Durham, where he hoped to get a loan. After asking about the purpose of the loan and the year of the car he wanted the bank to finance, the bank representative shrieked when T told her it was a 1926 maroon and black Cadillac. Not to be undaunted, T went to the Black-owned Mechanics and Farmers Bank and got the loan. He sold the car before he left for Harvard.

I was proud to be a member of the wedding party of Thomas E. and Delores Darden Malone. The wedding took place in New York on June 20, 1953, one month after Delores graduated from NCC with a major in psychology. T and Delores have two children: Shana, a housewife, and Thomas Jr., an anesthesiologist in Frederick, Maryland.

A pastime that T and Thomas Jr. have in common is flying. T took up flying in the Washington area, bought a plane, and flew for nearly fifteen years. Thomas owns two planes, a twin-engine Beech Baron and a World War II fighter plane. But before T's love affair with airplanes, he became enamored with judo. When he retired from NIH, a center at the agency was named the Malone Martial Arts Center.

In the early 1940s, I had little idea of T Malone's aspirations beyond graduating from Hillside High School, getting a job, and enjoying our circles of Gaylords and Gayladies. The likelihood is that both of us achieved measures of success beyond our expectations. I consider it a blessing that my friendship with T fifty years later is as solid as when I told him to put the baseball glove on his left hand because he would have to throw the ball with his right hand.

[14]

A Ray in the Forties: Charles A. Ray

WHEN I was discharged from the Army in November 1946, I was thinking seriously about pursuing a career in journalism. I knew that the journalism department at Lincoln University, a historically Black college in Jefferson City, Missouri, had an outstanding reputation. I learned this during my training stint at Fort Leonard Wood, some eighty miles from Jefferson City, Missouri. North Carolina College for Negroes (NCC), the school at which I had completed two years before my induction into the Army, offered neither a degree nor a course in journalism. The public White colleges in North Carolina offered journalism, but admission to a White university in the state was out of the question for African Americans in the 1940s.

Inasmuch as NCC is located in my hometown, I visited the campus when I was on furloughs or passes. I basked in the attention of former classmates—girls in particular—and in renewing acquaintances with faculty members. NCC was then on the quarter system, and I would be able to resume my studies there in mid-December after my discharge. I could hardly wait.

Charles A. Ray, a professor of English at NCC, was easy and refreshing to talk to. I stopped by his office to ask his assessment of Lincoln's journalism curriculum. I told him that I would take a course in journalism at NCC if the college offered one.

"An interesting coincidence, Mr. Brown," he said. "You'd like to take a course in journalism, and I'd like to teach one." He said he would talk with NCC's president, Dr. James Shepard, concerning our mutual interest, and he asked that I stop by the following week to get the president's response.

As president of the college, Dr. Shepard could approve or deny such

Charles A. Ray. *(Courtesy of James E. Shepard Memorial Library University Archives and Records, North Carolina Central University, Durham, North Carolina)*

a request even without the advice or consent of the faculty in whose department the course would be based. It was that simple. I thought things were supposed to be that way. I learned differently in courses in higher education that I took in graduate school. I was also to learn differently as a college faculty member participating in faculty senate deliberations on issues related to institutional governance.

When I talked with Professor Ray the next week, he was guardedly optimistic. He had told the president about his interest, and he was given approval with the proviso that at least fifteen students registered to take the course. Ray suggested that I check with him again, immediately after registration for the upcoming term.

The second quarter was under way when I went back to see Ray. He had fallen short of the recruiting goal—short by thirteen students! That was the bad news. He had been able to recruit one student other than myself, a sophomore French major whose name was Nathaniel Bond. As a young boy, Bond had been characterized as precocious, a fact borne out over his entire academic career.

The good news was that Dr. Shepard consented to permit Ray to teach the course with an enrollment of two students: Nathaniel Bond and Walter Brown. Professor Ray never told me about the extent of his recruitment effort. Upon reflection nearly fifteen years later, by which time we were faculty colleagues, I suspected that his efforts had been modest at best. I had learned by that time that young Professor Ray received preferential treatment from Dr. Shepard, probably because of Ray's genteel qualities, among his other attributes. I never got the impression that Ray wanted more than two students in the class anyway.

When I recount for St. Peter the experiences that made life on earth rewarding for me, this class in journalism will surely make the Final Four. What a privilege—a class of two students that met daily, Monday through Friday. As reporters, we were required to submit an article per day, whether or not we had time to critique them fully in class.

My greatest challenge came not from Professor Ray but from my classmate. Aside from my awareness of his reputation as a shy student of extraordinary intellect, I got a dramatic revelation of what lay ahead for me when Ray assigned us to write a news story about a fire that destroyed the house of a low-income family that included five children. The family had lost all of its belongings. I turned in my news story, as assigned. Bond turned in a news story and a moving feature article on the fire and the family. Such was the level of his performance for the entire quarter.

Nathaniel Bond and Walter Brown couldn't have been more different in temperament and disposition. He was the classic introvert. I won't say that I was the classic extrovert, but I was regarded as outgoing and, at least by some, gregarious.

I don't know that I enjoyed a course in my entire academic career more than I did this one. Contralto Marian Anderson and tenor Roland Hayes gave recitals at NCC during that quarter. On assignment for the class, I interviewed these internationally acclaimed artists in the B. N. Duke Auditorium (at NCC, not Duke University). Both stayed at the home of President and Mrs. Shepard. Durham's White hotels would not give accommodations to either of the artists.

When I interviewed Marian Anderson, I thought I was already in heaven. Such graciousness. Such charm. Such loveliness. My blood curdles each time I think about the Daughters of the American Revolution denying her an opportunity to sing at Constitution Hall in the spring of 1939 because of her skin color.

The interview assignment with Roland Hayes couldn't have been easier. I don't remember my first question to him. But it was as if I had asked him to give me his career history on a tape recorder, and he complied fully. Like every African American of his day, and mine, he had a story to tell.

Marian Anderson and Roland Hayes were celebrated artists about whom I had read and heard so much, and I interviewed both—one on one! Bond never even intimated that he wanted to interview them. For that I am eternally grateful. Nor did he want to cover the football game between NCC and Morgan State at the Polo Grounds in New York City. That was also my assignment. Talk about precious memories!

When Charles Ray and I became friends as well as faculty colleagues, he delighted in having me recount our conversation several days after the term ended, when I asked about my final grade. He particularly relished having me recount the conversation at social events. "Walter, tell [whom-

He embodied what he preached as an educator.
—preparedness, expectation of high standards 77 -

ever] about our conversation at the end of the journalism class," he would say. I always obliged.

"I asked him what was my grade," I would say. "And he replied without hesitating, 'Well, Mr. Brown, I grade on the curve, and Mr. Bond gets an A.'" The story evoked unrestrained laughter, especially from party guests who had had more than one drink.

Although I had asked the question, I couldn't have been less concerned about a final grade. A grade of B at the end of a curve with Nathaniel Bond was good enough for me. I had been one of two students taught for three months, five days a week, by one of my heroes.

Charles Ray's manner was relaxed. His critiques were instructive, and his compliments were good for my psyche. Nathaniel Bond kept my feet to the fire, not because we were in competition but because we were reporters for a phantom newspaper of high standards. I was determined to meet the newspaper's standards.

I asked a couple of Charles Ray's former colleagues and students how they would describe him. Neither had to search for words: "Great teacher, compassionate, high standards, loved his work, hated pretentiousness, a humorist, urbane."

Charles Arthur Ray and John Hope Franklin began teaching at NCC in the same year, 1943. Ray never tired of talking about our journalism class. And he almost always asked me, "Whatever happened to Bond?" In time, this turned out to be a rhetorical question, because I was never able to find out what happened to my classmate. Sometime in mid-2000, one of Bond's closest high school classmates told me that he was living in West Virginia when he died in the early 1980s.

Charles A. Ray died in 1986. I still find it hard to accept the reality of his death. He had been an icon of witticism, good fun, and urbanity. I was fortunate to have had an education experience similar to that described by President James A. Garfield when he praised his professor at Williams College, Mark Hopkins, with these words: "The ideal college is Mark Hopkins on one end of a log and a student on the other." A twenty-one-gun salute to this teacher, to my friend, on behalf of every person whose good fortune it was to have had him sitting at the other end of Mark Hopkins's log.

[15]

Paul Robeson in Richmond, Virginia

DURHAM'S NORTH Carolina College for Negroes (NCC) played a football game against Virginia Union University on October 25, 1947. As sports columnist for NCC's student newspaper, *The Campus Echo,* I traveled to Richmond to cover the game. Not long after I arrived on the campus, I learned that Paul Robeson was to appear in recital that same evening at Richmond's Mosque Theatre. The Beta Gamma Lambda chapter of Alpha Phi Alpha fraternity sponsored the concert. Robeson was a member of the fraternity, and I was fortunate enough to get a ticket from one of my Alpha brothers.

Robeson had made a pronouncement that he would refuse to sing in the American South before a racially segregated audience. For the Mosque Theatre concert, the management recanted its practice of separate accommodations based on race, and the audience was racially integrated.

During the recital, this tall, muscular, and athletically framed Black man moved majestically as he walked on and off the stage. And to see and hear him sing—oh, man! I was especially moved by the aria from Mendelssohn's *Elijah* and the excerpt from Modest Mussorgsky's opera, *Boris Godunov*, sung in Russian. George Harris, of the *Times-Dispatch*, wrote "After Robeson sang Mussorgsky's 'After the Battle,' there followed the 'Hasidic Chant,' an old Jewish lament of an oppressed people, this was introduced by hints made by the performer as to its application to his own people, and in it there was the great cry—'An end to this suffering!' It was deeply moving."

Following his dramatic recitation of the death speech from *Othello*, as I had anticipated, Robeson closed the recital with a diverse selection of Negro spirituals, rich in grace and depth of feeling. The audience responded with encores, repeated and sustained.

The *Times-Dispatch* review did not include Robeson's acknowledgement that he had been roundly criticized and called a Communist, nor his assertion that, "If standing up for the rights of my people makes me a Communist, then I suppose a Communist I am."

Paul robeson's father, William Drew Robeson, was born into slavery in Cross Road Township, Martin County, North Carolina. At age 15, his father escaped from slavery and made his way north to Pennsylvania. When the Civil War ended, William Drew Robeson matriculated at Lincoln University in Pennsylvania, where he earned a degree in Sacred Theology. Paul's mother, the former Maria Louisa Bustill, was a teacher whose father, Cyrus Bustill, helped to found the Free African Society.

Paul Robeson won a scholarship to Rutgers University and was valedictorian of his graduating class at Rutgers, where he also became an All-American football player. He was conversant in twenty languages.

He graduated from Columbia University Law School in the same class as United States Supreme Court justice William O. Douglas. When he was a member of a prestigious New York law firm, a secretary refused to take dictation from him because of his race. He quit the legal profession and achieved fame in the performing arts. His record-breaking performance of *Othello* in a Broadway production figured prominently in his being awarded the Spingarn Medal by the National Association for the Advancement of Colored People in 1945.

FBI director J. Edgar Hoover branded Robeson a Communist because of his outspokenness about racism in America and his admitted sympathies for prerevolutionary Russian serfs. In the wake of these actions, the McCarthy-led House Un-American Activities Committee also branded him as Communist.

I was unable to sleep for much of the night after Robeson's concert, thinking about his accomplishments against a backdrop of blatant racism in America: discrimination in education, housing, employment, health facilities, and the justice system. He was born April 9, 1898, exactly twenty-nine years before the day of my birth.

I have never deified a mortal being, but I have been close to it in my level of admiration of Paul Robeson. He died in Philadelphia, Pennsylvania, on January 23, 1976, following hospitalization in East Germany and an extended illness complicated by depression.

[16]

Joe Himes: God Sent Me His Way

I WAS IN awe of Joe Himes even before I learned about his credentials. It started when he gave the course overview and checked the class attendance from names he had written in Braille.

Joseph Sandy Himes was in his first year of teaching at North Carolina College in 1947 when I enrolled in his Principles of Sociology class. From the first day of class, I wished that I had known about sociology when I selected my college major. I took solace in realizing that my discovery in the first quarter of my junior year in college was better late than never.

Joe Himes had been blinded in an explosion caused by a chemistry demonstration at his high school in Pine Bluff, Arkansas. When the accident happened, young Himes was rushed to a Whites-only hospital, where he was refused admittance and told to go to a hospital for Blacks. The following week, his mother took him to Barnes Hospital in St. Louis, Missouri. His sight was never restored. Later, in 1923, his family moved to Cleveland, Ohio, where Joe attended East High School.

Joe's mother read his textbooks and other materials to him. He graduated in 1927 with the highest grade-point average in the school's history. In 1931, he graduated magna cum laude from Oberlin College, where he was inducted into the Phi Beta Kappa honor society. The following year, he received the Master of Arts degree from Oberlin. In 1938, he received the PH.D. from The Ohio State University.

Joe's wife, Estelle, also graduated from Cleveland's East High School, and she received baccalaureate and master's degrees from The Ohio State University. She taught foreign languages at high schools in Ohio and at North Carolina College.

Estelle was a role model in her own right. She was a pillar of strength as her husband achieved one milestone after another in teaching, research, and professional service.

I would probably write about Joe Himes under other circumstances, but in this instance, I salute him for being a major influence in my life at the very time when I became committed to serious study and scholarship. My story is like those of millions of men and women whose lives were somehow transformed from aimlessness to purposefulness while in military service.

In addition to the Principles course, I took three other courses Himes taught during my remaining undergraduate years: Social Psychology, Marriage and the Family, and Cultural Anthropology.

I was gratified to serve, albeit unofficially, as a student assistant to my mentor. Supplementary reading materials were rarely available in Braille when he needed them, and I read much of the material to him in a college library carrel. But my greatest satisfaction was in the appreciation he seemed to have for my comments on his writing.

Himes was deferential toward students who were veterans of military service. It was all the better, he later told me, when the veterans were critical and had analytical skills. In later years, when we were friends, Joe told me that he enjoyed the classes he taught immediately after the end of World War II more than at any other time. I took no small measure of pride in being a military veteran and one of his postwar students.

Joe's honors and awards included the Centennial Achievement Award and the honorary Doctor of Science degree from The Ohio State University in 1970. His books included *Racial Conflict in American Society* (1973) and *Conflict and Conflict Management* (1980).

When he resigned from North Carolina College in 1969 to accept the Excellence Foundation Professor of Sociology chair at the University of North Carolina in Greensboro, I was as happy for him as I was sad for the historically Black North Carolina College at Durham.

I MET Joe Himes's brother, Chester, when he visited Joe in Durham in 1951. Having read some of Chester's writings, which were typically filled with rage over racism in America, I expected to see fire in his eyes and hear anger in his speech. Neither was present in his countenance.

Chester Himes was a student at The Ohio State University until he was expelled for what I understand was a prank that resulted in his introduction to the underworld. In 1929, when he was nineteen, Chester was sentenced to twenty-five years in the Ohio State Penitentiary for armed robbery. During this incarceration, a prison fire killed 300 inmates. These grim events stirred Chester Himes to buy a typewriter and write stories while he was in prison that appeared in *Esquire* and other American magazines.

Chester was paroled after eight years. He worked at odd jobs, joined the Works Progress Administration, and eventually joined the Ohio Writers' Project. In his first novel, *If He Hollers, Let Him Go* (1945), Chester described the humiliation of a Black employee in a racist defense plant during World War II. He portrayed prison life in *Cast the First Stone* (1952) and family life in *The Third Generation* (1954).

Joseph S. Himes. *(Courtesy of James E. Shepard Memorial Library University Archives and Records, North Carolina Central University, Durham, North Carolina)*

Largely ignored for his literary talent in the United States, Chester moved to Europe in the mid-1950s. In Paris he joined fellow Black expatriates Richard Wright and James Baldwin.

When *If He Hollers, Let Him Go* was translated into French, Chester's career took a swing upward. In general, his works were well-received by his literary peers in France but did not bring him financial security. Nor did his nine detective novels, set in New York's Harlem, although they had international acclaim.

Chester published two autobiographies, *The Quality of Hurt* (1972) and *My Life as Absurdity* (1976). Samuel Goldwyn Jr., filmed two of his novels, *Cotton Comes to Harlem* (1970) and *Come Back Charleston Blue* (1974). These films gave him the financial security he had not known before.

In 2009 Dr. Carlton Wilson, chairman of the history department at NCCU told me that the department's records show that the university's chapter of Pi Gamma Mu Honor Society in the Social Sciences was chartered in 1954. I remember that in spring of 1952 when I was teaching at Bennett College and Joe Himes was chairman of the department of sociology at the North Carolina College at Durham, I attended what was to be the inaugural meeting for establishing the chapter. My attendance was at Joseph Himes's invitation. Dr. Wilson allows that it is not unusual for chapters to become established in one year and chartered in a later year. During my tenure and my emeritus status at the university, I have been honored by the chapter, particularly by its advisers Dr. Wilson and Dr. Lydia Lindsey, NCCU Associate Professor of History, and by their professorial colleagues Freddie Parker, Sylvia Jacobs, Beverly W. Jones, Percy Murray and Jerry Gershenhorn.

Joe and Estelle honored our family by becoming godparents to our middle daughter, Jacqueline, in the early 1960s.

Joseph Sandy Himes died in Greensboro, North Carolina, on September 4, 1992. Estelle Himes died in Greensboro on November 7, 1995. Chester Bomar Himes died November 12, 1984, in Moraira, Spain.

[17]

Henry Bayne Threw a Life Preserver

HENRY BAYNE and I kept in touch through occasional correspondence after I was discharged from the army. I graduated from North Carolina College at Durham in 1948. He would graduate from Brooklyn College a year later. My college sweetheart, Ozie Foster of Hartford, Connecticut, was also my classmate, and we had begun to talk about a future together. Her immediate plans were to return to Hartford, where she would live at home while seeking employment. I was exuberant about going to New York City, fortified with a letter of introduction from my college adviser and professor of sociology, Dr. Joseph Himes, to Lester Granger, executive director of the New York Urban League.

"Dear Lester," Himes' letter began, followed by complimentary statements about me as his student. He asked Granger as a "very special favor" to appoint me as a "beginning social worker" with the Urban League. I delivered the letter personally to Granger, who earlier had been one of Himes' cohorts in social work. The only question in my mind was how soon I would begin work after the interview with "Dear Lester." Icing on my cake was a telegram from Henry Bayne stating that his father would permit me to stay with them until I could make other arrangements to my satisfaction. A rosy picture, indeed.

Pain came in staccato succession. When I talked with Granger, he informed me that the minimum degree requirement for a beginning social work position in New York State had been changed to the master's degree in social work. It would take two years to earn the degree, one year of classroom work plus a year of internship. Granger said that his son had also hoped to gain employment as a social worker but didn't qualify because he only had a baccalaureate degree. He was gracious enough when he asked that I give his regards to "Joe" along with his "profound regret" that he was unable to honor my adviser's request.

Where would I turn? My journey to New York was not intended as a field trip. I had announced to the whole world—the world being family and friends in Durham, North Carolina—that I was going to be a social worker in New York City. I couldn't be a prodigal son. Like hundreds of African Americans who attended schools in the South, I had decided to seek my fortune up north. I was devastated.

One thing panned out, a room at the apartment of Henry Bayne Sr. and Jr. at 216 Bradhurst Avenue, in uptown Manhattan (Harlem). It was three blocks from the famed Polo Grounds, home of the New York Giants' National League baseball franchise. Bayne's parents were divorced, and Mrs. Bayne lived in the uptown area of Harlem. Bayne's father was an avowed Marxist who saw to it that I had a copy of the *Daily Worker* newspaper for my reading every day. This was a newspaper established by the American Communist Party in 1924 to reflect party views. Its publication was discontinued in 1957.

In the course of my stay on Bradhurst, I went several times with Bayne Jr. to visit his mother, the former Muriel Undine Walke, of Barbados, West Indies, a woman of striking elegance. I observed that Bayne's relationship with his father was one of respect but not of affection. His love for his mother was unbounded.

When the lead with the Urban League turned out to be a bust, young Bayne used his enterprising skills to help me get a job as a clerk with the Federal Reserve Bank of New York. I remained with the Bank for six months, until February 1949, when I enrolled in the School of Education at New York University. Ozie and I married the following September.

Henry Bayne's bachelor's and master's degrees are noted here mainly because they are benchmarks in his career as a biologist, first with the New York City Health Department and later with the United States Department of Agriculture in Albany, California. It was his collateral interest in theology that intrigued me. He commenced studies leading to ordination as a deacon in 1963 and as a priest in 1968. His education included courses in Spirituality, Old and New Testament Greek, The Prophets, Systematic Theology, and Story Theology. One of the last entries I have on his record is his position as associate rector of St. Mark's Church in Berkeley, California. An entry of particular interest is that he became proficient in the use of sign language and served in a ministry to the deaf at the Mission Church of the Holy Spirit in Berkley. Henry Godwin Bayne, Jr., died in Oakland, California in 2004. He is survived by his wife, Gloria, and three children.

Bayne's mother was a victim of Alzheimer's disease. She died in 1990. When my wife, Ozie, became victimized with Alzheimer's disease, my correspondence with Bayne through letters—e-mail and snail mail—and occasional telephone calls helped me gain strength as I coped with problems I could never have envisaged when I met him less than two months before my nineteenth birthday. I am persuaded that chronological age is not a requisite for effectiveness as a counselor. Henry Bayne proved it many times over.

18

Introducing Ozie Dowdell Foster

PRONOUNCE HER name correctly, please. The accent is on the long "Ō" as in ō'pen or cō'zy; not a short "Ŏ" sound as in "saw" or "all" or as in Ozzie and Harriet Nelson, who starred in the ABC sitcom that aired from the fall of 1952 to September 1966. Her name is pronounced Ō'zie.

Ozie Dowdell Foster was born in Americus, Georgia, and she lived with an aunt in St. Petersburg, Florida, for a substantial part of her childhood. Her most vivid memory of Florida was that Blacks were prohibited from sitting on mall benches in downtown St. Petersburg. Her mother left the South as part of the exodus of African Americans for jobs in northern cities in the late 1930s and early 1940s. When Ozie finished elementary school, she joined her mother in Hartford, Connecticut.

She graduated from Hartford's Weaver High School and enrolled in North Carolina College for Negroes, located in Durham, North Carolina. An uncommon reversal of fate in those years was that Blacks who graduated from high schools in the north frequently attended historically Black colleges in the South. The presence of relatives in Durham—Kennedys and Frasiers—was an incentive for Ozie to attend college in that city and for her mother to send her only child there.

In college, I was introduced to Ozie by Clarence Pittman, who was dating Johnnie Mae Taylor, a senior from Henderson, North Carolina, and one of Ozie's best friends. She was an attractive, soft-brown-toned coed with a slightly long neckline that made her slender, shapely body appear taller than her five-foot-seven height. I sensed right off that there was something special about Ozie Foster. Her countenance was suggestive of an inner peace.

I would later learn that her tastes were fashionable—neither faddish

Ozie Foster and Walter Brown, college seniors. *(Brown family papers)*

nor extravagant. A business education major, she was bright and well-spoken, with a pleasant manner. I well remember how she walked gracefully with upright carriage on "the sloping hills and verdant green" of our college campus.

On a lazy early fall day in 1947, Ozie and I walked to the Senior Bowl, a pocket between the old law school and the biology building, then to a bench just outside the Senior Women's Dormitory. When we arrived at the dorm, I reluctantly told Ozie that I could stay but a brief time because of my part-time job with photographer Carlin Graham. We had a wedding to cover. She said it was all right because she could go to her room and listen to *The Harvest of Stars*. The International Harvester Company sponsored this musical variety program on NBC Radio from 1945 to 1950. It featured a twenty-member choir and Metropolitan Opera star James Melton. Little did Ozie Foster know that when she told me she was going to her room to listen to a radio musical program on a lovely autumn afternoon, she left her mark on me for all time. I felt that this was an indicator that Ozie was different from other girls I had known. This resonated with me and became a trait by which I would determine the quality of future relationships.

Getting to know each other as late as our senior year in college evoked mutual ambivalence. On one hand, there was ever-increasing anticipation of graduation, seemingly days away. But there was also the awareness that we would be compelled to go separate ways after singing, "And from the path we'll never stray, our dear Alma Mater, NCC." Our decision was virtually instantaneous; it had to be. She would go home to Hartford, get a job, and be in touch, frequently. I would go to New York, get a job, and keep in touch as we contemplated longer-term aspirations, aided systematically by the U.S. Postal Service and the New York–New Haven Railroad. A permanent relationship was in our crystal ball.

19

Relatives Unbeknownst to Me

A MONTH OR so before we married, Ozie gave me a black piggy bank, about six inches tall, with the initials *OFB* and *WMB* painted on its back, and a pink snout and long eyelashes. On September 18, 1949, we repeated wedding vows, officiated by Rev. John C. Jackson in Hartford's Union Baptist Church. We left for New York City's Harlem soon after the ceremony and reception. I had reserved a room from a landlady who had rented the same room, in the same apartment, to two other young couples from Durham who had preceded us: Arthur and Mary Cole Goins, and Peter and Edith Scarborough Stanford. It was our first home, and it turned out to be a memorable one.

On the day after our wedding, I applied to the Veterans Administration in New York City for a change in dependency status from single to married with one dependent (my wife). In the preceding February, I had enrolled in the master's degree program in the School of Education at New York University (NYU).

As a veteran of World War II, I qualified for fourteen months of education benefits under the Servicemen's Readjustment Act of 1944, better known as the G.I. Bill of Rights. The time allotment for education benefits under the G.I. Bill was a period equal to the amount of time spent in military service. I would have been foolish to use my education and monthly subsistence entitlements for an undergraduate degree. Immediately after my discharge, I lived at home while continuing my education, and I had a pretty good part-time job, so I opted to postpone my entitlements, with confidence that I would attend graduate school some place other than North Carolina.

The G.I. Bill provided students a subsistence allowance of $50 a month for single veterans and $75 a month for married veterans. According to the Consumer Price Index, the 2009 equivalents of $50 and $75 were $458 and $688 respectively.

Had I received the increase in my subsistence check in October 1949, I would have considered it a miracle. But I was disappointed when I didn't receive a check at all. Ozie and I could hardly have had a more spartan lifestyle. We were renting a room in a Harlem apartment, did not own or rent a car, and winked at the rules of good nutrition in our daily bread. A fond recollection, however, is the visit by Ozie's cousin, Matthew Kennedy, who played the landlady's piano for our enjoyment. Matthew, then director of the famed Fisk Jubilee Singers, was studying at Juilliard on leave from his faculty position at Fisk University.

Mr. and Mrs. Walter M. Brown, newly-weds. September 1949. *(Brown family papers)*

No check came in November. I began to wonder if my pact with Ozie that I would not seek employment until I finished my studies made sense under the circumstances. Fortunately, the government had already paid my tuition for the semester. The problem was that no money was coming in for our subsistence.

No check came in December. Our savings were drying up. I got an advance from my folks. Ozie and I went to North Carolina for the Christmas holidays.

The midwinter change was pleasurable—Mama's cooking, introducing Ozie to my family and friends in Durham, Christmas service at West Durham Baptist Church, dances at the Algonquin Club and Hill Recreation Center, and house parties. My brother, Will, blessed us by making the loan for our trip a wedding present. Still, our pleasures were tempered by the nagging question of whether there would be a subsistence check—with retroactive pay—waiting for us when we returned to New York.

When we arrived at our apartment and surveyed the accumulated mail, we saw that our landlady had placed the letter from the Veterans Administration at the top of the stack. It was in a white, official envelope, not a brown one with a window: *Dear Walter Matthew Brown: Your wife and three children have filed a complaint with this office indicating that you have been receiving payments as a veteran with dependents but have not been providing for their support. You will receive no further payments until this matter is cleared. If you wish to contest this decision, you should report to the St. Nicholas Welfare Office, 133 W. 125th Street, New York, N.Y.*

I had read somewhere that an essential requisite of humor is time. It would take a lot of time to see humor in this episode.

The two people ahead of me at the welfare office must have arrived before dawn. When number *three* was called, I moved promptly to the receptionist's counter, forced a smile, and gave the receptionist my number. She asked how she could help me. I handed her my letter from the Veterans Administration and said I was there because a mistake had been made in sending that letter to me. She skimmed the letter, then turned and took it to an intake clerk. I saw the intake clerk scowl as she read the letter. She said something to the receptionist who turned and walked back to her counter—and me.

"You can go over there," she said, pointing to the intake clerk's desk.

When I reached the clerk, she gestured to the chair next to her desk without looking at it, or me. I sat, hoping for civility if not an indication of genuine interest.

"You Walter Matthew Brown?" she asked, expressionless.

"Yes."

"You a veteran?"

"Yes."

"Married?"

"Yes."

"You know why your wife says you not supporting her and your children?"

I was at the mercy of a huge woman with a lifeless demeanor. I noticed the name plate on her desk. "Miss DeWitt, I'm sure that in this instance someone has made a mistake," I said.

"What do you mean, mistake?" she asked.

I said the letter gave me a wife and three children, but I had been married only four months and didn't have any children.

She spoke with a hand on her hip and sounded off loud enough for everybody within earshot to hear. I sensed that was her intent. "Well, mister, all I know is the government says you got a wife and three children and you ain't doing nothing for them. Dudes like you come here every day. *Looking* all innocent! And *talking* all innocent!"

The gods were with me. A woman in her late forties or early fifties stepped from an office, walked to the intake clerk's desk, and spoke a cordial "Good morning." In a barely audible tone to Miss DeWitt, she asked, "Would you mind if I talk with Mr. Brown?"

She introduced herself as Marilyn Everett. Her handshake was firm as she invited me to sit. "I pulled your file before I came over to speak to you and Miss DeWitt," she said. Her brown eyes in deep wells accentuated a gracious manner. "I overheard a part of your conversation with Miss DeWitt," Miss Everett said. It was hardly a conversation, I thought but didn't say.

"Do you have my file?" I asked.

"I *have* your file, Mr. Brown. Now, let's start at the same point that Miss DeWitt started. Your name *is* Walter Matthew Brown. Right?"

I nodded as I replied, "Right."

"From Newark?" There was a studied pause. "Yes, Newark," she said. "Newark, New Jersey, Mr. Brown."

I told Miss Everett that I was from Durham, North Carolina, and that I had been to Newark one time in my life. She cut me off.

"You *are* a veteran, Mr. Brown?"

"Yes, I was in the army."

"What is your army serial number?"

I didn't have to check a document or wallet card: "44161665."

Marilyn Everett's countenance signaled what she was to express in words. She apologetically told me that the Veterans Administration had my records mixed up with somebody else's, a Walter Matthew Brown who lived or used to live in Newark, New Jersey. She said that I would need to clear this up with the VA downtown, politely adding that she hoped it could be done with as little inconvenience to me as possible.

She stood and said she guessed she could apologize for the system. We shook hands again. "At least I've cleared one hurdle," I said. I thanked her and left her office on my way to the Veterans Administration in lower Manhattan.

When I told the clerk why I had come to the VA, he smiled quizzically and shrugged his shoulders, but he agreed to see if they had files for more than one Walter Matthew Brown.

Ten minutes later—a short time for the precomputer age—he returned with two folders. In seconds, the records in one folder were identified as mine. There was another appropriate apology, this time on behalf of the Veterans Administration. My request for a dependency status adjustment would be processed "straight away," he said. He would walk it through himself. My spirits were uplifted when he said as I was leaving, "I wish for you and your new bride the very best."

The A Train to uptown Manhattan (Harlem), always fast, this time was not fast enough. I tried to read the same *New York Times* that I had purchased before I went to the welfare office. Words blurred as I rejoiced in anticipation of having a honeymoon of two or three days. The honeymoon began when Ozie saw my smile as I opened the door.

The subsistence check came the first week in February 1950—retroactive to September 1949. With our largesse of $375, we were rich!

The sign in the window at Carl's Market on Amsterdam Avenue read "Hamburger, 15 cents a pound. Pure Hamburger, 25 cents a pound." We bought some pure hamburger. We took a commercial tour to see New York City. We saw *Death of a Salesman* at the Morosco Theatre on Broadway, after which we had dinner at Longchamps.

We picked up the tab when our friends Jethro and Daisy Hooper went with us to the Baby Grand nightclub on 125th Street. It was a way of thanking them for good times at their impromptu Friday-night parties. I bought Ozie two classical music albums, a dress, a coat, shoes, and lingerie. She modeled the lingerie for me hours before putting on the rest of her clothes. Our honeymoon was still on. We made a monetary contribution to the Youth Outreach Project at St. Mark African Methodist Episcopal Church. Then we pondered the future that would commence in two weeks, upon the completion of my master's degree requirements at NYU.

I gave the effective date of my new address to the NYU Records Office. My diploma would be mailed three weeks later. By that time, Ozie and I would be further pursuing our destiny, this time in North Carolina.

20

Meet a Hero: Howard Roy

WHEN I applied for a faculty position at Bennett College in the summer of 1950, I gave Professor Howard Roy's name as a reference. He had taught me a year earlier at New York University (NYU), when I took two courses under him in Interpretation and Use of Tests in Guidance. During my interview at Bennett, Dean Willa Player said that Dr. Roy had recommended me highly. I was gratified.

In the fall of 1966, I attended my first rehearsal as a member of the Chancel Choir of Woodside United Methodist Church in Silver Spring, Maryland. The director introduced me to the choir as a whole, but there were no introductions to individual choir members. By the time I got home, one face in the tenor section was continually coming to the fore. I swore that I had seen the face before. Where? Whatever the occasion or circumstance, it had been one of gratification. But it had not been a recent occurrence. To whom did the face belong?

In addition to the Wednesday-evening rehearsals, Woodside's choir rehearsed on Sunday mornings at ten thirty, a fine-tuning for the eleven o'clock service. On the Sunday following my first rehearsal, I heard someone give the face a name: "Howard." Most of his hair had gone and there were lines from his cheeks to his chin. His face was still kind, and his five-foot-seven physique was still slight.

I asked Howard his last name. When he identified himself, I gave my name and said I was one of his students at NYU in 1949. The rehearsal was momentarily disrupted by two tenors in unrestrained jubilation.

Sometime between my attendance at NYU and the move of my family to suburban Maryland in 1965, Howard Roy and his family had moved to the same area. Howard was then on the faculty of Gallaudet College, a private, coeducational college for the deaf in Washington, D.C.

My family's friendship with Howard, his wife, Ethel, and their daughter, Karen, blossomed for the entirety of our stay in the Metro D.C. area. When Ozie and I celebrated our twenty-fifth wedding anniversary with a reception at Woodside Church, Howard saluted us and, of all things, read the grades of A for me from his NYU roll book.

Our friendship continued after my family and I moved back to North Carolina in 1980. A December 1995 letter from Ethel told of an episode the previous summer when Howard had "wandered from home and was lost for twenty-six hours before he was found with the assistance of a massive police search including dogs, a helicopter, and bulletins on television." When I talked with Ethel after the Christmas holidays, she said that Howard was attending an adult day-care center two days a week and was "very oriented to family but confused."

In February 2001, Howard Roy died of complications from Alzheimer's disease. This time, the letter was from Karen, who indicated that her father "was resigned to this eventuality from the beginning. He was gracious and gentle to the end," she said. She also said her mother's health was failing.

Writing this vignette was not difficult. Closing it was. Howard Roy helped to put me on a springboard of opportunity four months after my twenty-third birthday. Hallowed be his name.

To me, Dr. Walter Brown walked on water. Hallowed be his name.

21

Woody and Howard to the Rescue

I T WAS the middle of June 1951. The school year had ended two weeks
prior. I called Woodrow Edmonds at the waiters' quarters for the Martha Washington Hotel in Virginia Beach, Virginia, where he was working
for the summer. His wife, Vivian, who remained home in Durham, North
Carolina, unhesitatingly gave me his number when I phoned in despera-
tion, wanting to know Woody's whereabouts.

When I reached Woody on the phone, he expressed surprise and asked,
"How are things with the professor?"

"Not the best right now," I said. "S'matter of fact, I'm on my ass, and
I'm calling to ask for your help."

Woody said he'd help any way he could.

"Will you help me get a job at the beach for the summer?" I asked.

He said he'd see what he could do, and he asked if Vivian had told me
that Howard Fitts was also at the beach. She had. Woody called Howard
to the phone.

Howard came on and greeted me, laughing, as he said that Woody had
told him that I finally wanted to work for a living. He then asked how
much experience I had as a waiter.

"None. Zero," I responded and said I was willing to learn if he and
Woody were willing to teach me. I wasn't laughing.

Howard asked that I hold for a moment. I overheard conversation and
laughter.

Howard assured me that he and Woody would "work something out,"
and he asked when I wanted to come.

"Right away, tomorrow," I said with buoyed spirits.

Elation turned to indignation as I realized that my trip to Virginia

Woodrow "Woody" Edmonds. *(Courtesy of Kenneth Edmonds)*

would be as a passenger in the back of a bus. I didn't own a car, and the civil-rights revolution was a decade away.

The next day, during much of the six-hour bus ride, I relived my first year as a member of the faculty of Bennett College, a small liberal arts college for African American women in Greensboro, North Carolina. In 1951 it had a faculty of fifty and a student enrollment of 450. The college is affiliated with the United Methodist Church and has long been acclaimed for high academic standards and for developing cultural refinement in its students. The campus was postcard pretty, with colonial architecture and manicured lawns.

For the most part, I enjoyed the year at Bennett. I taught professional education courses, chaired the standing Committee on Testing and Evaluation, recruited students at selected Negro (the term in 1951) schools, and served on God only knows the number of other committees. I had worked for nine months—two semesters—on a twelve-month contract. My wife, Ozie, was also employed at Bennett within a week after our arrival in Greensboro. Her job as an administrative assistant in the college business office started before classes began. She worked until the following May, when she took maternity leave. By that time, I had become disenchanted with the college's president, David Dallas Jones.

I generally smile to myself when I recall a conversation that Charles Ray told me he'd had with W. Edward Farrison. Both were faculty members at North Carolina College at Durham (NCC).

"Walter Brown is going to teach at Bennett," Ray had told Farrison, who had taught at Bennett himself.

Farrison, well known in NCC circles—and many other circles—as a caustic wit, asked, "When is he going?"

"In September," Ray said.

"He will leave in October," Farrison jocularly replied.

Iᴛ ᴡᴀs ᴀʟᴍᴏsᴛ in disbelief that I learned that I would not get a vacation during my first year at Bennett. I assumed, naively perhaps, that a vacation entitlement was automatic. This vignette was written nearly fifty years after my time of employment at Bennett College. I was twenty-three years old when I began working at Bennett. At that time master's degrees were highly regarded, nearly as much as doctoral degrees are in 2010. Not only did I have a master's degree, but I was a military veteran, had lived in New York, dressed smartly, and had a modicum of courtliness. Add to this a trace of impetuosity, and it should not be difficult to appreciate how I comported myself in an environment that went against the grain of my temperament.

By the end of the second semester, I decided that I wanted to have my summers free. I could attend summer school each year to make my credentials more marketable. I asked for a change to a nine-month contract. In my letter to the president, however, I said a nine-month contract would enable me to better prepare myself for long-term service to the college. Two days after the letter was delivered to his office, Dr. Jones' secretary called to say the president wanted to see me. I made an appointment.

Pʀᴇsɪᴅᴇɴᴛ ᴅᴀᴠɪs ᴅᴀʟʟᴀs ᴊᴏɴᴇs, an African American of light brown complexion, was in his late sixties. He was dressed in a business suit whenever I saw him, and that was often. I never even imagined seeing him in casual clothes. He appeared to be in good physical condition, not tall, maybe five feet seven. He was stooped slightly at the shoulders and typically seemed to be in deep thought. His silver hair was parted at the side and pulled across the top to cover the bald spot where, one would surmise, there was once a full growth of hair.

He smiled faintly as we shook hands. Said he was glad to see me and invited me to sit down. I thanked "Mr. President."

The president's bearing abruptly became stern as he said he was going to talk to me as he would his own son. "We had high hopes for you when you came here," he said. "You were highly recommended and quite impressive in the interview. But now we have come to believe that you're not happy here."

"How so, Mr. President?"

"For one thing, you had hardly arrived on campus when you began to question some of our long-standing practices."

I waited a moment to see if he would be more specific. He wasn't. I surmised that he was referring to the time I asked for reimbursement of expenses after representing the college for three days at the 1951 spring conference of the North Carolina Teachers' Association in Raleigh.

The president was quick to tell me that Dr. Chauncey Winston, chairman of Bennett's Social Sciences division, had represented the college at that conference for years, and he never asked to be reimbursed for expenses.

I replied that I was not told the college would not reimburse me for my expenses and that Dr. Winston has been teaching for nearly forty years and—President Jones interrupted. He seemed agitated as he said, "Lo and behold, you even questioned our faculty evaluation measures."

"I questioned one criterion, Mr. President. I just said 'not in harmony with the philosophy of the college' is too nebulous to be used as a measure of a faculty member's effectiveness."

There was a perceptible pause. I sensed the president was even more agitated when he said, "Suppose we agree, Mr. Brown, that next year will be your last year here."

"Yes, sir," I replied.

"Better still," he parried, "suppose you take the summer off and come back in September."

"Yes, sir, Mr. President." Nothing more was said. The president stood. I followed suit. We shook hands. I thanked him, and left his office.

President Jones did not mention my service on a committee to which he had appointed me in the fall of 1950. The committee was to conduct a study titled "Factors Associated with Satisfaction and Dissatisfaction Among Members of the Bennett College Faculty." I was the only first-year faculty member on the team. At twenty-three, I was the youngest both in chronological age and in years at the college. We were to construct the survey instrument, i.e., develop the questions to be used by the team in conducting interviews of the faculty, analyze the responses, and write a report of our findings and recommendations.

One of the team's first tasks was to develop criteria for determining the validity of responses to the survey questions by each faculty member. The work session was going well, I thought, until the committee chairperson announced that President Jones wanted the team to use "not in harmony with the philosophy of the college" as an evaluation criterion.

I asked, "What is that supposed to mean?" I didn't get an intelligible answer. Later I realized that this criterion would be used to eliminate critical responses, with one exception: complaints about low salaries.

When I interviewed another faculty member in the social sciences, he warned that I was wasting time being involved in the study. "It's an act of chicanery by a despotic administrator," he said. "I don't know where I'll be next year, but I can assure you, I won't be here." I didn't argue with him. But neither did I forget what he said.

The outcome of our efforts was a glowing report that members of the faculty of Bennett College were highly satisfied in all areas except faculty salaries. Being members of a racially integrated faculty ranked highest on the list of satisfying factors. Other positive factors were the quality of students, Bennett's standing among colleges in the region, the beauty of the campus, and relationships with traditionally White colleges in Greensboro—principally Greensboro College, Guilford College, and, to a lesser extent, Women's College (now the University of North Carolina at Greensboro). I agreed with the findings on faculty satisfaction. I also agreed with some responses associated with faculty dissatisfaction, but these were dismissed as responses not in harmony with the philosophy of the college.

The report ended with a recommendation that faculty salaries be made more competitive with those of other private, four-year institutions, which was exactly what the president wanted. He used the report as an agenda item at the next meeting of the college trustees. He also used it as a support document in his appeals for financial contributions by philanthropic foundations. I regarded the whole thing as a leadership style characterized in part by sophistry and artistry.

Yet there was another matter equally disturbing to me. Four persons on the Bennett faculty were scholars who had come to America as refugees. They were among the wave of Jewish intellectuals who had fled the tyranny of Nazi Germany in the early and mid-1940s. President Jones was widely known for intimidating faculty members, whether in groups or as individuals, and the refugee scholars appeared to get the brunt of Jones's intimidation more than other faculty. He attempted to control faculty by threats to fire them if they complained about or questioned anything related to their work—teaching loads, inadequate instructional supplies and materials, attendance at vespers services, or salaries. Career opportunities were limited at best for Black professionals. But the mindset of refugee scholars was that their fate—in the short term *and* the long term

—was in Jones's hands. Jones knew this, and he used his position to be a puppeteer.

In February 2001, PBS aired a documentary on refugee scholars. Titled *From Swastika to Jim Crow*, the film showed that the scholars were respected by their peers and well-liked by their students. There were, however, numerous instances in which they faced hostility from citizens of the towns where they lived.

Many refugees were hired as professors in Black colleges, among them Howard University, Hampton Institute (now Hampton University), Morehouse College, Spelman College, Tougaloo College, Talladega College, and North Carolina College for Negroes (now NCCU). Their academic qualifications were coveted because of the importance of their credentials in helping an institution gain and maintain accreditation by state, regional, and national accrediting bodies.

In only a few instances were refugee scholars hired to teach in America's White or traditionally White colleges. Albert Einstein, who first visited Princeton in 1921 to deliver five Stafford Little lectures and to accept an honorary degree, was probably the best example of those who sought academic refuge at America's universities and colleges from the turmoil and persecution in Europe during the social unrest at that time.

One scholar featured in *From Swastika to Jim Crow* was Ernst Manasse, professor of German, Latin, and philosophy at NCC. James Edward Shepard, founder and first president of NCC, recruited Manasse. At NCC, I studied German under professor Manasse for two semesters in 1944 and 1945. His wife, Marianne, was an accomplished painter. I remember them as gentle and encouraging teachers.

BENNETT COLLEGE ALUMNAE who were students during David Jones's presidency well remember his performances at Sunday afternoon vespers services. More often than not, the sermons or speeches were by invited speakers, usually preachers. To me and to my closest faculty friends, Jones's patented performances immediately following the sermons were showy and entertaining.

The organist played softly for about fifteen seconds before Jones moved from his seat in the pulpit to the rostrum. He leaned on the rostrum, looked around, and spoke in somber tones as the music continued. "Beloved," he began, "now are we the sons of God [pause, music swells], and it doth not yet appear [pauses, removes eyeglasses, holds them in his hand] what we shall be: but we know that when He shall appear [takes out handkerchief, sniffles, another music swell], we shall be like Him; for we shall see Him as He is. [A longer pause.] And every man that hath this hope in him purifieth himself, even as He is pure. The Lord hath been [pause, heavy breathing] *mindful* of us. [A big music swell.] He will bless us." The president sat. The college choir sang. (Despite the fact that Bennett is a women's college, there were no substitutions of inclusive language for female gender.)

"I don't have a job for the summer," I told Ozie when I got to our apartment after my appointment with President Jones.

"We'll make it," she said. I fell in love with her again.

She listened, half infuriated, half amused as I spoke mockingly. "I wouldn't give that bastard the pleasure of making me grovel. I know he wanted me to break down and say, 'Please, President Jones, I won't have any income if I don't work this summer. And you know Mrs. Brown is pregnant.'"

In minutes, Ozie and I decided that she would spend the summer with her parents in Hartford, Connecticut. That would make it easier for me to fend for myself during the summer—plans A *and* B.

After six o'clock, when long distance rates were lower, Ozie called her mother and stepfather. "Nothing would make me happier than for my child to spend the summer with me while she is expecting my first grandchild," her mother said.

The next morning, Ozie took a flight from Greensboro's Triad Airport to Bradley Field in Hartford. A day later, I was on a bus to Virginia Beach.

The bus arrived in Virginia Beach shortly after seven in the evening, when Woody and Howard were serving dinner at the Martha Washington. Howard was driving when they came to the bus station a little before nine.

Our greetings were reminiscent of a small gathering at a college reunion. The celebration was held at Edna's Place, a small nightclub in the Black section of Virginia Beach called Crown Point. Woody told me that some African American workers at the beach went to Crown Point every evening to socialize. We were to visit Crown Point many evenings that summer.

Edna gave us a table away from the heaviest traffic. It shielded us from interruptions by customers who knew Howard and Woody, some from past summers. Woody was a science teacher at P.W. Moore High School in Elizabeth City, North Carolina. Howard was an instructor in health education at North Carolina College at Durham. Woody mentioned our good fortune in having summer jobs at the beach, and in particular at the Martha Washington. Howard and I concurred. We cursed the world that limited our summer job opportunities to jobs as domestics, waiters, or porters. For me, the discussion was reminiscent of poet Frank Marshall Davis's piece about his fictional character, "Giles Johnson, PH.D.," who had four college degrees and a knowledge of Greek and Latin classics but starved to death because he wouldn't teach and couldn't porter.

Woody and Howard had good news: the manager at the Martha Washington had agreed to hire me as a first-time waiter, on the strength of their recommendation. A bed had been found for me in the waiters' quarters. I couldn't find words to convey how much I appreciated what they had done on my behalf. A classic illustration of fellow Eagles coming to my rescue.

As grateful as I was for kindnesses that evening, I was overjoyed the next morning when Woody brought breakfast to my room on a big aluminum tray. I was to practice carrying the tray after eating and before going to see Elizabeth, the hostess at the Martha Washington, for briefing and scheduling.

It isn't likely that the Martha Washington has ever hired a waiter as inept as I was. I was in awe of my cohorts as they walked sprightly with laden trays held high on their fingers. Woody and Howard monitored my progress and served as a support team even as they were amused at my clumsiness. But my long suit while I learned to wait tables was a cost-saving practice for the hotel management—folding used but clean linen tablecloths precisely on the seams. Hostess Elizabeth said I reduced the dining room laundering costs by 10 percent.

I have always thought that if the federal government conducted a survey to learn what agency was valued most by consumers, Ozie would cast her vote for the U.S. Postal Service. She liked to receive mail even more than the post office managers did—priority mail or junk mail, so long as it was mail. By summer's end, Ozie was fully aware of what my adventure at Virginia Beach had meant to me: respite from a college president described by one of his own trustees as an artful despot, income greater than I would have earned working at Bennett during the same time, unofficial membership in the society of resort hotel waiters, and a never-to-be-forgotten lesson on the true meaning of friendship by fellow educators who worked as waiters at a beach hotel.

For most Virginia Beach workers, the season ended between mid-August and Labor Day. Howard provided transportation for Woody and me back to North Carolina.

I met Ozie at the airport in Greensboro on a balmy morning in late August. She was visibly pregnant and more beautiful than ever. We agreed that being separated for three months had made the summer seem interminable. I was happy to get reports that she and our expected child were in good health.

My reentry at Bennett was marked by updating course syllabi and participation in the college's faculty fall conference. I told Ozie that I would go about my work as if nothing had ever happened between David Jones and me and that I'd bet anything he would offer me a contract for the third year.

She said she'd stand with me in whatever I decided to do. "I'm not going to worry, and I don't want you to worry," she said. "We'll make out just fine." I thought: How many times can a man fall in love with the same woman!

When Ozie's labor pains started sometime between midnight and dawn on November 24, 1951, I called her obstetrician. Dr. George Evans was a caring African American physician whom everybody loved, and Ozie was certainly no exception. He instructed me to take Ozie to the hospital while he called to arrange for her admission. I am not sure that he even said the name of the hospital. He didn't have to. We were in the American South, and the L. Richardson Memorial Hospital was the hospital for African American patients in Greensboro, North Carolina.

Henry H. Holder, Bennett's chaplain and my best friend, took Ozie and me to the hospital. The Holders and the Browns were inseparable. Hank, as we called him, waited with me until Dr. Evans came out to congratulate me on the arrival of our first child, Judith Denise Brown. No baby was ever prettier than our angel of eight pounds, ten ounces. Hank and his wife Belva honored us by being Judy's godparents. Judy's christening was at Greensboro's St. James Presbyterian Church. (Two additional Brown angels, Jacqueline Dianne and Jennifer Delores, came on November 30, 1960, and May 16, 1965, respectively.)

Ozie's parents and mine were thrilled. Judy was the first grandchild

Howard Fitts. *(Courtesy of Howard Fitts)*

on either side. She was the darling of Bennett's campus. At a school of 450 students, everyone knew of her arrival, and it seemed that all of them were extended family.

I realize that herein I have made frequent references to racial segregation and discrimination. It could not be otherwise. Consider this episode: The advertisements of a Greensboro diaper service announced that the company picked up baby diapers once a week and left fresh ones. I tried to get the service, but couldn't get it. "We don't serve colored," a clerk told me. We swallowed pride and looked forward—as I had done in riding in the back of the bus from Greensboro to Virginia Beach.

Call it rascally if you like, but I could hardly contain myself when, in February 1952, I received a letter from President David D. Jones offering me a contract for a third year. In my reply, I thanked the president and said that the opportunity to teach at Bennett College had been a major milestone in my life. I declined the offer and wished the best for the college and the president.

The following September, I enrolled in the newly established doctoral program at North Carolina College at Durham.

WOODROW W. EDMONDS retired as principal of Grey Culbreth Middle School in Chapel Hill, North Carolina, in 1990. He died in 1992. His widow, Vivian, who died on Sunday, May 11, 2008, a graduate of NCCU, was editor-publisher of the *Carolina Times* newspaper, where their son, Kenneth, is general manager.

Howard Fitts retired in 1987 as professor of health education at NCCU. In February 2002, the Kate B. Reynolds Foundation contributed $25,000 to the endowed scholarship fund at NCCU in Howard's name. Howard had served the foundation as a member of its Charitable Trust Advisory Board since 1996.

In the 1952–1953 academic year, the year after he resigned from Bennett, Henry Holder took premedical courses at North Carolina Agricultural and Technical College (A&T College, now North Carolina A&T State University). In the evening, he worked as a waiter. In 1953–1954, he taught courses in science and mathematics, and he was head basketball coach at the Consolidated High School in Fuquay Springs (now Fuquay Varina), North Carolina. His wife, Belva, who had been his college sweetheart at Johnson C. Smith University, continued to work as an elementary school teacher in Greensboro. In September 1954, the Holders moved to Washington, D.C., where Henry entered medical school at Howard University. They subsequently moved to San Bernardino, California, where Hank was a practicing physician and Belva owned and operated the Mother Goose Nursery School.

[22]

Lead-Off Man in the North Carolina College PH.D. *Program*

WHEN I told Jim Blue that I paid $230 to have a watch renovated, his reply was quick. "Do you know how many Timex watches you can buy for that kind of money?" he asked. It was classic one-upmanship by a dear friend. But when I gave the rationale for my admittedly costly expenditure, Jim said he would have done the same thing.

I was elated when I opened the package and letter from Mrs. Louise Elder sometime in the late 1970s. The package contained a Hamilton pocket watch and a book, *Familiar Quotations,* edited by John Bartlett. The letters *AE* were engraved in bold flourish on the back of the watch. The book's first copyright date is 1882. Christopher Morley was editor of its 1946 version.

Mrs. Elder was librarian at Hillside High School when I was a student there. Her husband, Dr. Alfonso Elder, was the second president of North Carolina College (NCC). "I know Dr. Elder would want you to have these items," she had written in her note that accompanied the watch and book. "The watch was given to him by his parents when he graduated from high school." That was probably in 1916. Dr. Elder entered Atlanta University as a freshman in 1917.

Dr. Elder's first name is often misspelled: Alphonso, Alphonzo, and Alfonzo. I was a senior at NCC when Alfonso Elder was appointed president of the college in February 1948. He coined a phrase, "student self-direction," and appealed to students to make the concept a guiding principle in pursuing their goals. He also coined "Excellence Without Excuse" and proclaimed its significance throughout his tenure as college president. In varying iterations, the phrase has been the clarion call of his successors.

When I worked with Carlin Graham, then photographer for the NCC yearbook, I delivered Dr. Elder's photograph to his home and had a conversation with him and Mrs. Elder. I learned then that a visit with the Elders was an experience in graciousness and good taste.

Alfonso Elder was another academician whom I always called "doctor." He looked the part—a stately African American, taller than average, conservative in dress, with a quiet, gentlemanly demeanor. In his closing remarks to my graduating class of 1948, he invited us to visit the campus often. "And whenever I see you," he said, "I will be sure to ask one question: What are you reading?" That question is what I remember best from my college commencement.

My relationship with Dr. Elder as a colleague in professional education began in 1949, when I was in graduate school at New York University. My general adviser at NYU was Professor Alonzo Myers. In a conference with Professor Myers, I learned that he knew Dr. Elder as an innovative educator whose hallmark was excellence. I beamed with pride and could hardly wait to share the experience with Dr. Elder. While in New York I always communicated with Dr. Elder by letter, and I wrote to him on this occasion to say that I had heartening news. I shared with him the conversation with Professor Myers, and I ended the letter with, "What are you reading?" We raised that question with one another a number of times thereafter. I cannot recall the titles of every book that either of us mentioned. But I have a clear recollection of talking about three books: *Animal Farm* and *Brave New World* by George Orwell, and *Black Hamlet* by Wulf Sachs.

When I visited the Elders in the spring of 1952, Dr. Elder informed me that the North Carolina out-of-state aid program for graduate study in professional education would end in September 1952, at which time a doctoral program at NCC would begin. He suggested that I might want to consider applying for admission to the new program. I promised to let him know as soon as I reached a decision.

I talked with three persons about the possible opportunity to enter the doctoral program at North Carolina College at Durham: my wife, Ozie, my mother, and Henry Holder, who was in the second of his two years as a member of the faculty and college minister at Bennett College in Greensboro, North Carolina.

My mother was understandably subjective. She said that she would love to have my family and me at home in Durham. Holder, my bosom buddy and a graduate of Johnson C. Smith University in Charlotte, North Carolina, and Union Theological Seminary in New York City, couldn't see why

I was even pondering a decision. After all, NCC was the flagship institution of Black colleges in the state. It also had a reputation as one of the state's best colleges, Black or White.

Ozie gave assurance that she would be with me, whatever decision I made. We prayed for guidance. Our prayer was reminiscent of the African American spiritual, "Guide my feet while I run this race, for I don't want to run this race in vain."

Because I was an African American citizen of North Carolina, the state paid the tuition for my graduate study at a school out of the state in the summer of 1952 rather than permitting me to attend the University of North Carolina, located in Chapel Hill, twelve miles from my home in Durham. My experience was not unique. A substantial number of African Americans in North Carolina earned doctoral degrees at universities outside the state when the state's White colleges would not admit them because of discriminatory policies based solely on race.

In the summer of 1952, four of us shared the New York apartment of a family friend of mine who was elsewhere for the summer. Howard Fitts, a health educator at North Carolina College, was in school at Columbia University. Earl Artis, an elementary school principal in Roxboro, North Carolina, was at NYU. So was Richard Jackson, who was an elementary school principal in Culpepper, Virginia.

In 1952 articles and editorials about the new PH.D. program at NCC appeared in several issues of Durham's Black weekly newspaper, the *Carolina Times*. The articles announced the program. The editorials denounced it.

The first article, "North Carolina College to Begin Doctors Program in Field of Education This Fall," is dated August 30, 1952. It pointed out that the program would begin the following September 17th. It was to be the first doctoral program in any of the nation's predominantly Negro colleges. Officials at the University of North Carolina had pledged the "full resources of the university" to help the program at NCC get started, and officials of both institutions said the program would be "of the highest quality."

The second article, dated September 6, 1952, has a composite photograph of the six "Scholars Inaugurating [the] Doctoral Program at NCC" and a brief statement of the qualifications of each: Richard Beard, Rose Butler Browne, James Finney, Arnold King, Joseph Pittman, and W. Carson Ryan.

The headline of the first editorial, dated August 30, 1952 reads, "Sympathy Needed for Negro PH.D. Instructors." It said that the purpose of the program was to keep Negroes out of the University of North Carolina. The editorial also referred to the program as a one-way-street integration policy that "permits white teachers to grab a top ranking job in Negro colleges but bars Negro teachers from jobs in white colleges and universities." It "appears to us to be radically unfair and unjust," the editor said.

Dr. Rose Butler Browne. *(Brown family papers)*

The second editorial, also dated September 6, is headed, "The High Cost of Segregation in Education." It called on NCC president Elder to "confirm or deny" a report that one student was being paid $4200 to enroll, that is, $1800 in salary for his part-time work and $2400 per year for his wife, who would be employed full time on campus. That reference was to Ozie and me.

I have not felt the need to make a case for my decision to take advantage of the opportunities afforded my fellow students and me in NCC's doctoral program any more than I should make a case for attending Lyon Park elementary school, or Hillside High School, or North Carolina College for Negroes with its several name changes. Each was a Black school in the American South. Each was a proverbial card dealt to my peers and me in a racially segregated society. I wish it had been otherwise, but it wasn't. By taking advantage of such opportunities as I had, I met the qualifications for competitive opportunities in numerous racially integrated settings. In a number of these instances, I was the first of my race. I have written about this elsewhere in my memoir.

My major concentration was educational guidance, the same program I was in at NYU. My minor was psychology. As had happened at Bennett College, Ozie began working as an administrative secretary at NCC even before the first semester was under way. My mother kept Judith, our only child at the time, until she entered a preschool center at Durham's St. Joseph's AME Church.

I believe my graduate assistantship served the college as well as it did me. I established the college placement bureau and became its first director. I suppose it could be said that I was upwardly mobile in the positions I had after serving as director of the NCC placement bureau. But no position gave me quite the measure of fulfillment that I gained from helping young people, most of them first-generation college graduates, get their first professional job.

After about a year, Rose Butler Brown was named chair of the NCC Department of Education, succeeding Joseph Pittman. Carol Bowie, a clinical psychologist and educator, directed my studies in psychology. Arnold King, who held a joint professorship and graduate administration responsibilities at the University of North Carolina and North Carolina College at Durham, was my general advisor. My special advisor in educational guidance was Richard Beard. (See vignette 25, "Christmas Letters with Marginal Notes: Richard Beard.")

I took History of American Education under Professor King. (I had taken courses in History of Education before the Renaissance and History of Education since the Renaissance as part of the requirements at NYU, where I received the master's degree in 1950.) Before the first class meeting, Dr. King told me that my program at NCC would be more rigorous than it had been at NYU. As if to give credence to his prophecy, he assigned me to read the books and articles at the end of each chapter in the basic textbook. He topped it off by saying in a matter-of-fact manner that the textbook was merely the course outline. Also, I studied under Sing Nan-Fen (Comparative Education), George Kyle and Howard Wright (psychology), and Joseph Pittman (statistics).

I will always be grateful for the support and encouragement that Ozie and I received from every quarter during the three years of my graduate study at NCC. For instance, the answers to the two hundred or so items on my research questionnaire were scored by hand. Ozie and I hosted a party at which friends joined us in scoring the responses that I subsequently analyzed for my dissertation, "An Analysis of Teacher Responses to Sound and Unsound Principles of Guidance." Among the friends who assisted were former college mates George and Marian Thorne. In later years, George served NCC as vice chancellor for financial affairs, and Marian was a professor of business education.

I was to learn long after I finished my degree requirements that Dr. Beard was surprised at the drama that characterized my final oral exami-

The author receiving the first doctorate issued by North Carolina College, with NCC's president, Dr. Alfonso Elder. *(Brown family papers)*

nation. Eleven persons attended the exam, and most of them asked questions. They included faculty members and administrators from the education and psychology departments of both North Carolina College and the University of North Carolina. I must have been in a mildly hypnotic state because I was confident in my responses, although I hardly remember any of the questions. I was roundly complimented after the exam.

On May 22, 1955, in an article headed "NCC Finals Slated to Begin on Friday," the Durham *Herald-Sun* reported:

> *One of the highlights of the 44th commencement season will be the awarding of its first doctor of philosophy degree in education. The recipient will be Walter Matthew Brown, 28-year-old veteran of World War II, and a graduate of NCC in the class of 1948.*
>
> *A native of Durham and a graduate of Hillside High School, Brown received the M.A. degree at New York University in 1950, taught for two*

years at Bennett College in Greensboro and enrolled in NCC's Graduate School in education when the doctoral program was organized in 1952.

Dr. W. W. Pierson, dean of the Graduate School at the University of North Carolina and acting dean of NCC's Graduate School, last night authorized this statement: "This award of the degree of Doctor of Philosophy— the first to be conferred by a southern institution engaged in graduate education for Negroes—is a significant and historic event. Mr. Walter M. Brown, the recipient of this degree, has worthily and satisfactorily fulfilled the exacting requirements for this degree and is ready to take his place in the academic profession.

Next to that article was a picture of me receiving a cap and gown from Jaccie Conyers, manager of the college bookstore. The caption read, "Milestone for NCC."

Before the program was discontinued eight years later, the college would confer the doctorate on four others: Solomon Shannon, from Tennessee; Beulah Carr, Florida; and Minnie Forte and Lloyd Rufus Howell, North Carolina.

Lmy colleague

I DON'T KNOW that I ever told anyone, not even Dr. Elder, that my secret aspiration while a student at NYU was to become the first certified guidance counselor at NCC. But by the time I received the master's degree, the college had already appointed its first guidance counselor, Roger D. Russell.

Russell graduated from Virginia State College in Petersburg. He received the master's degree from Columbia University. I had completed course requirements for my doctorate when he went on leave to complete residency requirements for the doctorate at Pennsylvania State University. While writing my dissertation, I substituted for Russell as college counselor. It was a dream deferred, but a dream fulfilled.

When Dean George Kyle came to my office, rumor already had it that Dr. C. L. Spellman had resigned as the Department of Education's director of student teaching. "Spellman's leaving," Kyle said. "He's going to Maryland State." Maryland State College is a historically Black college in Princess Anne, Maryland. I had worked with Spellman for two years, assisting him in the supervision of student teachers and conducting seminars immediately preceding and following the six to eight weeks at their cooperating schools. He appeared to be pleased with my work, and I believed he would put in a word for me with Dean Kyle. By this time, my position description had been modified to include teaching in the Department of Education and chairing the committee on undergraduate recruitment.

I said I was glad for Spellman and would miss him. Dean Kyle then asked if I wanted the job. I said I didn't know, but would like to think about it. Then Kyle asked if I knew Spellman's salary. I believe my reply to that question was one of my finest moments. "It doesn't matter to me what he makes," I said. "There are other factors, chief among them job satisfaction, that I'll have to consider." Memory fails me in what the dean said as he was leaving my office, but he left on an amicable note. We had that kind of relationship. The following week, I accepted the offer, which subsequently led to an associate professorship in education and a springboard to horizons beyond NCC.

I HAVE A recurring thought that the decision by Dr. Elder's parents to give him a Hamilton watch as a graduation gift was influenced at least in part by advertisements in 1915 with a picture of White men in caps and gowns as they walked in an academic processional. The advertisement read: "For the event of his life get him a timekeeper for life. Make Hamilton His Watchword. The Hamilton Watch, by the service it performs, teaches the same lesson that school and college training gives—accuracy, precision and faithful performance of duty."

Dr. Elder was 76 years old when he died on August 7, 1974. An August 10th editorial in the Durham *Morning Herald* reads:

> *Dr. Alfonso Elder, who died this week, was not a civil rights activist in the generally accepted sense of the term. He once told a* Morning Herald *reporter: "I only marched but once and that was with a church group on a Sunday morning." But he always spoke with admiration of the Black men and women who actively pressed the drive for civil rights, criticizing them only when their activities led to violence and the destruction of property.*
>
> *Dr. Elder saw himself as having a different role. He said his task as president of North Carolina Central University was to prepare Black students "for the enjoyment of the rights they advocated." He worked hard at that task for 15 years until his retirement in 1963. The latter years of Dr. Elder's presidency of what was then called North Carolina College were*

Walker modeled Elder in his activism, attitudes toward roles, work and style of "gracious and modest"

turbulent years for race relations in North Carolina. He shepherded his college through those years with a firm insistence on the importance of education in Blacks' struggle for equality, but with an equally firm insistence that students were entitled to exercise their rights as citizens.

He was a gracious man and a modest man. He never tired of telling how his father, T. J. Elder, almost singlehandedly built a high school in Sandersville, Georgia, and served as its principal for 53 years. "I have often said I never accomplished with the facilities available to me as much as he accomplished with the meager facilities available to him," Dr. Elder once remarked. Dr. Elder's own accomplishments were solid ones. During his tenure as president, NCCU grew in size and stature. And he lived to see the day when the efforts of his predecessor [Dr. Shepard, founder and first president] and successor, Dr. Albert Whiting, have placed the predominantly Black university on the verge of overcoming the inequities it suffered and becoming a first-rate institution of higher education.

Dr. Elder leaves behind a model of service to his race and to education in North Carolina.

M RS. ELDER attended the Gate City School in Atlanta, the Atlanta University High School, and Atlanta University, where she earned degrees in chemistry and library science. She served as a librarian at Atlanta University before serving as librarian at Hillside High School in Durham. She died March 26, 1993. Funeral services for the Elders were held at Saint Titus Episcopal Church in Durham.

I do have a Timex watch—two, in fact: one with features for setting the date and an alarm in addition to the time. But the Hamilton watch given by Thomas J. and Lillian Phinazee Elder to their son, Alfonso, and given to me by Louise Elder nearly sixty years later, is guaranteed as a continuing source of inspiration—all the time.

[23]

A Noble Act, Not Intended

I COULD SPARE myself an embarrassment by not including this vignette in my memoir, but it keeps coming to mind, and I can resist no longer.

In the spring of 1958, Dr. Rose Butler Browne, chair of the Department of Education at North Carolina College (now North Carolina Central University), stopped by my office to tell me about what she regarded as an exciting opportunity for community service. The local television station, WTVD, would televise classes to teach adult nonreaders to read. Dr. Browne had been asked to help recruit volunteers to serve as facilitators at the several sites where classes would meet to receive the televised instruction. She said I was a natural for the project. I was flattered.

Classes were to meet twice a week, Mondays and Wednesdays, from six o'clock to seven, she informed me. Facilitators would preview the lessons for fifteen minutes. The televised lesson would follow for thirty minutes. Facilitators would then do a fifteen-minute review of the lesson.

One class would be held at McDougald Terrace, a low-rent housing complex four blocks from my house. The Laubach method of teaching reading skills to nonreaders would be used in the telecasts. Recruitment of students was under way. Employers, churches, area newspapers, and radio and television broadcasting stations heralded the places and times of classes. Claims were made that upon completion of the eight-week block, participants would be able to do things that most people take for granted—namely, to read such items as their mail, help-wanted ads in newspapers, food-market advertisements, traffic signs, church bulletins, and job application forms.

However, there was a hitch that I couldn't mention without at least a modicum of shame. I was second baseman for the Rangers, a team in the city's softball league for senior men. Our sponsor was the late Bill Jones, proprietor of the College Inn, Black Durham's counterpart to Mory's place in the Whiffenpoof song. League play started at 6:30 P.M., a little after the televised instruction would get under way, I thought. I accepted the radio station's invitation, mostly Dr. Browne's abbreviated invitation, to be a facilitator for the class at McDougald Terrace. But I did so in anticipation of being able to rush from the class and arrive at the park at about the time the teams finished infield practice. I would be able to start at the sound of "play ball" or very soon thereafter—the better of two worlds.

My letter of confirmation, complete with information about class schedules, orientation for facilitators, and the nobility of my commitment, came a few days after my conversation with Dr. Browne. Until that time, I had no idea that I had agreed to do anything that would require that I get up at five-thirty, six, or any other time near dawn, to teach anybody how to read or do anything else. The halo over my head was tilted. As it turned out, however, I kept my promise to teach adult nonreaders two mornings a week for eight weeks, and I taught two classes at NCC for much of the summer.

Dr. Browne, wife of the pastor of Mt. Vernon Baptist Church, a large church in Durham, told friends at her church, our faculty colleagues, and seemingly the whole world how proud she was that one of her young faculty members would be teaching adult nonreaders how to read. "It is a noble act on behalf of the Department of Education, and indeed on behalf of North Carolina College," she said.

The format was one in which I checked attendance, gave a preview of the telecast, viewed the telecast with the class, and reviewed the lesson, giving as much individualized help as possible within time constraints.

On the very first morning, there was a glitch. The television set in the housing complex was malfunctioning. A problem to be solved. I mentioned to the class members that I lived only a few blocks away, and as if by rehearsal, the students joined me in the living room of our home, where we saw the telecast and reviewed it in anticipation of the next class. The adventure went well and was the subject of a feature article in the local newspaper the following day.

Most adult nonreaders use a variety of compensatory practices, such as copying symbols from envelopes addressed to them, even though they may not recognize the symbols as letters and cannot see the symbols as words or associate them with sounds. In these instances, unlearning was a critical step before learning. I rejoiced that a few students did become functionally literate and that most of the others "finished" with a readiness to learn if the opportunity presented itself.

I accepted plaudits and a sterling silver letter opener from the television station and its project cosponsor, the Durham County Literacy Council. But my halo was tilted even as I received words of appreciation from my class of senior adults who declared that I had helped to transform their lives. Admittedly, the halo shines a little brighter now that I have written this vignette.

[24]

Before the Internet, There Was Norman C. Johnson

Norm chaired the NCCU Dept. of Ed when I started there in 1977.

I WAS ABOUT to whack on a nandina when Norman Johnson stopped by. "Prune the stems randomly," he said. "Cut some at the bottom, some about a third the height of the plant, some two-thirds the height, and leave some uncut." He asked for the shears. "Like this," he said, while deftly pruning one of my four nandinas. That was in 1982. It was the same lesson I got in 1998, when I was learning to become a Master Gardener in the Durham office of the North Carolina Cooperative Extension Service. I wondered how and when Norm had learned about this atypical way of pruning. I wondered for a long time how he got to know so much about so many things.

Norman and Pauline Johnson moved to Durham from Tyler, Texas, where Norm had taught mathematics, chemistry, and physics at Texas College. About the same time, Ozie, our firstborn, Judith, and I moved to Durham from Greensboro, North Carolina, where I taught history of education and educational psychology while I worked as a student personnel officer at Bennett College. Ozie and I were twenty-five. The Johnsons were thirty. It was the fall semester of 1952, the semester that Norm began teaching in the Department of Education at North Carolina College at Durham (NCC). I began study for the doctorate at NCC in the same department.

Pauline Johnson was born and reared in Jeffersonville, Indiana, a small town near the Ohio River. She was the first of her family to attend college. Norm and Pauline met at Indiana State Teachers College after Norm's four years of military service in World War II. "Norm and I married on the sixteenth of November 1948, in Mama's house on Carrolton Avenue in Indianapolis," she told me. Pauline said that her family was unpretentious, and it followed that their wedding ceremony had "no frills."

For three years, our families lived in a housing complex called Mutual Heights in south Durham. Our units were in Mutual Court, directly across from each other. Their daughters, Olga and Carol, were born during that time.

In 1955, our families moved from Mutual Heights to Plum Street, where the stork brought the other Brown daughters, Jacqueline and Jennifer. We were members of Asbury Temple Methodist Church, a small Black church on Durham's Lawson Street, in close proximity to McDougald Terrace, a federal housing development. Norm, Pauline, Ozie, and I sang in the church choir. Pauline sang alto, Ozie sang soprano, Norm sang bass, and I sang tenor. We provided our own musical entertainment at parties, some planned, most impromptu. *Norm's music skills*

A major milestone for the Johnsons during our stay in Mutual Heights was Norman's attainment of the doctorate degree at Indiana State University. He used a screwdriver to free stuck typewriter keys while typing his dissertation. Charles Gittens, another Mutual Court resident, and I once wondered what difference it would make in tasks Norm undertook if he had access to equipment in standard operating condition. The typewriter was only one case in point. Gittens would later become deputy director of the Office of Special Investigations at the U.S. Department of Justice.

On the doctoral qualifying examination, Norm scored at the ninety-ninth percentile in statistics, the highest score attainable. One year later, he helped me develop the statistical design for my dissertation.

Norm played the trumpet in his high school band. In college, he played in a jazz band, the Dukes. The band played at the Black junior prom at Indiana State University in 1942. Members of the band had ties either by birth or some other affiliation to Norm's hometown, Brazil, Indiana. The piano player was Norm's brother, Maurice, who also taught mathematics in the Indianapolis public schools. Other band members were successful in a variety of careers, including dentistry, teaching, mortuary science, and accounting.

After the Johnsons moved from Mutual Heights to Plum Street in Durham, Norman added a bedroom. Except for the electrical wiring, he did the work himself. The cabinets were a work of art. The city housing inspector approved the construction without a hitch.

Norm made a macramé shoulder bag that was one of Ozie's proud possessions. He was also an accomplished visual artist, with media concentrations in oil and photography. He played chess. I don't know how well,

I think I never appreciated, or even witnessed Norm's academic skills. Now, I wonder why.

but I suspect his game was on par with his performance in other areas. He taught himself to play the guitar. He also played a respectable golf game. He might have been better had he worn golf shoes instead of tennis shoes.

In 1965, my family and I relocated when I accepted a position with VISTA in Washington, D.C. Separating from the Johnsons was one of our few regrets.

In the early 1970s, Norm assembled a car from a kit containing parts and instructions. A close friend, William McDonald, campus engineer at North Carolina Central University, did the wiring. It was a two-seater sports car with a Volkswagen frame and a Ford engine. Norm was then chairman of the Department of Education. To the chagrin of the university chancellor, Norm drove the car about town as he would have driven any conservative model. The chancellor thought this unbecoming. My family and I were in Maryland at the time. Had we been living in Durham, I would have had the pleasure of riding with Norm in the other seat.

My colleague from University Associates in Washington, Milton Muelder, met Norm when he visited Durham with me in 1977. He was impressed with the car that Norm had assembled, but he was more than amazed at Norm's unadulterated modesty. Humility, unpretentiousness, even self-deprecation; these traits characterized Norman Johnson in virtually everything he did.

revised style

In the summer of 1980, my track record with the Office of Economic Opportunity in the U.S. Department of Labor, and my consulting positions with three firms—Fry, Lewin, and University Associates—paid dividends in the form of a professorship in the Department of Education at North Carolina Central University. Not only were Norm and I ace buddies, he was also my department chairman, a relationship that was never awkward for either of us.

On occasions when I introduced Dr. Norman Johnson to high school students at career orientation programs, I quickened their interest when I said that he was my colleague from Brazil. The students laughed when I followed with the announcement that he was born in the small Midwest town of Brazil, Indiana. There were more smiles when I added that he had graduated from Brazil High School.

NORMAN AND I were also fishing buddies. We fished mostly in farm ponds within a thirty-mile radius of Durham. Edward Allen, a neighbor

Walter + Norm were fishing buddies

who lived less than a stone's throw from us, fished at times on the North Carolina coast. We coveted Allen's saltwater catches, particularly when we were not having the best of luck in our freshwater fishing. Allen was my high school classmate and a detective in the Durham police department. When he invited us to go with him on an outing to the coast, we accepted the invitation with no hesitation. Allen knew the ropes. He would reserve a boat, set our departure time, guide us in what equipment we should buy, and brief us on the culture of coastal fishing.

We left Durham for Morehead City, North Carolina, at around one o'clock in the morning on a holiday weekend in 1958. It was Memorial Day or the Fourth of July, I forget which. Dawn had

Norman and Pauline Johnson
(Courtesy of Olga and Carol Johnson)

not yet broken when we arrived at the dock shortly after four thirty. It was quiet. The movement of fishermen and those in related occupations was yet to begin. Norm and I waited while Allen went to announce our arrival to the captain of the boat he had reserved three weeks earlier.

When Allen returned and was close enough for us to read his face, he didn't have to tell us that he had been victimized by the demon of racial bigotry. The boat captain had told him he did not rent his boat to colored and had said he "didn't know" he was talking to a colored man when he agreed to rent his boat to the Edward Allen party.

We walked the dock and tried to engage a different captain and boat. Some owners and service persons expressed disgust that we were denied the rental of a boat, especially under the circumstance that Allen described. The problem, we were told, was that on holidays every boat on the dock was reserved days in advance. There simply wasn't another boat available.

We were out of luck. Three men—two of whom were college professors, another a college-educated law enforcement officer—were denied the use of a fishing boat because of their skin color. Each had served in the army of the United States of America.

In 1982, the Johnson family moved from Durham to Atlanta, Georgia, where their daughters, Olga and Carol, and their families lived. In 2000, Norm's church sponsored his art in a one-man exhibition. In 2002, he was taking dialysis treatment three times a week, a fate that he talked about as matter-of-factly as if he had a hangnail. He was then eighty years old.

Norman Johnson's funeral was held three days after his death on February 24, 2004. His pastor, Derrick R. Rhodes, a graduate of North Carolina Central University, officiated. Norm and Pauline's grandson, Charles Matthew Bryant, offered some remarks, and at the family's invitation, I read some personal reflections of my own. It was a signal honor to salute a longtime best friend, an African American Hoosier from Brazil, Indiana, at the Hoosier United Methodist Church on Benjamin E. Mays Drive in Atlanta, Georgia.

Pauline Hardison Johnson died on October 27, 2008.

[25]

Christmas Letters with Marginal Notes:
Richard Beard

THERE ARE people whose names I wouldn't dare use without a title: Mr., Miss, Mrs., Reverend, Doctor, Professor, and so on. It's part of my upbringing. Titles sometime become a part of names, it seems. Take for instance, my relationship with my doctoral advisor, Dr. Richard L. Beard.

I received the doctoral degree from North Carolina College at Durham in 1955. Dr. Beard's family and my family exchanged Christmas greetings each year, beginning in 1956. I always inserted a note in my family's greeting card to inform him of my career status at the time. I am admittedly immodest in saying that the marginal notes in Dr. Beard's letters usually contained words of praise about me, first as a student, and later about my career profile. More than a few times, he was complimentary of the greeting cards I did in calligraphic art, and he once said that he and Mrs. Beard looked forward to what I would come up with each year.

In 1975, roughly ten years after I resigned from North Carolina College at Durham in 1965, the handwritten notes in Dr. Beard's Christmas letters indicated that he hoped that I would someday return to college teaching. He said my experience in government and private consulting firms would enrich my service in teaching or administration. As it turned out, I returned to North Carolina Central University in the 1980–1981 academic year.

I last saw Dr. Beard in the spring of 1980, at a retirement dinner in his honor at the University of Virginia. He joined the UVA faculty in the early 1960s, when he resigned from his joint appointment at North Carolina College at Durham and the University of North Carolina at Chapel Hill. There must have been a dozen of his former doctoral students at the dinner. I took great pleasure when, in the course of his remarks, he "proudly"

Dr. Brown wanted to be called Dr. Brown

The author with his doctoral
advisor Richard L. Beard.
(Brown family papers)

introduced me as the first of his ninety-two doctoral students. (Evidently, there was one to come after the celebration of his retirement.)

Dr. Beard may have tempered his introduction of me had he known that I didn't read his Christmas letters with careful scrutiny. I simply have never been able to muster enthusiasm for holiday epistles that recount the fortunes and adversities of generations about whom I know little or nothing. What I did look forward to with great anticipation, however, were my former professor's marginal notes. He generally wrote tidbits of recollections about his teaching stint in North Carolina and the personalities he got to know there. Invariably, he mentioned his admiration of Dr. Rose Butler Browne, who chaired the Department of Education at North Carolina College. He spoke fondly of the proficiency of my wife, Ozie, and he once mentioned "her calm and serene manner." Ozie was the department's secretary during Dr. Beard's time at NCC.

Sometime in March 1994, I asked Dr. Beard for a biographical sketch, to be filed among documents for my memoir. In a letter dated April 6, 1994, he promised to respond soon thereafter. A paragraph in that letter was heartwarming: "One thing is obvious; you were the first doctoral student of my list of ninety-three. I reminded the ninety-two that no one ever faced such a collection of important people, or such hard questions as you faced, or did so well as you. I am very proud of you. [None of] the other ninety-two did as well as you. . . . You will hear from me soon. I will prepare a new résumé. . . . Cordially, Richard L. Beard."

Dr. Beard's letter containing the biographical sketch was not dated. However, it is clear that it was sent between April 6 and June 10, 1994. In that letter, he said that Mrs. Beard was sorry he did not make a copy of the sketch. "I think she wants it for my obituary," he said.

We did not receive a Christmas greeting from the Beards in 1995. Two weeks into January 1996, I called the Beard home in Charlottesville, Virginia. Mrs. Beard answered. "I can hardly believe you are calling at this time," she said. She had mailed a letter to me that same morning. She said that Dr. Beard had had brain surgery on December 28th. He had been unable to stand or walk without falling. In surgery, it was discovered that his brain had been pushed to one side by fluids.

"And if that isn't enough, I regret to tell you that Dick has Alzheimer's," added Mrs. Beard. "He thought so much of you and spoke of you so many times through the years." I thanked her for the kind words and asked how she was doing.

She was "making out," she said, before speaking once again of Dr. Beard. "It is hurtful to watch," she added. "But it's been a good life, and I must find the strength to keep going." I said that I could identify with the problem more than she might imagine, and added that I would remember her and Dr. Beard in prayer and good wishes.

"I will tell Dick that you called, although he may not understand what I'm saying," said Mrs. Beard. "I will always be grateful for your call." Her earnestness was unmistakable. Even under the circumstances, the telephone conversation was a pleasure, never to be forgotten.

Mrs. Reva Beard's letter came the next day. I felt the same pain in her written words that I had felt in our telephone chat. I have felt the pain many times since.

It is not possible to recall the superabundance of motivational speeches, lessons gleaned from the literature, or other activities aimed at giving my peers and me a sense of purpose and determination to pursue worthy goals. But none of these yielded quite the measure of positive influence that I realized from Dr. Richard L. Beard's handwritten notes in the margins of his family's Christmas letters.

[26]

A Twenty-one-Gun Salute to
Marion D. Thorpe

THE ADMINISTRATION Building on the campus of Elizabeth City State University (ECSU) in Elizabeth City, North Carolina, is named as a memorial to Marion Dennis Thorpe Jr. It is unlikely that he had greater impact on the life of anyone associated with that university than he did on my life.

In the spring of 1965, Thorpe resigned as dean of students at North Carolina College at Durham to accept an appointment with a fledgling federal agency in Washington, D.C.: the Office of Economic Opportunity (OEO). Marion commuted on weekends until he found housing in Washington for his family. When he came home, he and his wife Lula usually gave a party, the kind that made you glad to be alive. Ozie and I were very much alive on those weekends.

At a party in mid-April 1965, Marion told me that I would get a call the following week about a job opportunity in Washington. Despite my eagerness for a career change—a dramatic change, if possible—and despite my curiosity about who would call me or why, I simply thanked Marion and let it go at that. I might have shouted at least one hallelujah, but I had seen too many persons disappointed when hopes based on insubstantial leads were dashed.

Although he was a fellow native of Durham, I had heard little about Marion before I met him during the 1956–1957 academic year. But from the time we met, I knew that he was bright, talented, and affable—a combination of traits that contributed to his effectiveness as a student personnel administrator.

Like many Americans, including me, Marion envisioned President Lyndon Baines Johnson's declaration of War on Poverty as a breakthrough for the nation's poor. He also saw it as an opportune time for new and challenging careers, particularly for African Americans with a liberal arts college education. He made his interest known to people in the right circles.

Marion was appointed assistant director of the Neighborhood Youth Corps in OEO. He was thirty-three years old. He had been in Washington only a few weeks when he was asked if he could recommend someone for another administrative position with the agency. He recommended me.

The call came the next week, as Marion had said it would. It was from Leo Kramer, director of recruitment and training for Volunteers in Service to America (VISTA), an OEO subdivision. Two days later, I was interviewed at OEO headquarters and was offered the position of special assistant for VISTA recruitment. When agency officials asked if I could begin work on the first of May, I told them that I was contractually obligated to complete the school year at North Carolina College (NCC). But I promised to see if I could get special dispensation from NCC to start at OEO in May.

My best bet, I thought, was for my department chairman, F. George Shipman, to permit me to close out the year before the first of May. I also hoped that Shipman would intercede on my behalf with the college president, Samuel P. Massie.

My letter of resignation evoked an immediate response from President Massie. He reminded me that I was on a nine-month contract and that I could be released from it only on Shipman's recommendation. Shipman was unequivocal: "If they want you badly enough, they will wait for you to complete the terms of your contract here," he said.

I might have expected a different reaction. The president of the United States of America had declared a War On Poverty. I wanted to believe that discerning Americans, especially those affiliated with human service organizations and institutions, would rally to calls for service. This was probably true of my department chairman and college president, except that I would have to satisfy the terms of my contract before going to war.

I have never regarded Shipman's position as untenable. After all, he was the department chairman, his doctorate from Peabody University was in educational administration, and he was accountable for carrying out the college's mission, for which the Department of Education had a prime responsibility.

Shipman relayed to me the suggestion from Massie that I take a leave of

Marion D. Thorpe. *(Courtesy of Mrs. Lula G. Thorpe)*

absence instead of an outright resignation. I was too brazen and too cocksure to consider it. But Massie's counteroffer was not altogether selfless. There was a groundswell of disenchantment among the faculty regarding what they perceived as Massie's ineptitude as the college's president, and Massie wanted to thwart any notions that tenured faculty would leave NCC because of dissatisfaction with his administration.

Although my resignation might have heightened perceptions of faculty unrest, I had a readiness for broadening my base of experience. Given the right opportunity, I would have resigned anyway. As a former colleague, Joseph Dempsey, used to say about career opportunities and retirement, "You know when it's time." Still, the big test was whether the OEO would hold a position for me for six weeks.

Walter would say this too!

I called Kramer and informed him of my dilemma. He promised to get back to me after several hours, and he kept his promise. OEO officials had agreed that my contract would be effective June 1, 1965.

Gestures of goodwill from colleagues and friends were gratifying. At the behest of chairman Shipman, the Department of Education sponsored a picnic for me. The university's chapter of the American Association of University Professors honored me with a reception. Douglas Moore, my pastor at Asbury Temple Methodist Church, wished me Godspeed on behalf of the church. In the marketplace, friends wished me well. And Ozie, Judith, and Jacqueline assured me that they would be on their way to Washington with baby Jennifer as soon as I gave the word.

ON THE MORNING of May 31st, my mother phoned me to cite the verse from Isaiah 26:3, which she paraphrased as: I will keep him in perfect peace, whose mind is stayed on me. The next day, I reported for duty at

VISTA headquarters, located in the Brown Building at 19th and M Streets N.W., Washington, D.C.

James Matthew Turner had been my friend since our boyhood and a classmate at Hillside High School in Durham. Our friendship was reaffirmed when he and his wife, Virginia, who then resided in Washington, gave me accommodations in their home on Tulip Street while I was becoming oriented to the nation's capital and looking for a place for Ozie and our daughters. It was an important prelude to noteworthy experiences in metropolitan Washington for the ensuing fifteen years.

In 1968 Marion Thorpe became president of Elizabeth City State College, after a stint in administration at Central State College in Wilberforce, Ohio. Ozie and I attended Marion's inauguration. He served as president until 1972, and then he served as chancellor of Elizabeth City State University from 1972 to 1983. The administration building at ECSU is a testament to his success at that institution.

In 2009 Marion Thorpe's widow, Lula, was living in Durham, North Carolina.

[27]

A Street Bus Named Desire

WHEN I moved from Northwest Washington, D.C., into Maryland, I joined the ranks of suburbanites who commuted from the Montgomery Hills section in Silver Spring to their jobs or other appointments in "the District." At the end of my first day as a commuter from VISTA Headquarters, I walked to the intersection of 16th and U Streets, N.W., the nearest metropolitan bus stop. As instructed by good-wishers who were helping me get oriented to my new environment, I dutifully waited for an express bus designated as Q-9.

The 5:59 P.M. was on schedule. As it approached my stop, I flagged it somewhat casually, anticipating that the driver would move from the middle lane to the curb lane, where I would get aboard. Sonofabitch! The driver neither moved to the curb lane nor acknowledged me with eye contact. The Q-9 zoomed by and I stood, waiting, alone.

I pulled the bus schedule from my pocket and noted the anticipated arrival time of the next Q-9—6:10 p.m. I could wait, not knowing what would happen if I waited. I could take a local bus, knowing it would take forever to get home. I decided to wait for the 6:10 Q-9.

No casual flagging this time. The driver made eye contact with me but pointed to the Q-9 sign at the base of his windshield and sped on. Then it occurred to me: this driver was trying to be helpful. His gesture was intended to tell me that I could not possibly be waiting for *his* bus. Only White people lived in the Q-9 section of suburban Maryland. By pointing to the sign, he was reminding me that I was supposed to take a local bus to wherever I was going in the District of Columbia.

Again I checked my pocket schedule. The next Q-9 was scheduled to stop at 16th and M at 6:16 p.m. A light came on: plan B. The pocket schedule indicated that the preceding express bus stop was at 16th and K streets, two blocks *opposite* the direction I wanted to go. Traffic at this corner—pedestrian and automobile—was heavy throughout the day and almost impossible during rush hours. I walked back to 16th and K, and I wedged myself into a mass of elbowing suburbanites boarding the 6:15 Q-9.

As I stepped from the curb into the bus, the driver cupped his hand over the fare box and announced, "This bus goes to Silver Spring."

"Thanks," I said, with fare in hand.

"This is a 'spress bus," he said with visible annoyance.

"Exactly what I want," I said, with feigned calmness.

"I don't discharge passengers in the District," he added, obviously flustered by my insistence on riding *his* bus, and probably more flustered that I was holding up the phalanx of passengers behind me.

"I don't want to be discharged in the District," I said. "Now, may I put my fare in the box?"

I didn't read the Q-9 driver's expression as he moved his hand from the fare box. I didn't care what he felt or thought. I was finally on my way home.

[28]

An Officer in the War on Poverty

IN VIGNETTE 26 ("A Twenty-one-Gun Salute to Marion Thorpe"), I observed that in 1965 I resigned from the faculty at North Carolina College at Durham to accept a position with President Lyndon Johnson's War on Poverty. I became a Washington liaison officer with Volunteers in Service to America (VISTA). It was a dramatic career change that I regarded as something akin to a gift from a genie's bottle. Later I would recall the saying that the grass may be greener on the other side, but you still have to mow it.

Roughly three months after I was assigned as a special assistant to VISTA's recruitment and selection division, I met Tom Powers, a former Washington attorney and then VISTA liaison officer for Hull House in Chicago and the University of Maryland School of Social Work in Baltimore. When Tom was about to complete his last cycle with these centers, he recommended me as his successor. I took the baton.

Hull House was named in memory of Chicago philanthropist Charles J. Hull, a wealthy real estate developer. In 1889, the house, which was vacant, was leased to Jane Addams and Ellen Starr for $60 per month by Helen Culver, cousin and business partner of Charles Hull and inheritor of his estate. Jane Addams became a widely acclaimed pioneer social worker and peace activist. She is remembered for having helped thousands of Chicago immigrants and others gain self-sufficiency and respect. In addition to her work with the poor, she was instrumental in shaping labor-reform laws that governed working conditions of children and women, and she was a charter member of the National Association for the Advancement of Colored People (NAACP). The VISTA training center was organized under the auspices of Hull House and named in memory of Jane Addams. I was proud to have the opportunity to serve as VISTA's Washington liaison officer for this center.

During a session with the training center staff and a VISTA project officer from Washington, I was handed a note that read, *Some trainees are waiting in the hall to see you. Looks like it's real urgent.*

I must have had a puzzled expression when I excused myself and left the room. I wondered what could be so important that I should leave the session where the qualifications of trainees were being discussed in relation to available service projects. Between fifteen and twenty VISTA trainees, roughly three-fourths of the trainee contingent, awaited me in the hall. A young man of less than average height, with a stubby beard and stringy hair to his shoulders, stepped forward. The young man (who was obviously the spokesman) said the trainees knew that we were making decisions about project placements, but he also wanted me to know that he and his fellow trainees were "refusing to go anywhere as government workers."

"You're about to finish your training but you are refusing to accept a project placement? Do you mind if I ask why?" I asked.

He replied that it was about the mandate that they sign a loyalty oath to the United States government. "We just ain't gonna sign your loyalty oath," he added with greater intensity. He then turned to the crowd and asked, "What say you, my friends?"

Some murmured. Some yelled. Some talked. One shrilled. I asked the spokesman to step forward. I asked his name, and he told me it was Barry. I extended my hand, and probably before Barry realized it, we were shaking hands while facing the crowd together. I said I didn't see that it would serve a useful purpose for me to try to have a conversation with all of them at the same time. I said I would ask Barry to select four others and join me in ten minutes in the conference room to see if we can agree on next steps. I then asked Barry if that was all right with him. Barry said it was all right.

I tried to conceal consternation when I met with the delegation of five. "You were supposed to sign the oath during your first week of training," I said. "Now here we are in the sixth and final week of your training, and—" I was cut off.

"We were asked to, and we refused to sign then," a young woman trainee said. Another said, "We told Mr. Mulligan—the training center director— that we wanted that requirement waived."

"And?"

"Mr. Mulligan asked us to wait it out until we could talk with the people in Washington."

"I suppose I'm the people in Washington," I said. "Let me tell you this—" I was interrupted.

"It's not just the oath, but the *mandate* that we sign it," Barry said.

I told them that I identified with them more than they might imagine, and to the best of my recollection, I added, "Whenever I find myself in an audience that is asked to pledge allegiance to the flag, I get squeamish. I manage to mumble the words, but when I get to 'with liberty and justice for all,' I do not say the words." I said that their circumstance was different. That they had made a commitment to serve some of the nation's poor, and they had successfully completed training toward that end.

I went on: "Those people asked for you to come to their communities even though they've never seen you. They're waiting for you to help some Head Start children and their families: children who can learn to read and do simple arithmetic if they get a lot of tutoring and a little love, elderly persons who are sick and despondent—the needs are unlimited. And you are telling me that we'll just have to tell them you will not honor your commitment because you refused to sign an oath that you knew you were obligated to sign as federally subsidized volunteers. What do you think they will say? Well, I'll tell you what they'll say. They'll say you weren't sincere when you promised to help them in the first place."

The ten or twelve seconds of silence seemed interminable.

An older trainee, a woman, said she "hadn't thought of it that way."

I saw others nod affirmatively.

Barry spoke: "Maybe you should give that line to everybody."

I said it was not "a line" and asked that they relay my message to their fellow trainees. I asked further that they talk about it until they reach a decision, and we'd have to meet again very soon.

Barry suggested that that the delegates meet with the other trainees that same evening and with me the next morning.

"Not tomorrow," I said. "An hour from now."

No one objected. The delegation left the room.

I mulled over the loyalty oath: *I do solemnly swear (or affirm) that I will support and defend the Constitution of the United States against all enemies, foreign and domestic; that I will bear true faith and allegiance to the same; that I take this obligation freely, without any mental reservation or purpose of evasion;*

and I will well and faithfully discharge the duties of the office on which I am about to enter: So help me God.

For the next hour, a stream of thoughts rushed in and out of my mind as I imagined repercussions if trainees resigned en masse as a protest against the requirement that they sign the oath before serving as Volunteers in Service to America.

As I awaited the meeting, my imagination ran wild over potential developments during the next few days, including a possible newspaper headline:

CHICAGO POVERTY WARRIORS DESERT
RATHER THAN FIGHT: VISTA VOLUNTEERS
BOLT BECAUSE OF LOYALTY ACT REQUIREMENT.

Congressional investigation into why volunteers completed training without taking loyalty oath. Rumblings at VISTA *headquarters in Washington: Why didn't Walter Brown call our legal counsel for backup? After all, he's not a lawyer. He probably didn't have time under the circumstances. A congressional staff person called to relay a constituent's complaint that the volunteers are anti–Vietnam War protestors under the guise of helping poor people. Do you think they were trying to use Walt as a pawn? We haven't had this problem with the other training officers. And so on.*

The delegation returned with a couple of minutes to spare. Barry wanted me to know that they had voted to go to their sites for service and to thank me for my guidance. His expression was solemn. The others looked relieved. A young woman trainee was smiling.

I said I thought Jane Addams would have made the same decision that they made, wishing I had interjected her name at our first meeting.

A trainee, smiling, said they wanted me to come to their graduation party that same night.

"We'll have bells and whistles," another said.

It was a lively party, indeed. Most, if not all, of the trainees and training staff attended. But what I remember best was the table centerpiece: a scale model of Chicago's Cabrini-Green housing project made by the several trainees who did field work at that training site. The model was made with butter pats. I was glad to have been associated with such a bright, creative, and—yes—caring group of Americans.

Roughly two weeks later, Tom Powers accompanied me to the University of Maryland School of Social Work for a transition meeting with VISTA training center director Ernie Kahn. Matthew Rubin of VISTA's recruitment and selection division came along for enlightenment. The School was located in a drab and uninviting section of Baltimore. Kahn allowed as to how they would miss Tom as their training officer. Tom made a complimentary statement about me as his successor.

Kahn evidently assumed that Tom and I wanted a speech. He spoke about the training curriculum, staff, field-placement sites, and straddling the U of M and Washington bureaucracies. We said good-byes until the opening of the next training center, when I would return. Then we went to lunch.

I don't remember how we decided to eat at this restaurant, but I do remember that I didn't like the ambience from the moment we entered: smoke-filled, heavy odor of beer and whiskey, and din such that nobody's words were distinguishable. We took a table and waited to be served. And waited, and waited some thirty minutes as we observed orders by others in our vicinity taken and filled—until Tom asked the waitress why she was not taking our order. "I can't take a order from your table," she said. "Just can't."

"Why can't you?" Tom asked. "Is it because of Walt here?" He was pointing to me.

"That's right," she said.

We left the restaurant without further incident. I was outraged. I was also disappointed that Tom and Matt did not seem as angry as I. The next day I filed a complaint with the U.S. Department of Justice. The restaurant's food-service license was revoked. Their license to serve alcoholic beverages was not.

My family and I enjoyed several attractions in Baltimore during our stay in the metropolitan Washington area, among them the Baltimore Museum of Art, the National Aquarium, historic Lovely Lane United Methodist Church, Orioles professional baseball, Colts professional football, and Bullets professional basketball. I attended several exhibitions of medieval calligraphic manuscripts at the Walters Art Gallery, and I visited friends at Morgan State College. I even took a workshop in Lithuanian Egg Decorating in a community of ethnic Lithuanian concentration. But the refusal of a restaurant to serve me because of my race, at a time when I was committed to help make America a better nation, still tarnishes my thoughts of Baltimore, Maryland.

THE VISTA training center in New York City was one of two centers for which I reviewed proposals from community organizations seeking help from volunteers sponsored by the Office of Economic Opportunity (OEO). On the day when a delegation from Harlem Team for Self Help (HTSH) presented a proposal, I was struck by the familiarity of a face, following introductions. It turned out to be that of Frank Jones, whose father, David D. Jones, was former president of Bennett College, where I had taught sixteen years earlier. It was good to make Frank's acquaintance.

The HTSH presentation was impressive. There was, however, a sticky item in their proposed budget. Their requested daily subsistence rate of $3.25 (2009 equivalent $21.91) for trainees was higher than the daily subsistence rate of $2.50 (2009 equivalent $16.85) allowed by OEO policy. HTSH insisted that the cost of living in New York City was substantially higher than in other cities and that the standard trainee subsistence was inadequate.

One man in OEO administration was authorized to approve requests for subsistence costs higher than the standard rates: contracts officer Milton Fogleman. The word around VISTA headquarters was that, when asked to bend the policy, Fogleman was like the proverbial tree planted by water—he would not be moved.

Before the coffee break, I was authorized by the representative from the VISTA director's office to speak to Fogleman on behalf of the HTSH.

Fogleman received me without an appointment. He was not a bogeyman. I explained the HTSH proposal and its rationale. I will probably never know what evoked Milton Fogleman's concession, but I saw the change in his countenance when I said that I had lived in Harlem when I was a student at New York University. We agreed on the higher subsistence rate requested by HTSH.

VISTA headquarters staff were discernibly impressed. The HTSH delegation was visibly appreciative. The proposal was approved. I was gratified. I was also assigned as the agency's training officer.

My work with HTSH was relatively stress-free. The agency had an able staff of administrators and seminar leaders, a sound curriculum, and satisfactory field placements. It was good to be in Harlem again.

My next major challenge: working as training officer for the VISTA training center under the joint auspices of the Southeastern Regional Office of the National Urban League and Atlanta University.

One of the top political appointees in VISTA was a man whom I will call Herman Nockman. It was Nockman who engineered the plan to establish a training center in Atlanta. The National Urban League and the historically Black Atlanta University had long histories as agencies of social change and in higher education. VISTA officials regarded them as logical institutions to train volunteers in the South.

The institutions named the training center in memory of Eugene Kinkle Jones, who helped found the National Urban League and served as its executive secretary. Jones also was the "Seventh Jewel" among the seven organizers of Alpha Phi Alpha Fraternity, founded in 1906, and coincidentally the fraternity I had joined in 1945.

As the division's only Black training officer, I was probably regarded as a natural for working with the new E.K. Jones Training Center. Once the paperwork was completed in Washington, Nockman and I went to Atlanta to meet with the Urban League staff. I went first and met with the staff for a full day. By the time Nockman arrived, the staff and I had agreed on the main features of the training design. Nockman said he liked what he heard, with a single exception: he did not want the trainees to live in the community during their field-placement experiences. He told a joke about a man whose wives had died and were buried in the same cemetery, with space for one grave between them. He quoted the man, saying, "I done figured how y'all would do it, but won't y'all put me just a little closer to Mary than to Sadie?" Nockman guffawed.

Then Nockman added, "I know you all have heard our conflicting suggestions, but won't you come closer to mine?" Another guffaw. He said they didn't have to decide right then but to think about it, and we'd talk again later, "when you're ready to come closer to my side." Last guffaw.

I was not piqued by the alternative suggested by Dr. Nockman—he insisted on being referred to as "Doctor," even in casual interactions—but the chemistry between us was not good. For example, Nockman had gone about the country making speeches and indiscriminately inviting people to come to Washington to work in staff positions in the War on Poverty. People came, there were no slots for them, and Nockman labeled staff members as incompetent if they didn't find ways to hire the job-seekers. Another example was the occasion of a division meeting at which Nockman presided, and a staff member who happened to have earned a PH.D. in clinical psychology asked a policy question. Nockman barked, "I will not comment on such a question at this level."

Once again, the gods were kind to me. Nockman did not return to Atlanta during either of the training cycles while I served as training officer there. But that is not to say I didn't need backup help with some knotty problems. One problem stemmed from an allegation that VISTA officials, in assigning the new enrollees to Atlanta, did not tell them that Atlanta University was a historically Black university. We got through that. Another was trainee dissatisfaction about the food. We resolved that one. The biggie—the episode that probably took a few years off of my life— happened at the field-placement site in Dougherty County, Georgia, three and a half hours south of Atlanta. (I describe that experience in vignette 31, "An Unplanned Curriculum for VISTA Volunteers.")

As I MOWED the grass on the new side, several results were satisfying:

- I was not boxed into nine-to-five office hours, although, travel included, I worked considerably longer than forty hours a week. I had been accustomed to this pattern in college teaching and administration.
- When VISTA's recruiting teams planned large-scale recruitment drives, they solicited the participation of other headquarters staff to join them in travel. The carrot for our participation was the opportunity to choose the places we preferred to visit, provided it was on the master schedule. I chose the University of California at Los Angeles, San Francisco State University, Seattle University, and the University of Utah in Salt Lake City.
- I was a member of the agency's speakers' bureau and represented VISTA on several occasions in the Washington, D.C., area.
- I was privileged to have colleagues who were bright, innovative, and eager to make a difference in the world.
- In 1967, two years after I began at VISTA, I accepted an opportunity and challenge as chief of the division of training and technical

assistance for the manpower division of the United States Department of Labor. I then recalled a phrase coined by James Russell Lowell more than a century earlier: "New occasions teach new duties."

The presidential election of November 1967 signaled the beginning of strategies to dismantle most federally subsidized programs in the nation's War on Poverty. Appropriations were severely cut, and few of the programs survived, including VISTA. In 1980, however, a new advocacy group was formed: Friends of VISTA. VISTA is now an integral part of AmeriCorps, the national service network.

[29]

Neighbors Closer Than Neighbors

MY FAMILY met Saul and Nellie Oberzanyk when we moved next door to them at 1709 Flora Lane in Silver Spring, Maryland. It was summer of 1965, and we hadn't been there more than a week when I saw tattooed serial numbers on the Oberzanyks' arms. I learned from another neighbor, who was Jewish, that these were identification numbers that had been permanently marked on their skin in a Nazi concentration camp. Saul and Nellie earned their living as tailor and seamstress in their small shop on Seventh Street in Washington. Their shop burned down on the night of April 4, 1968 — the night of rioting in more than a hundred cities nationwide following the assassination of Martin Luther King Jr.

Ozie and I were privileged to attend the wedding of the Oberzanyks' daughter, Gail. At their request, I wore a kippah (yarmulke) on my head in the synagogue. I was to learn later that it is traditional among some Jews to cover the head as a way of being encouraged to think about what is above: God.

I have often wondered what Saul and Nellie told Gail about the reasons why numbers were tattooed on their bodies in Germany and their shop was burned down in America. I hope they were better able to explain such inhumanity to Gail than Ozie and I have been able to explain it to our daughters, Judith, Jacqueline, and Jennifer.

Nearly thirty years have passed since we last saw the Oberzanyks. Yet I think of them whenever I read or see films about the persecution of Jews in Nazi Germany. A recent and painfully vicarious depiction is given in Martin Goldsmith's book *The Inextinguishable Symphony*. In many ways, the biography of Goldsmith's family is analogous to stories of man's inhumanity to man throughout the history of humankind. That realization, however, makes the pain no less intense.

[30]

Not Just Any Endodontist

I WAS WEARING my feelings on my sleeve when I visited Larry Gandel, DDS, sometime in 1974. That is when he told me I needed a root canal and the longer I put it off, the worse my problem would become.

"Damn," I responded in exasperation, but followed with quick resignation. I said I'd like to get it behind me as soon as possible, and I asked when I should make the appointment.

"I don't do root canals," Dr. Gandel replied. "That requires the work of an endodontist. I can make a referral, or I can give you names and you can make the appointment yourself."

"Which would you recommend?" I asked.

He said there were only five endodontists in Silver Spring, and he wouldn't recommend any of them over the others.

I remembered that one of my golfing buddies, Herb Kenny, had had root-canal work done by an African American dentist named Jenkins. I also remembered that Jenkins's office was in Silver Spring.

"Only five in Silver Spring?" I asked. "What are their names?"

Dr. Gandel called five names. Quiet rage came over me. I thought: *This man claims that there are only five endodontists in Silver Spring. There are at least six, because he didn't mention the one whose name is Jenkins.*

Dr. Gandel couldn't have known what I was thinking when he said, "You can ask my receptionist to make the appointment for you. Or, as I said before, you can call and make the appointment yourself."

Smoldering, I said I would make the appointment myself. I thanked him without being thankful.

When I reached my office at Lewin and Associates, I called Herb. Yep, it was Dr. Jenkins who had done Herb's root canal. Yep, his office was in downtown Silver Spring, in a complex of offices on Colesville, east of

Georgia Avenue. Hell yes, Herb understood why I'd be pissed. I made an appointment with Dr. Preston Jenkins for three days later.

Dr. Jenkins was a man in his late forties, graying at the temples. His handshake was firm and his aura friendly. As he approached me with a mouth mirror in hand, I waved the imaginary ethnic flag.

"You'll find this interesting," I said to Dr. Jenkins. "My dentist, who happens to be White, told me that there are only five endodontists in Silver Spring. He gave me five names, but yours wasn't one of them. I can hardly wait to see his face when I tell him that my root canal was done by a Silver Spring endodontist whose name he didn't even—"

I was interrupted. "I'm not an endodontist," Dr. Jenkins said, "but I do root canals as a part of my practice."

I was dumbstruck! Hadn't I one-upped my White dentist who I thought had withheld the name of an African American endodontist when he gave me only five names? I squirmed and may have even mistaken Dr. Jenkins' hand mirror for a claw. "Doctor . . . Dr. Jenkins . . . uh . . . I really don't want a root canal," I said. "Not now, anyway. Would you just do an x-ray and give me the negative? Would that be all right?"

In a seemingly empathetic manner, Preston Jenkins, DDS, replied. He said he'd have his assistant take an x-ray of the problem area and give me the negative.

I called Larry Gandel's office and asked his receptionist to give me the name of an endodontist—any endodontist—to whom Dr. Gandel made referrals. She gave me the name and office address of Dr. John Mattocks, and she wished me well. I thanked her, called Dr. Mattocks's office, and made an appointment.

"Dr. Mattocks will be with you soon," his receptionist said as I gave her the completed patient information form. My wait wasn't long.

"Mr. Walter Brown? Dr. Mattocks will see you now," Mattocks's dental assistant said.

The assistant led me down the hall and into an examination room where she leaned me back in the dental chair, asked how I was doing, and said Dr. Mattocks would be right in.

Two minutes later, my endodontist entered. My back was to the door. He spoke before I saw him. "Mr. Brown, I'm Dr. Mattocks." He walked into my field of vision and extended his hand. "Glad to meet you."

I couldn't help but wonder what he saw in my countenance. John Mattocks, DDS, was youthful, soft-spoken, urbane, and unmistakably African American.

[31]

An Unplanned Curriculum
for VISTA Volunteers

IT WAS the summer of 1966. I was making a visit to the VISTA training center in Atlanta, Georgia, and I was accompanying the center's four staff members and trainees to a field placement site in Dougherty County, Georgia. The entire contingent had turned in for the night—I thought. What little sleep I had been able to get ended abruptly around two o'clock in the morning, when a battery of fists pounded on my door. Hallway lights blinded me as I opened the door. It appeared that the entire contingent of thirty-five VISTA (Volunteers in Service to America) trainees was in the hall. They were talking at the same time. I read tension in most of their faces.

"Sorry to wake you . . ." "Sure hope this doesn't mean we won't be able to stay . . ." "Maybe it wasn't such a good idea . . ." "Somebody blew it . . ." "What can be done to stop him?" "Maybe we should've called the police." "Are you out of your mind?" "That guy had as much a right . . ." "How were we to know?" "Anybody with half a brain . . ."

Now I was fully awake. "Hello, hello, hello. One at a time, please. Young lady in the denim jacket, sorry, I don't remember your name. Yes, Gretchen. Would you tell me what all this is about?"

"Well," she gulped, "right after we checked in this afternoon, five of us went outdoors for a stretch break: Paula, Jeanne, Harold, Mike, and me. This Black guy came up and introduced himself. Cal. Cal Grady. Said he lives around here."

"And then?" I asked.

"Cal said he was available to help us learn our way around the county, and he asked where we planned to have dinner. We told him our plans were flexible. He suggested we join him for dinner at a restaurant across town."

"Better talk fast, Gretch. Time is crucial," came an admonition from an unidentifiable trainee.

"Yeah, like any minute now," said another.

"Okay, okay," said Gretchen with less composure. "One of us, I don't remember who, said it might not be a bad idea. Then somebody, I think it was Harold, said, 'We don't have any training activities this evening. Why don't we go to dinner with Cal?' So we said all right."

"And?" I asked.

"And we went," said Jeanne. "Look, we felt we needed a break after the three-hour drive down here. And that bus wasn't exactly a recreation vehicle."

"How'd you go wherever you went from here?" I asked.

"In Cal's car. It was a little tight, but we managed," Mike chimed in. "We went to a restaurant called 'Trucker's Friend' on Highway 17, about five miles from here."

"A trucking station?" I asked with an inflection that suggested disbelief. Grins on some faces. Astonishment and smirks on others.

"Yeah," Mike replied. "I'm not sure what we thought the restaurant would be like, but that wasn't quite it." A chorus of laughter broke the tension momentarily.

"Cal told us to go on in and get a table while he parked his car. And that's what we did," said Paula.

Gretchen spoke again: "After we were seated, the waitress came to take our order. We told her a friend would join us in a minute or two, and we would place our order as soon as he arrived. She said okay and left. She hadn't been gone more than a minute when Cal came in and took a seat with us. We're sure the waitress saw him because she was standing not far from our table. But when Cal sat down, she left right away."

Gretchen began to cry. Jeanne tried to comfort her with a reassuring arm around the shoulder. Jeanne spoke. "The waitress didn't come back. A man came instead, a big man with a big scowl. The proprietor or manager, maybe. He looked at Cal and said, 'Boy, you know I don't serve niggers.' Then he turned to the rest of us and said, 'And I don't serve nigger-lovers either.' We were dumbfounded. I know I was."

"The stuff had hit the fan," yelled a trainee I hadn't heard before. Murmurs were punctuated with laughter.

"Why didn't you tell him you were VISTA volunteers so he would back off?" another asked derisively. More laughter.

"And then?" I asked, intent on having some measure of decorum.

"And then Cal jumped up and left the room shouting, 'I'll be back. I'll be back tonight. And when I get back . . .'"

"As soon as Cal got outside, the proprietor ran to the door and shouted, 'Just be sure you do come back, Black boy. That'll be just the favor I need from you.'"

"So what'd y'all do then?" came a question.

"Whadda you think we did? We got the hell out of there," responded Harold. "I mean we *moved*."

"Y'all lucky a posse didn't follow you," another unidentifiable voice.

"Tell me about it," Mike said. "But mainly we wanted to catch Cal and see what was on his mind."

"Besides, Cal had the transportation," someone quipped.

Mike looked through the crowd to where he thought the comment came from. He continued, "When we got in the car, Cal had started the motor. He was fuming and beating his hands on the steering wheel. As soon as he took off, he said, 'I'm gonna take y'all home first, and then I'm going home to get my gun. And I'm going back to that place and kill that sonofabitch. Tonight!'"

"We were trying to tell him how sorry we were about the incident. We said we would report it to the authorities and all, but he wasn't listening," Paula said.

Another spoke, Harold, I believe: "We kept saying, don't do that, Cal. You'll just make matters worse, a whole lot worse. But he just ranted. 'I don't care what y'all say. That bastard's gonna meet his maker this night what's here.'"

"Well, he did bring y'all back, didn't he?" came a question from the back.

Again, Harold: "Yeah, he let us out and muttered something like, 'Nice meeting y'all. Now I got some business to take care of.' And even while we were getting out of the car, we were begging him not to do what he said he was going to do. But he didn't say anything else. Just sped away. There was nothing we could do at that point but to come in and try to regroup."

"Regroup?" I echoed.

"Yeah, we came in and woke up some of the other trainees and told them what had happened. Then the word spread like wildfire. Next thing we knew, just about everybody was in the hall."

"Did you alert any of the training staff?" I asked.

"Are you kidding? Why should we call on them with our Washington representative on the scene?" Laughter.

"Jeez, you're a smart-ass, Chip." It was a girl's voice. Nervous laughter.

By this time, the training center staff, all four of them, had worked their way to the front of the group, very near the door where I was still standing.

"There he is. Here he comes." Gretchen and a couple of other trainees were shouting, waving their arms as if trying to hail a New York City taxi during rush hour. "It's Cal. Ohhhh God, what a relief. Oh Cal, are we ever glad to see you. Cal, this is Dr. Brown from Washington. The one we were telling you about. Dr. Brown, Cal Grady."

Calvin Grady reeked of liquor. I extended my hand, wondering if he had been drinking at the time he met the trainees. "Glad to meet you, Cal," I said. Some trainees crushed forward.

"You too," said Cal Grady. Our eyes met, but only momentarily. He turned but not to look at anyone or anything.

"Come in, Cal. I think we have something to talk about," I said. I stepped aside, and Cal entered my room. He didn't speak to any of the trainees. It was as if they were not there. His "okay" was barely audible as he slid by me, sauntered across the room and sat on the side of the other bed, which was still made up.

The trainees crushed toward my door. From the din, I understood someone to say, "We want to be in on this."

"Oh no. No, no," I exclaimed. "I'm going to talk with Cal myself. Okay?" My eyes spanned the faces. "I ask you to return to your rooms, get some sleep if you can, and let's see what tomorrow brings. Please . . . thank you. Thanks. . . . Oh, he'll be all right. . . . Thank you. . . . See you in the morning."

They left, a few reluctantly. Gretchen and Mike waited. I gave a gentlemanly smile and closed the door. Politely.

I sat on the side of my bed opposite Cal. His chin was almost touching his chest. He appeared to be staring, but I sensed that he wasn't seeing anything, including the floor. He was younger than I had imagined: nineteen or twenty, maybe. A modest Afro, buff-colored long-sleeved shirt open at the collar. Bell-bottomed denims. He took the last cigarette from a Lucky Strike pack in his shirt pocket and patted himself looking for a match.

"Put that one back and have one on me if you can deal with a filter cigarette," I said. "You're sure to need it later." I lit up a Carlton. His whiskey breath was loud. "You don't seem to be feeling any pain, brother." He took the Carlton and lit it from my match.

Smoke whirled. "The VISTA volunteers seemed surprised when you walked up," I said. "How about telling me what happened?"

"All I got to say is that that White man will have to tell his grandchildren that a Black man whupped his ass," said Cal Grady. But hadn't the trainees reported that he'd said he was going to kill the man? When? Where was the gun?

"Did you kill him already? Or do you intend to do that when you leave here?" I asked.

"I shoulda done it last year. That bastard. I shoulda done it then. Took money outa my check to pay for a damn chair he said I broke. Then fired me 'cause I told him I wasn't goin' to work no more till I got all my money, chair or no damn chair."

"Fired you?" I asked incredulously. "Are you telling me that you used to work at that restaurant?" I asked.

"Yeah, he didn't hardly pay nothing noway."

"The kids who went with you to dinner, did you tell them you used to work at that restaurant?"

"Naw, I didn't say nothing 'bout that. We were going to integrate that place. They were all for it, till he come raising hell. My folks take that kind o' crap. Me, I ain't gonna take it."

"Cal, I don't know what those kids told you about our reason for coming to Dougherty County. But let me tell you something. A delegation from this community went to Atlanta and asked the National Urban League to let VISTA Volunteers come here for their week of field training. They're supposed to be assigned to work in Head Start centers, nursing homes, and the county's Community Action Agency. I think you call it here the CAA. The League has arranged for the local sheriff and some community leaders to welcome the volunteers to the county tomorrow morning. We're talking about a few hours from now. Look man, there are a lot of people who would like for you to beat that White man's ass so they will have reason to get every last one of these volunteers out of here even before they can get started with their work. Yes damn it, a whole lot of people."

Cal said nothing. He snuffed the cigarette. Again, our eyes met. Again, he looked down. "Didn't know all that," he said. I shuddered to think of what would happen in Dougherty County, Georgia, if he were to assault his former boss. But I also knew that Cal's ego was at stake, having boasted to the trainees that he was going to kill a man.

"Listen, Cal," I said. "You just lie back on that bed and get some sleep. And we'll deal with this some more when you wake up. Okay?" No reply. "Come on, man. Okay?"

Cal awoke three hours later, shortly after six o'clock. He broke my snoring. "Hey, Doc, I'm sorry I've caused so much trouble. Look here, I just want to split without talking to nobody else." I said I understood and wished for him the best. We shook hands.

I watched as Cal climbed through the window of my room. I would call a meeting of the training center staff to decide how best to capitalize on the first night's experience as an unanticipated case study. Two days later, I returned to Washington, the outline for my site report well in mind.

After the week of field training, the volunteers and training personnel returned to Atlanta for the final week of seminars. I was to return to Atlanta about the same time with a colleague from the VISTA headquarters field project division. He conducted the meeting in which decisions were made regarding the volunteers' project assignments during the remainder of their two years of service. Whitney Young, executive director of the National Urban League, was the graduation speaker. He praised the volunteers for their commitment and thanked them on behalf of the League. I thanked them "on behalf of VISTA Washington and the president of the United States but most of all on behalf of all the people whose lot they would be working to improve as VISTA volunteers."

James F. Tucker Defied Life's Odds and Won

W HILE SERVING with the U.S. Army in Europe, James (Jim) Tucker was also the anchor runner on the Mediterranean track relay team in its meet against the European relay team in Italy. When Jim was handed the baton, his team had a lead of ten strides. But on his lap, Jim pulled a muscle, "a charley horse," he said. He reached down and forced his leg to keep moving until he fell across the finish line one yard in front of his nearest competitor.

Writhing in pain, Jim rolled into the grass and onto his back. When he could open his eyes and focus, he looked up to see two pearl-handled pistols on the hips of legendary general George F. Patton, who was standing over him. The general looked down at Jim and said, "They call me 'Blood and Guts,' but in this race you showed more blood and guts than I ever have. Congratulations, soldier." I don't have the foggiest notion of how long General Patton remembered this scene. When I talked with Jim Tucker in February 2003, he remembered it well.

While I marvel at Jim Tucker's athletic achievements, I believe the most remarkable thing about the man is the adversity he overcame to achieve what is often referred to as the American dream. He was born in Brooklyn, New York. His mother died when he was eighteen months old, and he was taken to Philadelphia to live with his grandmother. His grandmother died when Jim was five years old, and Jim was then taken to Houston, Texas, to live with his aunt and his great grandmother.

In 1935, the director of the National Youth Administration (NYA) in Texas visited the high school in Houston where Jim was an NYA work-study student. The NYA provided financial assistance to students who worked part time as clerks or maintenance workers, and to nonstudents who worked on public projects such as highways, roadside parks, schools, and public buildings throughout Texas.

The principal invited Jim to be interviewed by the state director. When the director asked Jim what participation in the project meant to him, he replied that it meant he earned "a hundred percent" as much as his aunt got in her monthly welfare benefits—six dollars a month. Young Jim Tucker didn't have a clue that he was helping to educate the NYA director who would become the nation's thirty-sixth president, Lyndon Baines Johnson.

Jim was recruited by historically Black Prairie View State College on an athletic scholarship. In 1943, following

James F. Tucker. *(Courtesy Mrs. Caroline Tucker)*

his sophomore year at Prairie View, he was drafted into the army, where he was a member of a unit with a cooperative training arrangement with Howard University in Washington, D.C. After serving with the 92nd Infantry Division, Jim enrolled at Howard, where he earned the bachelor's degree in 1947 and the master's degree in economics in 1948. He then returned to Philadelphia—where he had lived with his grandmother until he was five—and entered the University of Pennsylvania, where, in 1957, he earned the PH.D., also in economics.

There are few things as satisfying to me as a job offer from someone I hold in high esteem. I went to the U.S. Department of Labor (USDL) in 1967. "Dr. Tucker" was then director of operations for the department's Office of Manpower Administration in Washington, D.C. I had been a training officer at VISTA for nearly two years when Jim offered me a promotion to chief of the division of training and technical assistance for the USDL. Actually, it was more a notice of opportunity than an offer. The job had to be advertised. Only then could I make a formal application.

A panel from the human resources division would evaluate my qualifications against those of other applicants. Jim said the description of minimum qualifications mirrored my career profile: *Advanced college degree; concentration in psychology and career counseling preferred. At least three years of teaching and administrative experience in education and state or federal government. Experience in employee supervision. Good skills in oral and written communication.* An interview was required. The "offer" was made, and I accepted.

Jim Tucker was a jewel of a supervisor. For a while, we had lunch together almost every day, mostly in his office. He gave me crash orientation sessions in departmental policies and governance, and in the personalities and styles of office managers in Washington and the department's nine regional offices. Not the least important was exposure to the personalities of some congressional aides whose bosses supported the federal government's War on Poverty. I did not expect to find such arrogance and condescension from staff persons in an arena where programs were designed to help people get out of the poverty mire. This, in addition to the election of Richard Nixon in 1969, made it easy for me to accept another job, as a senior consultant with the Washington, D.C., office of Fry Consultants.

Nearly twenty-two years later I attended the retirement party for Janice Payton Perry, who had served as my secretary in the Department of Labor. Janice received numerous accolades at the party; I remember best the one for her having risen from an entry-level clerical job to division chief through years of continuing education and meritorious performance.

At the same party, a man who was an employee of the department when I was hired revealed to me something I had not heard during or after my employment there. He said that Mark Battle, an African American in one of the highest positions in the department, had complained about the lack of other African Americans in top managerial positions.

"At one executive meeting, Mark was told that the department could not find qualified persons for such positions," he said. "Mark told them that maybe they weren't looking in the right places. They told Mark right then, all right, you find them and we'll hire them. Not too long after that, Dr. Thorpe, Dr. Tucker, and you were hired. I was so glad, I didn't know what to do," he said, "and I know Mark was. Best thing though, was you all did the department and yourselves proud and kept on going up."

Marion Thorpe, Jim Tucker, and I were colleagues at North Carolina College. Marion was the first of us to leave the college for a position in Washington. From the Department of Labor, he went to Central State University in Ohio as a vice president, and later to Elizabeth City State University in North Carolina as president.

Jim Tucker also moved on and up. In 1968, he became president of Virginia State College in Petersburg. Next he was a professor of economics at Virginia Polytechnic Institute and State University from 1970 to 1974. In 1978, he graduated with honors from the Stonier Graduate School of Banking at Rutgers University. He served as a vice president of the Federal Reserve Bank of Richmond, from which he retired in the early 1990s. After he retired, he continued to serve as an arbitrator for the National Association of Securities Dealers of the New York Stock Exchange and the Municipal Securities Rulemaking Board. He has also been a member of governing boards of numerous organizations and institutions, including his undergraduate alma mater, Howard University.

Jim and I took no small measure of pride as workers in President Johnson's Great Society programs. But the feature I remember best about him is that he characteristically helped his colleagues move up the career ladder even as he was moving up. I was one of his beneficiaries. So was a U.S. Army track team fifty-eight years earlier. And so was a certain former director of the National Youth Administration in Texas.

[33]

The Guys

THE STANFORD Warren Library in Durham, North Carolina—formerly known as the Durham Colored Library, the second Black library in the state—has the county's only copy of golfer Charlie Sifford's 1992 autobiography, *Just Let Me Play*. He was born June 2, 1922, in Charlotte, North Carolina, and began caddying when he was thirteen. Even at that age Sifford played well enough to hold his own with adults who were seasoned golfers. Until he turned professional in 1948, he competed professionally in leagues that Blacks organized for themselves. "Professional" in this context meant that the door opened for limited play in tournaments sponsored by the White-dominated Professional Golf Association. He was subjected to racist taunts from fans, threats of abuse, and ostracism by White players on and off the course.

Charlie Sifford endured the displays of racial hatred, particularly in the American South, and in 2004 became the first African American inducted into the World Golf Hall of Fame. The incomparable Tiger Woods, who had the advantage of excellent instruction in golf from his father and advanced educational attainment, commented that it was "wonderful" that Sifford overcame tremendous obstacles and still entered the World Golf Hall of Fame.

Until now, it never occurred to me that I would recommend that readers see the video at this Web site: http://www.youtube.com/watch?v=5VtQLjLW9lg. But even for readers who have never touched a golf club or seen golf and have no inclination toward golf in any venue, I am recommending the viewing of this video, the 2006 graduation exercise at the University of St. Andrews, Scotland, United Kingdom. I concede that in part the video may have struck chords with me because of my participation in so many such events and having served as a university marshal, but I venture to say the video depicting the university's award of the honorary degree of Doctor of Laws to Mr. Charlie Sifford will arouse the emotions of every discerning person who sees it. The citation reads in part that Sifford "is awarded the honor in recognition of his achievements as a golfer and his perseverance in the face of injustice."

Alas, I cannot give a plausible explanation of golf's attraction to me or anyone else, and I smile when I hear the game referred to as "a good walk spoiled." Yet as I write at age 82-plus, I still go to courses where it is not unusual to see young golfers no taller than their golf bags and senior golfers aged ninety or older.

Author as "Sr Games" Gold medalist in golf. *(Photographer Wendell Hull)*

The addictive game of golf has had as much positive impact on my mental health as has any individual, any group, or, conceivably, any institution. In this vignette, in addition to my recognition of Dr. Charlie Sifford, I salute the golfers with whom I have played at least several times—primarily in North Carolina and metropolitan Washington, D.C.—and a few regulars with whom I have played more times than I can count. I am vain enough to write that they are members of my Golf Hall of Fame.

Reginald Allred—Employee, Newton Industries

Joe Alston—Union Organizer and Supervisor, American Tobacco Co. (retired)

John Amey—Administrator, U.S. Department of Agriculture (retired)

Franklin Anderson—CEO, Custom Molders (retired) and Consultant

Edward Boyd—Athletic Coach and City Recreation Official (deceased)

Cornell Brandon—Building and Landscape Contractor

Floyd Brown—Attorney, Athletic Coach, and Physical Educator, NCCU (North Carolina Central University) (deceased)

Oliver "Zeke" Brown—Medical Technician, Duke University Hospital (retired)

James Carter—Public School Administrator, Orange County, N.C.

Willie Covington—Register of Deeds, Durham County, N.C.
Fredrick Davis—Minister, First Calvary Baptist Church, Durham, N.C.
James Davis—Employed by IBM (retired)
Wendell Davis—Deputy County Manager, Durham County, N.C.
Harry "Choker" Edmonds—Head Athletic Coach (deceased)
Stewart Fulbright—Tuskegee Airman and Professor, NCCU School of
    Business (retired)
Nathan Garrett—Certified Public Accountant, Attorney, and Professor,
    NCCU School of Business
Willie Hayes—Three-Sport Letterman and College Golf Coach
James "Jim" Horton—Attorney, U.S. Department of Labor (deceased)
Nathaniel "Skeet" Johnson—Equipment Operator, American Tobacco
    Co. (deceased)
William "Bill" Jones—Business Manager, NCCU (deceased)
Herbert Kinney—Member of the Original Ink Spots Singing Group
    (deceased)
George Lipscomb—Public School Teacher and Professional Athlete
Irvin McCollum—Professor of Mathematics, NCCU (deceased)
Milton "Milt" Muelder—University Administrator (retired)
Michael Palmer—Office of Community Affairs & Government Rela-
    tions, Duke University
Willie Patterson—Community Leader; CEO, Patterson Enterprises
George Quick—Finance Director, Durham County, N.C.
George Quiett—Head Football Coach and Physical Educator, NCCU
    (deceased)
Lowell Siler—Durham County Attorney, Durham, N.C.
"Fill" Smith—Engineer and Auto Racer (retired)
William Smith—Athletic Coach and Physical Educator
Lawrence "Larry" Suitt—Durham County (N.C.) Hospital Administra-
    tor (retired)
Lawrence "Larry" Swain—Supervisor, Department of Corrections,
    Washington, D.C. (deceased)
Frederick Terry—Chaplain, U.S. Air Force (retired); Minister
Samuel Vaughn—Director of Intramural Athletics, NCCU
LeRoy Walker—Chancellor, NCCU; President, U.S. Olympic Committee
    (retired)
Phail Wynn Jr.—Vice President for Regional Affairs, Duke University;
    President, Durham Technical Community College (retired)
James Young—PE Professor and Tennis Coach, NCCU (deceased)

[34]

God Is a Helluva Golfer

IT ALL started at a cookout that Ozie and I hosted for Brenda Thompson and a number of her closest friends. Brenda had just graduated from Howard University's Medical School in Washington, D.C., and she wondered if we would permit her to celebrate the occasion with a backyard party at our home in Silver Spring, Maryland. We assured her of our delight and looked forward to the event along with our daughters, Judith, Jacqueline, and Jennifer.

Our families had lived on the same street, less than a block apart in Durham, North Carolina. Brenda's father, Ray, and I had been faculty colleagues in the Department of Education at what was then named the North Carolina College at Durham. Her mother, Clara, a teacher in the city's public school system, had been a family friend through the years. Of particular interest to me was that Brenda and I had both graduated from Durham's Hillside High School, although I was ahead of her by twenty-nine years.

Among Brenda's guests at the cookout were her longtime friend Cleopatra Broadnax—called "Cool" by close friends—and her friend whose name I faintly recall as Eli somebody. Eli chanced to see a stray golf ball that I'd used while chipping in the yard, and he poked fun, saying I was tearing up the yard with my wedge. He wanted to know if I played golf, and if so, the courses I played on. I named them: mainly Rock Creek, Langston, Northwest Park, and the University of Maryland course at College Park. His eyes and forehead furrows registered surprise when I said I had membership at the University of Maryland golf course. I didn't tell him that I'd been sponsored by a golfer who was a former co-worker in the U.S. Department of Labor.

In a matter of minutes, Eli Somebody and I set a golf match for the following Saturday. We would play the University of Maryland course. "I'm always ready to take on chumps with my AWs," he said with more than a touch of arrogance.

At his invitation we went out to his '71 Lincoln Continental with white sidewall tires. An encased spare tire was on the back end. He was grinning as he opened the car trunk and pointed to a set of golf clubs. "Friend," said Eli Somebody, "these are my AWs."

I was familiar with most of the then-popular brands of golf equipment: Spaulding, McGregor, Hogan, Wilson, and Ping. I noticed that his were a set of Lynx clubs, very expensive. "Damn nice clubs," I said. "But what are the AWs you keep talking about?"

"*Ass* Whippers, man! These are the clubs I'm gonna whip your ass with Saturday," came his reply. I shrugged my shoulders, half-smiled, and simply okayed Eli Somebody's dare.

When we rejoined the party, Eli was laughing as he told Cleo and other guests that I turned "cherry red" when he showed me his AWs. He was a big man. His sport shirt and trousers seemed tailored for his muscular frame. Some of the guests laughed when he announced how he would beat me in our golf match—and with what instruments. I faked a laugh.

I'd been playing golf for only six years. African Americans were prohibited from playing on golf courses—municipal or private—in most of the South, including my home town. And I never caddied a day of my life. But in 1964 a privately owned nine-hole course let down the color barrier, and I believe the owner took in more money than he'd ever envisioned, including mine. When I left North Carolina for metropolitan Washington, the legendary Olympic track coach LeRoy Walker gave me the set of clubs that I had borrowed from him until that time. I doubt that he ever knew or had heard of Eli Somebody.

Yet I knew what every veteran golfer knows all too well: on any given day, a golfer's game can go sour. And on any given day, a golfer can play over his head. I thought: how utterly foolish for a man to boast that he is going to beat someone he's never met or whose skill level he knows nothing about.

Ozie picked me up at National Airport on the eve of my match with Eli Somebody. I had come in from a site visit to Kansas City, Missouri. Characteristically, Ozie listened to the playbacks of my latest skirmishes in the War on Poverty. She then said that what I needed was a relaxing evening at home and a round of golf the next day. I said amen to both prescriptions and was surprised that I had given little thought to the scheduled golf outing.

Eli and I met the next morning at the University of Maryland's course. I don't remember seeing him until we were on the first tee. Nor do I remember the preround warm-ups, the putting practice, or any one-upmanship bantering.

What I do remember is that I played golf like a man possessed. It seemed that each time I took a club in hand, an unseen force took over. Tee shots were well positioned. I was on or near greens in regulation. Chip shots rolled within inches of the pin, and putts rolled into the cup like remote-controlled spheres. *I* did not play Eli Somebody. God did. I have always maintained that golf is a game invented by the devil. This time, God beat the devil at his own game.

Not since that Saturday morning has God played such a round of golf in my stead. Maybe it's because there are so many demands on His time. I suspect, however, that it has something to do with the sin of vindictiveness, because I decided then and there that I would never play Eli Somebody again. The way I figured it, his AWs might just work next time, or God might well be somewhere else. I often find myself wondering if Eli Somebody is telling golfers everywhere how his mouth did him in when he thought he was playing golf against me back in 1972. God knows I do!

In 2009, Brenda Thompson was living in Merriville, Indiana. Her medical practice was located in Gary, Indiana.

[35]

Fry to Thompson to Lewin

My ADMINISTRATIVE assistant at the Department of Labor, Janice Payton, had entered the name, date, and telephone number on the call pad: *While you were out, you received a call from Art Mandakas.* I don't remember the exact date, but the year was 1968.

"He said he knew you from VISTA. Said it's urgent." Mandakas's name was familiar. The telephone number wasn't. "Mrs. Brown called a few minutes after the call from Mandakas," Janice said. "Wants you to call her as soon as you can. She's at home."

Ozie's voice was cheerful, but I could tell she was baffled. "Art Mandakas called here for you. I remember meeting him when you were with VISTA. He sounded desperate." Art had told Ozie that he was calling me at home because he thought I might be out of town, and if I were, he'd appreciate it if she'd relay the message.

I knew that Art was no longer with VISTA, but I didn't know where he was at that time. My gut feeling was that he was looking for a job. Either that or he wanted to broker a contract that could help him get on with a consulting firm. I wanted to call him, but I simply wasn't up to saying "no" to a friend who I thought needed help. Within minutes after I got home, the phone rang.

He wasn't job hunting, not exactly. He was with an executive search firm and was calling on behalf of a client to offer *me* a job. I thanked him for calling, apologized for not getting back to him right away, but said I wasn't in the market for a job.

I had had three jobs in the past four years. Besides, I had completed three years of probationary employment at government service grade 15, the highest civil-service grade attainable. Any grade higher had to be

Walter was classicly ambitious.

by political appointment, and I didn't imagine that was in the cards. Art Mandakas hadn't called to hear me boast about my job security, and I refrained from doing so.

"Would you just hear me out, Walt?"

I agreed.

He said that a coworker had been assigned to find a person for an executive opportunity but hadn't found anyone who met the qualifications. "I've seen the order, and the more I think about it, Walt, the more it sounds like you."

"Executive opportunity? With whom or what?" I asked.

"A consulting firm," he replied. I sighed heavily. Art and I were not on the same page. A number of friends in Washington had a dim, stereotypical view of consulting firms: hustlers in the federal marketplace, con artists with expense accounts, robbers of opportunities that should be given to government workers. To some, these were the good points about consultants.

"Hold on, Walt," Art insisted. "The firm I'm talking about is from an entirely different cut of cloth." He assured me that he would not waste his time or try to mislead me on a matter vital to my career and my family. I asked the name of the firm.

"Fry," he replied. "Fry Consultants, Incorporated. One of the top ten management consulting firms in the country. Headquarters in Chicago. The Washington office is their newest. On Connecticut Avenue, near the Peace Corps headquarters. Small staff. Real sharp. No nonsense, but friendly."

Art went on to say that he couldn't give me a job with Fry if he wanted to, or if I wanted him to. All he wanted was for me to agree to talk with them if he arranged an interview. I agreed, but not before Art Mandakas said that he had made a deal with his associate that they would split the commission if Art found the right man. "I'd be able to take a cruise that I've wanted to take for a long time," he said. I promised to think about it and call Art. That wasn't quite good enough, he said. He'd call me.

Fry? I had heard the name, but it didn't ring any bells when I was talking with Art. Fry? Then I remembered: It happened when I was chief of the Division of Technical Assistance, Office of Manpower Administration (OMA) in the U.S. Department of Labor. Early in 1968, Secretary Willard Wertz issued a directive to the OMA saying that its contracts with consulting firms had proliferated so much that they had gotten out of hand. He ordered the OMA to cut back the contracts to a number and date that I didn't remember. I did remember, however, that the secretary had no preference regarding firms to be kept or eliminated. That, he said, was OMA's problem.

I also recalled that when the meeting of the OMA senior staff began, Joe Kilgallen, chief of the Concentrated Employment Program, said, "The only contract I have that is automatically exempt is with Fry. The others are on the table for review."

What in hell makes Fry untouchable? I wondered. There was no discussion of the firm at this meeting. Kilgallen had spoken with finality about a matter in his Division. *He* was the one accountable, so we went on with the rest of the agenda.

Art called again the next week, at home. He asked me to call Fry, and I agreed to but didn't say anything about my recollection of Fry's reputation in the Department of Labor.

When I called Fry, I was connected with Larry Lewin, principal in the firm's Washington office. I agreed to visit the office and to reserve time for lunch and conversations with some of the staff.

The last person with whom I talked was Robert "Bob" Thompson, vice president of Fry's Washington office. I remember two things from that conversation: The first was Thompson's unmistakable reverence for Vince Lombardi, legendary coach of the Washington Redskins and the Green Bay Packers. I felt that Thompson had said it many times before when he quoted Lombardi as saying, "The difference between a successful person and others is not a lack of strength but rather a lack of will."

The second thing I remember from this conversation is the cleverest job offer I could have imagined: "A long-standing policy in Fry is that we do not raid our clients," Thompson said. "I can't offer you a job because you are with the Department of Labor, and they are one of our clients. *But* if you should ever leave Labor, I'd like for you to give me a call." I thanked him, glanced at a bigger-than-life poster of Mr. Lombardi, and returned to my office at the Department of Labor.

On November 12, 1968, Richard Nixon was elected president of the United States. No one had to tell me that the social programs spawned by the John Kennedy and Lyndon Johnson administrations would soon be in peril. Although I had achieved permanent civil-service status, I was more concerned about job satisfaction than job security. I reasoned that a move to the private sector, provided it offered the desired level of satisfaction, might well be worth the risk. Two weeks after the presidential election, I called Fry.

This time, they asked me to visit their headquarters office in Chicago for interviews and "further orientation." Within a week, I went to Chicago. Not only was I interviewed by three or four members of that office and given the "orientation," as they described it; I was also given a battery of standardized tests that included the Minnesota Multiphasic Personality Inventory and what I believe was a variation of the Wechsler Intelligence Test. At the end of the round with Fry Chicago, my calm was a façade.

A weekend passed between my visit to Chicago and my return to my office at the Department of Labor. My resentment was at a boiling point when I called Fry. Larry Lewin asked how it went in Chicago. I replied without hesitating, "You didn't tell me that I'd be asked to take a battery of tests, and I resent it. You can't imagine how much I resent it." Lewin said he understood and asked if I would come and talk it over with him and Thompson. I complied.

Thompson said he called Fry Chicago on my way over and was told that they tested me because they test prospective executives when requested to do so by Fry's clients. They said they also thought Fry D.C. would appreciate it if they tested me. More was said, all supposedly in an apologetic vein.

Fry Chicago reported that they regarded me as an outstanding candidate. Yet I struggled with conflicting questions of whether to give the job back to Fry or to take it and prove my mettle. Then I recalled that Art had said that Fry had offices in seven cities and not one black professional in any office. Two days later, I went again to Fry D.C. and announced that I accepted their offer pending my resignation from the Department of Labor.

Memory is hazy as to how much advance notice I gave to Labor, two or three weeks probably. Memory is not so hazy about the bon voyage lunch party given for me by co-workers. My mother came up to see and hear what people in the U.S. Department of Labor thought of her oldest son—at least what they said they thought of me.

In 1969, when I joined the Washington, D.C., office of Fry Consultants, Inc., the D.C. staff included:

- Lee Franklin—Williams College; MBA, Harvard University
- Edward Hanley—BA, Colgate University
- Gary Jonas—Columbia University; MBA, Harvard University

- Vello Kuuskra—North Carolina State University; MBA, The Wharton School of the University of Pennsylvania
- Lawrence Lewin—Princeton University; MBA, Harvard University
- Robert Stross—Fordham University; MBA, University of Chicago
- Robert Thompson—West Virginia University; MBA, Harvard University

I say this was pretty good company for a boy from the West End in Durham, a North Carolina Central University Eagle.

I had been at Fry nearly two years when Thompson hired Richard Lowery, a young African American fresh out of Harvard Business School. Thompson was excited about his newest draft pick (Lombardi lingo). When I read Rich's résumé, I was probably more excited than Thompson. I was absolutely in awe when I learned that Rich had graduated from the Boston Latin (High) School and Boston University.

Ever since I first studied the history of the American secondary school, I have had a mystical fascination with what was first the Boston Latin Grammar School. It was established in 1635 as a private school with a classical curriculum that prepared boys mainly for entrance to Harvard College. In 1638, it received public funds from the city of Boston and became the Boston Latin School, the nation's first public high school. Five of its former students were among the signers of the Declaration of Independence: John Hancock, Samuel Adams, and Robert Treat Paine from Massachusetts; Benjamin Franklin from Pennsylvania; and William Hooper from North Carolina.

The hiring of Ellen Wormser, an executive with the federal government's Office of Management and Budget, was a step toward closing Fry's gender gap. Ellen and Rich joined the firm about the same time. I was also pleased when Ellen was hired.

Before I went to Fry, I wondered how it was that this band of MBAS chose to work with a firm whose clients were in the public sector instead of the private—or, more specifically, big business. Thompson explained that each of them had turned down offers from other corporations because they wanted to work with an organization that had as its mission improving social conditions.

Until the early 1960s, Fry's clients were primarily commercial. Some were major corporations like Gillette, Whirlpool, and Radio Corporation of America. As Thompson put it, "Fry's corporate board decided to diversify its practice by establishing an office that would concentrate on social programs. The board also decided to put the office in Washington." Fry appointed Bob Thompson to head the Washington office. Lawrence "Larry" Lewin was appointed office principal. They further explained that my track record in education and government complemented their qualifications. I would be a senior consultant, my first senior *anything*. I was forty-one years old.

Early in my second year with the firm, Bob Thompson severed his ties with Fry and set up his own firm. I was taken aback, to say the least. Here again, he made a veiled offer to me. "I can't ask you to join me. It would be a violation of ethics," he said. *"But* if you should resign from Fry, I would make you an offer right away." The entire Fry D.C. staff accepted the same offer when the firm became Thompson, Lewin and Associates.

Within another year, Lewin bought out Thompson. The rest of the team remained pretty much intact except that Gary Jonas, who was part of the Fry D.C. staff when I joined, left to take a top managerial post with University Research Corporation (URC). Still later, Gary became president of URC, also located in Washington. In 2009, we still have a close friendship.

For the five years that I was with Fry and the organizations it spawned, I worked on teams whose assignments included:

- Evaluation of the national training network for training Head Start staff
- Evaluation of the third-party custodial project with the District of Columbia Department of Corrections
- Design of an implementation plan for carrying out the J. Skelly Wright decision on the equalization of schools in the District of Columbia
- Evaluation of a parent involvement pilot component in an Anacostia neighborhood school (Washington, D.C.)

It would be foolish to suggest that my contribution to Fry was a one-way venture. The firm's standards were high and the work ethic rigorous. It was as if Thompson's idol, professional football Hall of Famer Vince Lombardi, were coach and general manager of two teams, the Washington Redskins and Fry Consultants, Incorporated. I grew as a professional in ways I had never imagined. I increased my skills in developing strategies for addressing organizational problems, report writing, working on management study teams, and making client presentations. My confidence grew in proportion to the development of my skills and my effectiveness with the organization.

With one exception, Lewin hired persons as needed for particular studies rather than full time. The exception was Obie Pinckney, a graduate of South Carolina State College and American University, who was hired full time. Obie and I used to say that as graduates of historically Black colleges, we balanced the firm's ethnic profile. There was an imbalance in the gender profile, with Ellen Wormser as the lone woman consultant. Joyce Hughes, the firm's African American administrative assistant with lightning-fast typing speed, helped the profile with gender as well as ethnicity.

After little more than two years with the firm, Obie resigned and entered Georgetown University Law School, and graduated four years later. In 2009, I did not know how he was using his law credentials although I do remember that he was at one time mayor of Glenarden, Maryland in Prince George's County.

For a long time after my family and I moved back to North Carolina in the fall of 1980, I was asked if I missed Washington. My answer was that Ozie and I always missed places where we had lived. And as much as we enjoyed our return to North Carolina, my experience with Fry Consultants figured prominently in how much we missed the metropolitan Washington area.

[36]

University Associates

Ann collins was a program officer in the United States Office of Education (usoe, the forerunner to the Department of Education). We had first met in 1950 at Bennett College, where she was a student and I was on the faculty. In February 1974, Ann asked if I would make a site visit to Union College. I thought she meant Union College in Schenectady, New York. "Not *that* college," she said, laughing. Ann knew that I wouldn't want to go to upstate New York for anything in the middle of winter. "I mean Union College in Barbourville, Kentucky," she said.

"Come onnnn, Ann," I pleaded. "Isn't there a college in Florida that should be visited at this time? California? Hawaii?"

She said there was no such place on the visitation schedule, and if there were, the director would probably go herself.

The usoe paid a hundred dollars per day plus expenses for site visits. Payments were made directly to individual consultants. My ceo at Lewin and Associates, Larry Lewin, did not like this practice because payments to individuals did not include firm overhead costs. Larry acquiesced when the firm's fiscal officer said he could itemize the visit as a marketing expense. I agreed to make the site visit for the usoe.

Union College in Barbourville, Kentucky, was founded in 1879. It is affiliated with the United Methodist Church. At the time of my visit, the college had an undergraduate enrollment of 290 men and 275 women. Fifty-four were enrolled in graduate courses, eighteen men and thirty-six women. Eighty-eight percent of the student enrollment was White, 6 percent Black, and 1 percent Hispanic. The other 5 percent were Native American and Asian "nonresident aliens."

The college offered twenty-two majors in eight departments. Several departments combined disciplines under one chairperson. "Union College is a place where intellectual and environmental adventurers have been blazing new trails for centuries," a note in the college's public-relations literature proclaimed.

One of Union College's major benefactors was Col. Harland Sanders, of chicken restaurant fame. The college received a grant from the USOE under the Higher Education Act of 1965. The purpose was to improve its capability in program planning and management, and in some curriculum areas. I interviewed administrators, faculty, staff, and students. I checked for congruence between the college's working documents and its reports to the USOE. In all areas, the college fared well.

My exit interviews were with President Maylon Miller and members of the faculty, including Kevin McCullen, an assistant to Miller and assistant professor of political science. After the interviews, McCullen asked if he could talk with me before I left the campus. I thought he wanted to offer me a job at Union College or wanted me to help him get a job in Washington. Instead, he gave me insights that were to change the direction of my life for at least the next five years.

He asked if I had heard of a firm called University Associates. I had. It was in southwest Washington, D.C., on L'Enfant Plaza, the same plaza where my firm, Lewin and Associates, was located.

McCullen said Union College had been getting technical assistance from University Associates for four years. He described it as a small firm, staffed with former college professors and administrators, and he added that it was the odds-on favorite to get a big contract from the Office of Education. The contractor would give technical assistance and do project evaluations of grantee institutions throughout the country.

McCullen leaned forward, put his forearms and hands on the table, and looked me straight in the eye. He said University Associates did not have a single Black person on its staff, and he added, "They have some big guns going for them, but I know that unless they hire some professionals who are minority persons, their chances of getting that contract are zilch. I'm sure they know it too!"

McCullen said that he had been watching me as I went about my work there, and that I was the kind of man that University Associates needed, whether they got the contract or not. He further said that if I were interested, I should find a way to talk with them soon. "You already have an entrée, having visited one of their clients—us," he told me. I tried to conceal my excitement.

He went on to tell me that the chairman of the board was Frank Rose, a former president of the University of Alabama. Rose was president there when George Wallace tried to keep the university from becoming racially integrated, and he added that Frank Rose was bringing Black students into the university through other doors while Wallace was howling at the front door.

By this time, McCullen was as excited about what he was disclosing to me as I was. He further informed me that the president of University Associates was Luther Terry. The name didn't register. I was informed that Terry was the U.S. surgeon general who had ordered that labels be placed on cigarette packs indicating that tobacco may be harmful to smokers' health.

I thanked Kevin for the intelligence, shook his hand, and said I looked forward to connecting with him again.

During the return flight to Washington, I decided on the strategy I would use to get a foothold at University Associates, a strategy I began using eight days later.

I called University Associates and asked to speak to Dr. Rose. The receptionist put me through to Rose's administrative assistant, who, as I'd expected, said Rose was "not in at present" and asked if she could give him a message. I told her that I had made a site visit to Union College for the USOE, and I was willing to talk with Dr. Rose when it was mutually convenient.

The tone of the assistant's "Yes, yes, I will," let me know that she would follow through—pronto. My strategy was working.

The next morning, University Associates' program officer, Dennis Smith, called to say Dr. Rose had asked him to get in touch with me. He wondered if I would mind coming over to talk with him, and he marveled that our offices were just across the plaza from each other. I said I marveled, too. We agreed that I would visit his office two days later.

My heart stopped when I saw the receptionist at University Associates. I only remember Barbara's first name. She was in her early or middle thirties. Her smile accentuated the beauty of her oval face and Greek features. Her coal black hair hung to the small of her back. I tried to feign unaffectedness and said I had an appointment with Dr. Smith.

Dennis Smith came to the front immediately when Barbara announced that I was there for his appointment. We shook hands and exchanged glad-to-see you pleasantries. I glanced at a bouquet of red roses on Barbara's desk as I was leaving with Smith for his office. I had not noticed the roses before.

I told Smith that I had already submitted my report on my Union College site visit to the Office of Education. He seemed a good deal more interested in making an assessment of me than in anything I had to say about his client. When we had talked for about twenty minutes, he asked that I wait in his office "for another minute or two." Five minutes later, he returned. "Dr. Rose would like to meet you."

Rose had a corner office on the second floor of the west building in L'Enfant Plaza in southwest Washington. On one side, the office overlooked the waterfront on Maine Avenue. On the other side, it overlooked the plaza. Rose wore tailored suits that looked smart on his six-foot-two frame. His shirts were also tailored, with the initials *F.A.R.* embroidered on his French cuffs. A chain smoker, Rose was in his late sixties and had most of his hair, most of it gray. His demeanor was pleasant.

Smith stayed in Rose's office as we talked about the Washington scene and how the federal government could assist small colleges in carrying out their missions. As one might expect of three transplanted southerners, our meeting ended amicably, with promises to stay in touch. Rose was the chairman of the board for University Associates. He said he wanted me to meet the firm's president when it could be arranged.

A month passed before I heard from University Associates again. I wanted to be in touch but didn't want to appear too eager. Dennis Smith called to ask if I'd come over. He said the firm anticipated being awarded the contract that Kevin McCullen had told me about. He also said that Rose had in mind Dr. Wiley Bowling for a top administrative position on the contract and asked if I knew Dr. Bowling. I did.

Wiley Bowling was an African American on the School of Education faculty of Georgia State College. He and I had met in the mid-1950s when he was on the faculty of Clark College (now Clark Atlanta University) and had taught consecutive summer sessions at North Carolina College at Durham. I was then the director of the college's career guidance and placement center. Bowling had done consulting for University Associates, and they were pleased with his work. But Smith was certain that Wiley would not give up his tenured position at Georgia State for a consulting job of questionable duration. In that case, "the firm will need a good man, experienced in consulting and familiar with government operations and higher education." Smith knew that I knew he was talking about another African American of proven experience. I surmised that he also knew that I knew he was talking about me.

Then Smith surprised me. He said that Frank Rose had told Dr. Willa Player, director of the USOE, that he was considering offering me the senior consulting position on the project staff. Player had been dean of instruction at Bennett College in 1951 when I was on the faculty there. Rose had asked Player if she had ever heard of me, and if so, her impression. Not only did Player say she knew me but added that I would serve both University Associates and her office well. She also said that I was "a little impetuous" when I had worked under her supervision at Bennett College, but that I was very young at the time.

Rarely have my spirits been so buoyed as when I learned twenty-five years after I worked under Willa Player that she would be pleased if I held a position of leadership on a major contract for her office. I later learned that Smith, at Frank Rose's behest, had asked the president of my firm, Larry Lewin, for permission to talk with me about joining University Associates. It was clear to me that I was not the only player in the cast with a working strategy. Ann Collins insisted that her part in this scenario was purely coincidental.

I was on board at University Associates three weeks before I met Dr. Luther Leonidas Terry. The former surgeon general divided his time between an adjunct professorship in medical affairs at the University of Pennsylvania and the University Associates presidency. He was sixty-four years old and had distinguished himself as a pioneer in medical administration and public service. I wouldn't have thought that Terry was a man who would mandate anything, certainly not that health warnings be put on cigarette packages. He was soft-spoken, stooped at the shoulders, and unassertive. His title as University Associates president was more titular than operational. Frank Rose, chairman of the board of directors, was also the firm's chief operational officer.

University Associates' offices were located in the U.S. Postal Service headquarters building at L'Enfant Plaza in southwest Washington. Barbara, the receptionist parked her blue 1974 Mercedes 450SL in the postal service garage. The only other UA staff person who parked there was Frank Rose. The rest of us rebelled at what we regarded as exorbitant rates for parking. The whispered word was that Barbara's sugar daddy paid her parking bills. Whether or not that was true, we knew that he sent her flowers to commemorate dates that I had long since forgotten, such as the December 16, 1773, date of the Boston Tea Party. Yet the most beautiful thing about Barbara was her personality.

A UA colleague, Harry Blanton, once said that Barbara had slipped out of heaven and brought her personality with her. I would have watched the 1976 Super Bowl on television anyway, but when Barbara told me she was going to the game, I watched with particular interest. Lo and behold, there she was. The television camera people had zoomed in on her. I called Ozie and the girls in adjoining rooms, but before they could join me the camera was back at the action between the Dallas Cowboys and Pittsburgh Steelers. Colleagues Harry Blanton, Calvin Crawl, and Dick McCarthy also watched the game and saw Barbara. No one at University Associates said anything about the Steelers' victory over the Cowboys during the following week. It was all about seeing our Barbara on TV for a fleeting moment.

In the three years I had worked at Fry Consultants followed by three years at Lewin, I had developed solid consulting skills. As blues singer and Orange and Durham counties homeboy Willie Trice had put it, I knew the sun was "gonna shine at my back door one day." I was a star at University Associates.

Wiley Bowling and I were responsible for recruiting the staff persons who assisted in evaluating the reports, supervising the staff, and ensuring the quality of their work. We were the key staff persons in scheduling and planning cluster workshops, and in writing periodic reports for the U.S. Office of Education. My work with fellow UA staff and the USOE was gratifying. Visiting grantee colleges throughout the country was particularly enjoyable, although the travel was taxing at times.

This scenario began when I reluctantly agreed to make a site visit for the USOE in the bleak of winter, to a place I had never heard of, and a stranger pointed me toward new horizons. It is reminiscent of Plato's counsel that the beginning is the most important part of the work.

WILLA PLAYER's death on August 27, 2003, was reported in a front-page article in the *North Carolina Christian Advocate* on September 9, 2003. She was 94 years old at the time of her death. The article credits Dr. Player with opening a major civil rights chapter in Greensboro, North Carolina, when, as president of Bennett College, she welcomed Martin Luther King

Jr. to speak at the college when other colleges in the area would not open their campuses to him.

Willa Player was born in Jackson, Mississippi, and raised in Akron, Ohio. She earned degrees from Ohio Wesleyan University and Oberlin College before receiving the doctorate in education at Columbia University. Dr. Player was president of Bennett from 1955 to 1966, when she went to the Department of Health, Education and Welfare as director of its Title III Program for Postsecondary Institutions.

Milton Muelder: World Class by Any Measure

M OST OF the personalities who made a major imprint on my life did so in my early years. My relationship with Milton Muelder was an exception. I had been on the staff of University Associates (UA) in Washington, D.C., for roughly a year when we met in 1976. He was sixty-nine years old. I was forty-nine. I perceived that he was a learned man with a liberal stance, a great sense of humor, and an enthusiasm for many sports, not the least of which was golf.

His influence on me as a fellow consultant with the U.S. Department of Education was long-lasting. I admired his work ethic, his zest for life, his appreciation for arts and letters, and his clear sense of social justice. When I learned about his family background and his academic career, it was easy to discern how he had acquired and cultivated these attributes.

Milt's academic credentials included degrees from Knox College, Columbia University, and the University of Michigan, and membership in Phi Beta Kappa. Knox College conferred on him an honorary doctor of laws degree at the same ceremony at which his two older brothers were awarded honorary degrees.

During World War II, he was a naval officer on loan to the army for developing the postwar military government in Germany, and he was awarded the Legion of Merit for leadership in a variety of educational and cultural programs in Europe.

A citation awarded to him by the Michigan State University Board of Trustees noted his forty years of service as an instructor in history and political science, department chairman, dean (twice), program director, and vice president of the university (also twice). It further noted that "he gave expertise to dozens of nations on five continents."

Milton Muelder was born in Boody, Illinois, not far from Decatur. His father, a Methodist minister with a PH.D. in philosophy, and a divinity degree, studied Greek and Hebrew, and could read, speak, and write German.

His mother was a registered nurse and a church deaconess. There were seven children: four boys followed by the three girls. Milt was the third oldest. The three older boys were listed in Who's Who in America, each with the PH.D., each with a Phi Beta Kappa key, and each having completed studies in the humanities. A younger brother was completing his PH.D. in science at the University of Iowa when he contracted tuberculosis and passed away. Two of the girls earned degrees in the humanities. The third and youngest became a medical missionary, as was her mother's first ambition.

Milt's excellent work ethic was demonstrated early when, at age twelve, he was hired as a farm hand and used a sulky plow pulled by three horses to plow an entire forty-acre field himself. At thirteen, living in Burlington, Iowa, he lied about his age to get a job in a glass factory. He lied about his age a year later to get work with white-hot boiler rivets in an iron factory.

Particularly poignant to me were Milt's comments that his mother sewed clothes and the boys argued about whose turn it would be to get a new shirt. To make their own baseballs, he and his brothers cut out the leather from ladies' discarded high-laced shoes. They then covered hard rubber balls with the leather and stitched it.

Milt often accompanied his father on visitations made by horse and buggy, which were rented for one dollar. "For a kid, such religious visitations can be very boring," he said, "especially the extended prayers at the end of the encounters, but at least I got to drive the horse and buggy after the ordeals."

Milt's wife, Kathleen Dietrich Muelder, was a scholar and classicist in her own right. She had a PH.D. in biochemistry and nutrition and worked in these areas at Michigan State. She and Milt had met when Kathleen was writing her doctoral dissertation and needed an article in German translated. As he has done for so many others, Milt translated the article for his new friend. The friendship blossomed into marriage in 1939.

After a heart attack in late 1979, Milt moved from Washington, D.C., back to East Lansing, Michigan. He regained his health and has followed a strict regimen of proper diet and exercise—swimming in particular—ever since. He has followed the arts and sports just as intently.

Milton E. Muelder. *(Brown family papers)*

I was saddened when, on February 11, 1995, Milt called to say that Kathleen had passed away. She had been blind for the past ten years of her life because of macular degeneration, and at age ninety-three, she died from an advanced case of pneumonia. She dedicated her body to science. Of Kathleen, Milt said, "She was the smartest person I have ever known, and happily my most severe and honest critic, which was a big boon. We had compatible tastes in literature and art and in the enjoyment of music. In our last years, we patronized the Wharton Center [Michigan State University's cultural arts center] more than anyone else."

In July 1998, Ozie and I received a letter saying we were among a "few close friends" being invited by MSU president Peter McPherson and his wife, Joanne, to a celebration for Milt. The occasion was Milt's ninetieth birthday, August 27. Ozie was unable to attend for health reasons. The celebration took place with a luncheon at the University Club and an evening cookout at the McPhersons. Milt visibly enjoyed it all.

Milt's golfing days were behind him by that time, but I played the next day—a Friday—with a group of his former golfing friends. On Saturday, I was Milt's guest along with his brother, Walter, and his assistant, Beth Schwartz, at a football game between MSU and Colorado State. The only damper during the entire celebration was that MSU lost the football game, 16–23. A small measure of solace for MSU faithfuls, however, was that it was a nonconference game.

I was the only nonrelative to attend the celebration from outside Michigan. Milt had to share center stage with his brother Walter who, at ninety-one, was a year older than the birthday honoree. I delighted in meeting Milt's friends and relatives, especially his sister, Ruth, from Kenosha, Wisconsin, and his brother, Walter, from Boston. But when Milt and I found time to chat, he told me how much he missed Kathleen.

A conversation with Walter Muelder was yet another memorable experience during this visit. He was dean emeritus of Boston University School of Theology and a social activist. He had also served on the doctoral committee for Martin Luther King Jr. In the "small world" department, at Boston University Walter Muelder was the graduate adviser to Douglas Moore. Twelve years earlier, Moore had been Ozie's and my schoolmate at North Carolina College at Durham, and he was our minister in 1957 when we joined Durham's Asbury Temple Methodist church. Walter Muelder was also the doctoral advisor for my friend, C. Eric Lincoln. Lincoln's dissertation was subsequently published and widely acclaimed as *The Black Muslims in America*. Lincoln later became professor of religion and culture at Duke University's Divinity School.

Milt, a major financial benefactor to MSU, contributed substantially to establish the Japanese Garden at MSU in partnership with the University of the Ryukyus in Okinawa, Japan. I attended the opening of the garden in 2002. During this visit, I was the guest of Milt and the McPhersons in the president's box of the MSU–University of Michigan basketball game— won, incidentally, by MSU, by a score of 71–44.

My friendship with Milton Muelder has continued far beyond the years when we were colleagues at a consulting firm in the federal marketplace (1976–1979). More than once, I have heard Milt tell friends in East Lansing that I had contributed significantly to his life. There is no question that he contributed to mine in equal or greater measure.

[38]

KVWs in the Whitley Family

I T S E E M S that Black males have always been regarded as an endangered species. In 1994, for instance, the Indianapolis Commission on African American Males issued a report in which it concluded, "Black Males' Future Looks Bleak." Voyce and Katie Whitley either missed such reports or were undaunted by them in raising their sons, Karl, Kenneth, and Kyle.

When Karl Vinson Whitley was in the ninth grade, he began to scribble his name and add "M.D." to it. He enjoyed being man of the house when Voyce was on travel. The oldest of the Whitley sons, Karl graduated from the University of Maryland and received the medical degree from George Washington University Medical Center in Washington, D.C., in 1990. In 1994, he was appointed chief resident in otolaryngology at Temple University Hospital in Philadelphia, Pennsylvania. Karl is married to Kim Smith Whitley, a graduate of Duke University Medical School. She is a pediatrician and fellow at Children's Hospital in Philadelphia.

With the encouragement of a master cellist, Kenneth Vernon Whitley, second son, decided in the seventh grade that he wanted to be a cellist. He loved working jobs to make his own money. Katie once offered to pay Kenneth the same amount of money he was making as a carrier for the *Washington Post* because he had to make deliveries in inclement weather at five-thirty in the morning. He declined the offer. Kenneth received undergraduate and graduate degrees from the University of Michigan. He is a performing cellist and former conductor of the Washington, D.C. Youth Orchestra, and the Mount Royal String Orchestra in Baltimore. Kenneth is presently the director of the Bryn Mawr middle school music program in Baltimore. He is married to Jane Cromwell Whitley, a graduate of Peabody Conservatory of Music at Johns Hopkins University. A performing

Voyce and Katie Whitley
with the author. *(Brown
family papers)*

violinist and teacher, she worked with Kenneth as assistant director of the Mount Royal String Orchestra.

Kyle Victor Whitley, third son, "was a real challenge," said Katie. "He always showed entrepreneurial interests. When he was two years old, he thought he knew everything." Kyle is marketing manager for Sprint's call center technology services in Plano, Texas. He received his undergraduate degree in marketing from the University of Maryland and his master of business administration degree from the University of Michigan. He is married to Helisa Horton. Helisa is accounting manager at Mary Kay's headquarters in Dallas.

Voyce Preston Whitley and Katie Porter Whitley live in Silver Spring, Maryland, where each of their sons attended the Montgomery County public schools. Voyce retired from the U.S. Department of Health and Human Services as director of facilities and administrative management. He attended public schools in the racially segregated school system of Luling, Texas, a small town between San Antonio (a little less than sixty miles west) and Houston (about 140 miles east) and situated just north of I-10. Its population in 2000 was just over 5,000.

When Voyce was in the eleventh grade, some of his closest friends volunteered for service in the U.S. Army. The friends were seventeen or older. Voyce was fifteen. He said that he didn't want to be left in Luling, Texas, without his friends, so he dropped out of school and started saying he was seventeen. In May 1946, he was inducted into the army. After his honorable discharge in May 1949, Voyce returned to school and graduated with the class which, by that time, he had caught up with in chronological age.

Voyce received his undergraduate degree from Huston-Tillotson College in Austin, Texas, a historically Black institution affiliated with the United Methodist Church and the United Church of Christ. He did graduate study at Howard University, Washington, D.C.

Katie attended the public schools in her native New Orleans, and after graduation attended Xavier University in New Orleans, the only college in America that is both historically Black and Catholic. Following a career of thirty years with the federal government, she retired from the Department of Health and Human Services in 1990.

Since the late 1960s, Voyce and Katie have been active members of Woodside United Methodist Church in Silver Spring, which was racially integrated a few years before they joined. Voyce is chairman of the church's board of trustees and treasurer of the Huston-Tillotson alumni chapter of Metropolitan Washington. Katie is president of the United Methodist Women at Woodside, where she has served as chair of three committees: Education, Staff-Parish Relations, and the Administrative Board. She is also secretary for the county's chapter of the National Council of Negro Women, and she is a member of the Ladies Board of the House of Mercy in the District of Columbia.

When asked about their child-rearing practices, Voyce and Katie were responsive and explicit. They did not have strict rules about television, but they monitored the programs their children saw and encouraged the viewing of current events and news programs. They studied with the children instead of merely insisting that they observe home study periods. Voyce was the key resource parent in math and science. Katie's strengths were in language and writing skills.

The boys made their own career decisions, although the parents hoped early on that Kenneth's interest in music would be a merely avocational interest. "We lost on that score, but he is happy and we are too because we are filled to the brim each time we hear him play or see him conduct an orchestra," said Katie.

Summers with grandparents in Texas gave the boys a sense of adventure and independence from their parents.

Membership in the African American youth organization Tots and Teens supplemented the boys' education in the county's predominantly White public schools. Voyce and Katie agreed that the boys' lives were enriched socially, intellectually, and spiritually through Tots and Teens, and they made lifelong friendships through the organization.

Child-rearing practices aside, their children were endowed with good native intelligence. "They had an inherited gene from Voyce," Katie said deferentially.

The Whitleys attended Woodside United Methodist Church regularly, and the boys were active in youth groups. Kenneth was the cross bearer on Sunday mornings.

The family almost always had dinner meals together. Blessings and Bible verses were said at each meal. Kenneth's special verse, encouraged by Katie's mother, was "Let brotherly love continue." He started saying this verse when he was six years old and still says it at family gatherings.

Voyce and Katie were in full accord on the benefits their boys derived from participating in the home regimens of cooking, cleaning, washing, ironing, and entertaining. They enjoyed the cooking and entertaining, but the other requirements were integral parts of Homemaking 101 for Guys, they told me. Katie seemed especially delighted to add that the extended benefits of their homemaking skills now accrue to their wives and children.

Music of all kinds—classical, jazz, rhythm and blues, pop, and country—is a perennial interest and activity with the Whitleys. On occasions when gifts are exchanged, items pertaining to some aspect of music are given—books on music history, albums, tapes, and compact discs.

More often than not, role models are viewed as adults worthy of emulation by children and young people. The Whitleys were my family's closest friends during our years in Maryland and the metropolitan District of Columbia. Their lifestyle influenced our lifestyle. With their friend, Marian Hayden, we commiserated together, worshipped together, and partied together. My favorable impression of the Whitley family led me to write a story about them and submit it for publication in a popular black-owned magazine. I was naive enough to expect the editors to wedge it somewhere between stories about "fabulous" seasonal fashions, celebrated entertainers, "eligible" bachelors, and slick advertisements.

I thought: This is the kind of story that subscribers—families in particular—should read and contemplate at least once in a while. My submission was neither published nor acknowledged. It often occurs to me that only our Maker will understand when we sing the words of the Negro spiritual, "my soul looked back and wondered how I got over."

Going Home: In Defiance of Thomas Wolfe

T HE YEAR 1980 turned out to be as momentous for me as 1945 had been thirty-five years earlier. Not long after the new year was under way, I applied for admission to the Institute for the Management of Lifelong Education at Harvard University and was accepted. The Institute would only run for two weeks, but it would also be something different, and the anticipation was exciting.

At different times in my travels to colleges, first as a federal employee and later as a consultant, I was offered jobs in administration, although I admit that offers were sometimes in response to my discreetly made inquiries. I also admit that in each instance, Ozie's response was, "Humph, I don't want to go there." But in the spring of 1980, when I was offered a full professorship at North Carolina Central University (NCCU), effective the following fall of the 1980–1981 academic year, Ozie was smiling as she said, "I'd like that." Decision time: What would I do about the summer institute at Harvard? Wouldn't I need to be at home to attend matters incidental to the sale of our house, closing out my work at University Associates, and getting a house in Durham? Would our daughters be amenable to leaving Silver Spring for Durham? At first blush, two weeks might seem to be a short block of time, but time is such a relative apportionment, especially when momentous decisions are to be made.

Enter Ozie Foster Brown, unquestionably explicit: I should attend the Institute and not lose sleep over conflicting options or responsibilities. Meanwhile, she would attend to matters related to selling our house in Silver Spring. And we would keep in touch about getting a house in Durham, with the help of my mother, who lived in Durham. The girls would be all

Walker returns to NCCU in 1980

Celebrating something. *(Brown family papers)*

right. And after all, I had no proprietary interest in University Associates. It was simply a cultural phenomenon in Washington.

I did attend the Institute and earned a certificate from it. The experience merely broadened my horizons, inasmuch as I never used it to negotiate a possible career opportunity. But my self-directed study at the Gutman Library for Harvard's School of Education yielded considerable payoff in planning for the courses I would teach in Historical, Philosophical, and Social Foundations of Education, beginning in the fall semester at NCCU. My resignation from University Associates was accepted "with complete understanding" and enough effusiveness to last for many moons.

Judy had taught in the Washington metropolitan public schools, and she chose to stay in the area, where she soon became a teacher at Georgetown Day School. In 2009, she was still teaching there.

Jackie had just graduated from Montgomery Blair High School in Silver Spring, and she chose to remain with Ozie while our house in Durham was under construction. Ozie had negotiated with the buyers of our house to rent it from them until our place in Durham would be ready—roughly six weeks.

Jennifer had just finished the ninth grade at Sligo Junior High School.

Sweet though she is, I am not certain that Jennifer has ever forgiven us for the move that prevented her from going to Montgomery Blair High School, where she qualified to be a member of its pom-pom team, and instead required her to attend a school that didn't have one at all. Nevertheless, Jennifer and I moved to Durham, where she attended Jordan High School and I began my new job at NCCU. We moved in with my mother as we awaited completion of our house and the arrival of Ozie and Jackie.

Six weeks later, the family, minus one, was in our new home. Senior faculty in the university's Department of Biology remembered Ozie from her time with them sixteen years earlier, and they were delighted that she was rejoining the department as its administrative assistant. She held that position until she retired in 1992.

Jackie landed a job as wait staff supervisor at Swensen's restaurant in the city's Brightleaf Square complex. After the restaurant went out of business, Jackie was in a state of depression until she was rehabilitated by professional services and the family's love. She earned certification in early child development at Durham Technical Community College, and in 2009 she is a teacher at Durham's Triangle Day Care Center.

Jennifer subsequently earned a bachelor of arts degree with a major in political science from North Carolina Central University. In 2009, Jennifer is a senior claims officer with Monumental Life Insurance Company in Durham.

For the next twelve years, I was engaged in teaching and research for NCCU's Department of Education, intermittently consulting for the U.S. departments of Education and Labor, teaching calligraphy for the university's Art Department, and serving as the university marshal. Then came the appointment of Dr. Tyronza Richmond as NCCU's chancellor, the system's approval of a proposal for the university to establish a School of Education, my appointment as interim dean of the new school, and then my appointment as permanent dean—a misnomer if there ever was one—two years later.

ON JULY 6, 1989, the university provost, Dr. Mickey L. Burnim, announced my appointment as dean of the School of Education in a memorandum to the school's faculty. The memorandum included the following:

The written recommendations and comments.that were submitted to me revealed that Dr. Brown is well respected within the Department of Education. He was nominated for this position by several faculty members and has been endorsed for it by all of the other top candidates. As nearly as I can determine, he possesses all of the qualities outlined by the faculty as being desirable. These include the following: (1) a very selfless attitude with respect to the department, (2) good knowledge of accreditation bodies and processes, (3) good working relationships with the established educational community, (4) good breadth and depth with respect to educational issues, problems, approaches and initiatives, (5) strong sense of fairness, and (6) lots of common sense.

Dr. Burnim ended the memorandum by asking the faculty to rededicate themselves to the progress of the school and to "work diligently" with me toward that end.

My letter dated July 6, 1989, to the School of Education faculty read:

Dear Colleagues:

Experience has shown that a new administrator must be careful in writing the first letter to his/her colleagues. "First" letters are generally read with careful scrutiny. Readers look for evidences of egotism or self-centeredness. ("Did you count the number of I's and me's in his letter?") Some make judgments as to whether there are evidences of timidity or apprehension. Some are alert to signs of pedantry or shallowness. Still others take note of whether the newly appointed administrator tries to be a jester, or is too cute in his remarks. It appears, therefore, that a hazard in writing the initial letter is that it either will make no lasting impression or that it will turn everybody off. (The next paragraph should be easier to write.)

I can do Robert Fulghum one better in his claim that "All I Really Need to Know I Learned in Kindergarten." I never attended kindergarten but much of what I really need to know, I learned at my mother's knee. It should be understandable, therefore, that I will place a premium on fairness in administering the office and in carrying out our mission. What I hope to achieve is a judicious blend of fairness, adherence to established university policies, and efforts to further strengthen our offerings in education and the human sciences.

To promise or even envision Camelot as a work setting would be folly

The author as university marshal.
(Brown family papers)

in the face of the awesome challenges in public education and problems associated with racism, sexism, political chicanery, abuses of the environment, abuses of children and the elderly, crime, unemployment, and so on. When we add our own day-to-day adjustment problems, Camelot becomes even more elusive. Yet, to the extent that a healthy work environment contributes to our capacity to cope with stress-inducing situations, I hope that each of us will strive to establish and maintain such an environment.

Take note that I have treaded gingerly in making an appeal to support me in my efforts, etcetera, etcetera. . . . Rather, the appeal is for us to be solid professionals. Our challenges are formidable both for the immediate and longer term. This would be so even if we were not cutting our teeth as a newborn school. But we can meet the challenge. We must. There is too much at stake, not the least of which is the welfare of the students entrusted to us for instruction and guidance.

Godspeed, WMB

The school's highest priority was the forthcoming (1992) accreditation visit by teams from the North Carolina State Department of Public Instruction and the National Council for the Accreditation of Teacher Education (NCATE). We were constantly reminded by the accrediting body that the standards were more rigorous than at any previous time, and we heard disquieting stories about the failure of some schools to meet the standards.

I believe that one thing in my favor was my determination to retire three years later, at age 65. With this awareness, I worked at a pace that I couldn't have kept beyond the three-year timetable. I walked alone each morning before the work day officially began, thinking through creative solutions to daily and longer-term problems. At the end of each walk, I recorded letters, memoranda, strategies, and ideas, and gave the tape to

Walter was much beloved by his colleagues.

Chuck Alcorn,
Carolyn Whitted, and
the author. *(Brown family papers)*

my secretary, first Vernell Massey and later Joan Morrison, who succeeded Vernell, when I reached the office.

Drs. Carolyn R. Whitted and Charles L. Alcorn were the School of Education's associate deans. They, along with Dr. Cecelia Steppe-Jones, who coordinated the student advisory services for our graduate programs, worked as if their lives were on the line in the tasks they were assigned or took on voluntarily.

Carolyn was associate dean for instruction. Her field of concentration was guidance and counseling. She held degrees from Hampton University, Boston University, and the University of Wisconsin, and she had been on NCCU's faculty for twelve years. I consistently tested my brainstorms on her. She was unusually adept at making good ideas better and applying the brakes when the ideas seemed far-fetched or untimely.

Chuck (the name Charles preferred) was associate dean for administrative services. His degrees were from Grove City College, Harvard University, and the University of North Carolina at Chapel Hill. He was gifted at ensuring that bureaucratic requirements were met on time and in the orderly flow of business. He had been at NCCU for twenty-one years.

Dr. Cecelia Steppe-Jones held degrees from NCCU and Southern Illinois University. Her field was special education. A tireless and indefatigable worker, Cecelia saved the day for the School of Education when she managed the transition of student personnel functions from the College of Arts and Sciences (CAS) to the School of Education. She had been on NCCU's faculty for seven years.

I had thirty-nine years of experience in higher education, the federal government, and the private sector when I was appointed acting dean. Not

Heady days
w/ a good team (handwritten annotation)

in all those years had I been a member of a team where the chemistry was as good and the efforts so rewarding as when I worked with Carolyn Whitted, Charles Alcorn, and Cecelia Steppe-Jones. Also, the faculty generally responded positively to the leadership team's efforts.

Carolyn and Chuck took on some of the duties in my job description while I wrote a grant proposal to the U.S. Office of Education. The proposal was funded and resulted in a number of benefits, including:

- a personal computer for each faculty member who wanted one, a significant accomplishment in the early 1990s;
- funds for faculty visits to public schools or school systems with exemplary programs in different parts of the country;
- funds to start and purchase materials for a curriculum library; and
- funds for limited capital improvements in the building that housed the Department of Education. (Construction of a new building to house the School of Education was begun five years later.)

An accreditation standard that evoked intense interest was the accrediting agencies' requirement that each institution adopt a unifying principle that could make its teacher education program unique. This unifying theme was to be called the "Knowledge Base." We adopted two different concepts before coming up with one that was to be NCCU's Knowledge Base: Educators for Diverse Cultural Contexts. I developed and presented to units across the University a "Conceptual Model of the Knowledge Base Theme for North Carolina Central University's Teacher Education Program—Educators for Diverse Cultural Contexts." I could not have been more pleased with the response. At a banquet for the university's Teacher Education Council and the School of Education faculty, Chuck delighted me with the presentation of the theme literally etched in stone. Insofar as I have discerned, the School of Education continues to use this Knowledge Base for program planning and operations. The ten-pound stone is now displayed in the School of Education's lobby.

Several key factors fueled the drive toward our forthcoming accreditation visit. Dr. Mary Townes, then dean of the CAS and a personal friend since the late 1940s, cooperated fully in improving working relations between her unit and the School of Education. We worked together to ensure that CAS faculty who were teaching education methods courses were appropriately rewarded when they wore two caps well, one in CAS and the other in the School of Education.

I took advantage of existing opportunities and created others to impress upon other administrators that the outcome of the accreditation visits would reflect on the entire university, not merely the School of Education.

As the university's chief academic officer, Dr. Burnim was aware of the school's shoestring budget and found ways to assist where we had severe constraints, such as our need for funds to hire adjunct faculty and clerical support staff, and to close gaps in our library holdings.

The accreditation teams were on campus March 1–4, 1992. They were vigilant in carrying out their charge to determine whether the institution in general and the teacher education program in particular met the prescribed standards in curriculum, general education, professional studies, clinical experiences, relationships with public schools and graduates, advisory services, qualifications of faculty, faculty load, faculty development and evaluation, governance, and resources.

Well in advance, we were informed that the measure for each standard would either be "met" or "unmet," with no provisional ratings. This in itself was enough to heighten our anxiety.

On the fourth and final day of the visitation, Dalton B. Curtis, chairman of the NCATE accrediting team, notified vice chancellor Burnim's office that he was ready to present the teams' findings to the dean of the School of Education and the associate dean for instruction. No other persons were to be included.

The conference was held in my office. Carolyn and I sat patiently, wondering.

I FELT THAT chairman Dalton Curtis was moving tantalizingly slowly as he reported whether the School of Education met the eighteen accrediting standards in five different categories. This is what the chairman reported:

Category I   Knowledge Bases for Professional Education (design and delivery of curriculum, general education, specialty studies, professional studies):   MET

Category II   Relationship to the World of Practice (clinical and field-based experience, relationships with graduates, relationships with schools):   MET

Category III   Students (admissions standards, advisory process):   MET

Category IV   Faculty (qualifications, teaching load, development   MET
opportunities, evaluation criteria):

Category V   Governance and Resources (organizational struc-   MET
ture, due-process provisions, budget alloca-
tions):

Chairman Curtis extended congratulations. We exchanged expressions of appreciation and wished each other well. When Curtis left our office, Carolyn and I exhaled sighs of relief and embraced before going to the auditorium to meet with the education faculty and vice chancellor Burnim. We knew that they were as anxious as we had been.

I began by saying that Dr. Whitted and I were delighted to announce that the visiting teams would recommend to their respective organizations that our School of Education be fully accredited. Burnim gave a down-ward thrust of his arm as he exclaimed, "Yes!" There were cheers until I interrupted and announced that Dean Whitted had an additional word. Carolyn then announced that "all standards were met." Even the doors and windows smiled.

I called Ozie and told her the good news. She had retired as admin-istrative secretary to the chairman of the Biology Department a month earlier. When we celebrated that evening, I reassured her that I, too, was looking forward to retirement three months later, at the end of June 1992.

THE CHANCELLOR of NCCU during my tenure as dean was Tyronza Richmond. In a letter to me dated May 19, 1992, he wrote:

> *Although you informed me of your decision to retire on July 1, 1992, more than a year in advance, it is only now that I have accepted the fact that it will occur as you planned. Prior to my decision to return to a full-time faculty position, it had been my intention to use every persuasive tactic in my power to try and convince you to delay that decision. . . .*
>
> *With the trailblazing success you have had in so many different educa-tional arenas, you represent the standard of excellence by which we judge outstanding students, faculty and administrators. While there are many things that are surely special from your very distinguished NCCU career, I*

am sure that you will always have fond memories of how you orchestrated a successful NCATE *review with a newly formed school and crumbs for resources. . . .*

With your literary skills, I am sure that you will devote some more time to writing. You have a lot to say, and there is an interested audience.

In 2009, "Educators for Diverse Cultural Contexts" continued to be the Knowledge Base and the underlying theme for the School of Education's practices in admissions, curriculum planning, and evaluation.

Mary Doris McLean Townes, distinguished emerita professor of NCCU, died January 14, 2003.

Charles L. Alcorn, emeritus professor of education, died October 23, 2008.

[40]

Germany the Second Time Around

I WISH I could say that my college sophomore courses in German were taken in anticipation of spending time in Germany. However, in the school year 1944–1945, I had no way of knowing that in 1945 I would "visit" Germany as a private in the United States Army, or that I would visit again in 1990 as an educator, three years before my retirement. In the main, I studied German as an alternative foreign-language course to meet the basic curriculum requirement at North Carolina College at Durham. Both experiences—the courses and the trips—broadened my horizons appreciably.

In June 1990, I enthusiastically joined twelve other faculty and administrative persons from four historically Black colleges and universities as participants in the Phelps Stokes New Horizons Project. The German Marshall Fund sponsored the project. The mission of the German Marshall Fund of the United States was to stimulate an exchange of ideas and promote cooperation between the United States and Europe in the spirit of the postwar Marshall Plan. The Fund was created in 1972 by a gift from the German People in appreciation of the original Marshall Plan aid.

I was dean of the School of Education at North Carolina Central University (NCCU). The other participants from NCCU were Mickey L. Burnim, vice chancellor for academic affairs, and Eugene A. Eaves, director of international programs. In addition to NCCU, the institutions were Clark Atlanta University and Spelman College, both private and located in Atlanta, Georgia, and Lincoln University, a state institution in Chester, Pennsylvania.

The timing couldn't have been better. The reunification of West Germany (the Federal Republic of Germany) and East Germany (the German Democratic Republic) was the single most important issue in recent decades for our host countries. We would have opportunities to observe the dynamics between two nations, at the same time culturally similar and dissimilar, as they weighed the consequences of becoming a single political and geographic entity.

The author at the dismantling of the Berlin Wall. *(Brown family papers)*

Two aspects of education in West and East Germany were of particular interest to me—the relationship between church and state, and whether there were equal educational opportunities.

In West Germany, church and state existed almost as a single educational entity, at least in the perception of many German citizens. I had an opportunity to observe these perceptions when I visited a *Gymnasium*—a school primarily intended to give students the qualifications needed for admission to the university—as a guest of one of the school's teachers. I was struck by the fact that the school was located in a Catholic church. I questioned the reason for this integration and was surprised at the imperturbability of my host's reply. It was as if there was no basis for questioning the relationship between these two institutions in supporting public education. In his view, it was all rather simple. Educational practices varied locally, according to the *Laender* in which a school was located (a *Laender* is a distinct politico-educational region that establishes educational policy in its area). Some *Laender* were predominantly Catholic; others were heavily Protestant. Where one group was dominant, it exerted the greatest influence in shaping educational thought and practice—in governance and administration, curriculum development, instruction, and teacher education.

In some *Laender*, primary schools were divided according to the religious denomination of the parents. About 44 percent of the population in the Federal Republic of Germany was Roman Catholic. The nature of relationships between church and schools was established by consensus

The author at the entrance of Karl Marx Universitat. *(Brown family papers)*

between the parties and approved by the Vatican. Secondary schools were generally Christian community schools. In them, religious instruction was given according to the denomination of the pupils. My own view is that church and state should be separated on matters pertaining to public education. This visit heightened my appreciation that separation between the two is a historical fact in the United States and is undergirded by the U.S. Constitution.

The educational system in the German Democratic Republic (East Germany) was controlled by a central government with underpinnings that reflected socialist ideology and Marxist doctrine. When the GDR was established under Soviet rule in 1945, three key principles were decreed: (1) education was to be the exclusive responsibility of the state, (2) religious instruction was to be the responsibility of religious corporations, and (3) public education was to be the same for boys and girls—a democratic *Einheitschule*, it was called (an *Einheitschule* is a comprehensive school with grades one to ten).

I concur with the view that in the GDR, the state *was* the religion. Socialist ideology pervaded the curriculum and daily instructional activities. Even in the universities, students received compulsory instruction in Marxism-Leninism.

Until World War II, Germany had a two-track system of education. There were minor variations between school systems, but generally speaking one track was vocationally oriented to prepare students for work, and the other was classically oriented to prepare students for study in the university. After the war, West Germany modified the system at the behest of the United States, but the national pattern of dividing students according to ability during grades five and six continued.

When schools in East Germany came under the control of the Soviet Union, the concept of a multiple-track educational system was abolished in favor of a single ladder from the primary school to the university. This action is consistent with the view that educational opportunity should never be based on students' socioeconomic conditions. It is also consistent with the GDR's constitutional provision that "every citizen of the German Democratic Republic has the same right to an education. The integrated socialist educational system guarantees every citizen a continuous socialist education, training, and further training."

I enjoyed the hospitality of the German people in their schools and universities, their public agencies, in their shops and homes.

In West Germany, I was particularly moved by the contrast between the cities in ruin that I had seen in 1946 and the gleaming, bustling cities I saw in 1990. Streets were clean. Flowers were everywhere, in window boxes and in garden plots. I had never imagined that there could be a place so beautiful as the Herrenhausen Garden in Hannover. I sent postcards to relatives and friends from Hannover and Bonn, Cologne and Leipzig, Dresden, Berlin, and Munich. A side trip to Salzburg was reminiscent of the movie *The Sound of Music*. A boat ride up the Rhine and a wine festival in Pommern blended with our fantasy worlds.

Fully 90 percent of our study group's activities centered on education in Germany—a conference with a representative of the Ministry of Economic Corporation, lunch with journalists in Bonn, and presentations and discussions on Germany's economic systems. We visited schools and universities; held conferences with teachers, students, and administrators; and were observers in several schools.

In East Germany, signs of a failing economy were evident in the decay of public buildings. Color tones everywhere were like mixtures of burnt

The author with East German educators. *(Brown family papers)*

umber and ochre on an already dirty palate. This was strikingly incongru-
ent with the festive air of a midweek dance at the student center at Karl
Marx University in Leipzig, although Leipzig is also East Germany.

When I learned that our train was routed through Göppingen, Germany, I announced with fanfare that I had been stationed there as a member of the United States Occupation Forces following World War II. Like
wildfire, the word spread all the way to the head conductor and engineer.
For me, the train stopped in Göppingen so I could step onto the ground
for a matter of seconds. It was a dramatic step indeed. Eugene Eaves tells
about the experience with gusto.

At Humboldt University we discussed higher education in Germany
with about twelve faculty members. Also in Leipzig, we attended the opera
Carmina Burana by Carl Orff, a magnificent production unlike anything
we expected based on impressions gained from some FRG officials about
the overall culture of East Germany. Our visit to the Paul Robeson Archives in East Berlin was profoundly moving for me. A Robeson medallion
purchased at the archives is among my most treasured memorabilia.

I am haunted by the memory of our visit to Bergen-Belsen, the museum on the site of the infamous concentration and prisoner of war camp

in Lower Saxony, "dedicated to the children, women and men who were humiliated, tortured and murdered in Bergen-Belsen." An excerpt from a memorial publication reads:

> *Time is a great healer, a popular saying goes. For those who were imprisoned in Bergen-Belsen and in other concentration camps, this saying was never true. The survivors of National Socialist persecutions continue to suffer from physical and psychological consequences. "Some wounds never heal," wrote Werner Weinberg, one of the survivors from Bergen-Belsen. "The suffering of the victims makes it our duty to remember them first and foremost." We will remember the dreaded Berlin Wall as more than a tourist sight from which we would obtain pieces to be taken as souvenirs, but as a dreaded symbol of oppression, which gave greater meaning to the concepts of unification and freedom.*

I recall this quotation each time I see the piece that I chipped from the Berlin Wall, and I suspect the other participants have a similar reaction when they look at their souvenir pieces.

I would never be the same after this experience, not as an educator and not as a citizen of the world. But in neither of the Germanys did I find answers to the multiplicity of problems in American education. By way of illustration, when I returned to my home in Durham, North Carolina, there was in the mail an article that had appeared in the May 27, 1990, issue of the *Guardian Weekly,* a Manchester (England) newspaper, entitled "Thirty Years On and Durham High School Is Still a Blackboard Jungle."

WHILE THE English reporter may have overstated some of what he learned during a visit to Durham and other cities in the United States, it signals the broad range of problems to which we returned and are still compelled to address. In the two Germanys, there was anxiety over unification. In my hometown, there was anxiety over the proposed merger of a predominantly African American city school system and the predominantly White county school system. Merger of the Durham systems has been a fact since 1992. But there remain in this city and throughout America problems in education related to governance, achievement gaps between ethnic minority (mainly African American) students and White students, and the pervasiveness of racism and poverty. The worst thing that can happen is for concerned persons to be overcome by despair.

[41]

Bonding with Jack Bond

IN AUGUST 2009, the Southern Piedmont Chapter of the National Forum for Black Public Administrators (NFBPA) sponsored its fifth John P. "Jack" Bond III Memorial Golf Tournament in Charlotte, North Carolina. The event is a scholarship fundraiser for students in public administration, African American students in particular. Jack was one of the founding members of the NFBPA; he received its Marks of Excellence Award in 1988 and served as its president from 1989 to 1990.

A key to the city of Winston-Salem, North Carolina, hangs in my study. It was presented to Ozie and me by Jack on our twenty-fifth wedding anniversary. I met many people in the fifteen years in which I traveled for government agencies and consulting firms in Washington. Jack was the only person I met in those years with whom I developed an enduring friendship.

In 1971, Jack Bond was Winston-Salem's assistant city manager, the first Black person to hold a top position in the city's administrative echelon. I was then with Fry Consultants, a management consulting firm that had a contract with the city of Winston-Salem to provide technical assistance for a project jointly funded by the city and the U.S. Department of Housing and Urban Development (HUD).

The federal agency designated the program a Community Development Block Grant. Participation of area citizens across socioeconomic lines was a major HUD requirement. Its aim was "to ensure decent affordable housing for all, and to provide services to the most vulnerable in our communities, to create jobs and expand business opportunities." I believe the Winston-Salem program was successful to the extent that social programs

John P. "Jack" Bond III. *(Courtesy of Carol S. Bond, Phillip S. Bond photographer)*

can make a difference in the face of funding limitations and changes in political parties.

Jack Bond and I hit it off right away. We were both graduates of what are widely referred to as historically Black colleges and universities. So were our wives, Carol and Ozie. Our schools were Morgan State University for Jack, Howard University and Winston-Salem State University for Carol, and North Carolina Central University for Ozie and me. The families' favorite professional football team was the Washington Redskins, although Jack was far more zealous about the Redskins than the rest of us. Also, Jack and I were both members of Alpha Phi Alpha fraternity. (Later, we would also become members of the Alpha Tau Boulé, Sigma Pi Phi fraternity.)

Perhaps the coincidence that started the bond between Jack and me was the revelation of friendship between our families and historian John Hope Franklin. Jack's father, John P. Bond Jr., and his mother, Willard Phillips Bond, were among Franklin's closest friends when Franklin was at St. Augustine's College in Raleigh, North Carolina. At that time, the older

Bond was a National Youth Administration administrator. On December 23, 1937, Franklin was visiting the Bonds, who were then living in Washington, D.C., the night that Jack was born. After Jack's parents, Franklin was the first person to hold infant John P. Bond III.

Jack's public-service career began immediately after he received the bachelor of arts degree and was commissioned as a second lieutenant in the U.S. Army in 1960. He served the next seven years in Korea, the Military District of Washington, Italy, Fort Monmouth, New Jersey, and Vietnam. He resigned his commission in 1967 and took a management position with the Community Action Agency in Monmouth, New Jersey. His career in Winston-Salem began in 1971. During my work with him, I met Orville Powell, the city manager and Jack's immediate supervisor. Powell was later city manager of Durham, North Carolina.

Jack and I kept in touch after he left North Carolina in 1978 to take a position in Florida. Over the next six years, he was city/county manager in Miami and Tampa, Florida, and was city manager of Petersburg, Virginia. I was on the faculty of North Carolina Central University in Durham when, in 1984, Jack became county manager of Durham.

Jack and Carol bonded closely with Ozie and me during his stints in Durham. We attended social gatherings, had meals at each other's homes, went fishing, and had other good times together. We also watched our children grow up, although my family saw less of their son Phillip than of their daughter Johnna. Phillip was a midshipman at the U.S. Naval Academy for four years. He was commissioned ensign upon his graduation in 1987 and served six years in the navy, based primarily on the West Coast; he visited his family in Durham only when he could get leave.

One of Jack's characteristics was his readiness for new career opportunities, some of which he made for himself. He considered every challenge presented to him by consultants who were hired to find persons—African Americans in particular—with outstanding track records in municipal management. In 1990, he resigned his position as Durham's county manager to accept an offer from the mayor of Washington, D.C., Sharon Pratt Dixon, to become city administrator and deputy mayor for operations. I attended Durham County's farewell social hour for Jack along with his cohorts in county administration, area politicians, members of Jack's family, and friends. It turned out, however, that conditions in the District of Columbia municipality were in such turmoil as to make improvements and rational management practices virtually impossible. As explained by Kay McFadden of the Durham *Herald-Sun,* "Instead, [Jack] found himself mired in the internal troubles of a staff that seldom agreed and with responsibilities that fielded questions about the city's handling of protests and riots that erupted in D.C.'s Columbia Heights. The situation deteriorated . . ."

Jack severed those ties in early 1992 to return to Durham to form his own company, Jack Bond & Associates, Inc. (JBA). The focus of JBA was management consulting, drawing on Jack's years of experience in county, municipal, and state government. JBA facilitated minority participation in the construction contracts of several major Durham projects, including the Durham Bulls' ballpark. He was employed at the same time as chief operating officer for Construction Control Services Corporation, a firm that specialized in engineering and project management. Two years later, he became the deputy chief auditor for the state of North Carolina.

In the spring of 2000, Jack was appointed by North Carolina Governor James Hunt to coordinate services for rebuilding the historic town of Princeville in eastern North Carolina. Princeville is the oldest town incorporated by African Americans in the United States. It was established in Edgecombe County by freed slaves after the Civil War and incorporated in 1885. The municipality was inundated by floodwaters in the fall of 1999 after hurricane Floyd dumped catastrophically large amounts of rain on coastal North Carolina counties, destroying property and displacing hundreds of residents. At the same time, Jack was a lecturer for the School of Business and consultant to chancellor Julius Chambers at North Carolina Central University.

Jack's challenges in Princeville were compounded when he began to suffer a recurrence of an earlier bout of cancer and was compelled to take radiation and chemotherapy with the hope that he could thwart the disease, even as he commuted daily to eastern North Carolina. By May of 2001 my friend learned that more aggressive treatment was required, and by the end of June he was hospitalized for the management of pain. Although a valiant fighter, Jack lost his battle with cancer on August 16, 2001. I was at his bedside in Durham Regional Hospital the day before he died, and I knew then the end was near. I believe Jack also knew it.

There were chords of sameness in the recollections of Jack's life, the same kinds of observations I made about him at the office of Fry Consultants at least twenty-five years earlier:

- His management style was a blend of formal training and experience, congeniality, and good instincts. During his tenure in Winston-Salem, he earned the MBA from the Babcock School of Business at Wake Forest University.
- He was a tireless worker whose work day frequently began with breakfast meetings and planning sessions.
- He was an astute but low-keyed political strategist.
- He was a pioneer in the use of communications technology in management practices.
- He was an avowed practitioner of affirmative action in searching for and hiring qualified ethnic minorities and women.

During Jack's tenures as Durham's county manager, deputy state auditor, and the governor's representative in Princeville, he and I communicated by telephone, e-mail, or both nearly every day. When we missed a day, Jack customarily began our next exchange with something like, "Where've you been, Bro?" The range of topics was limitless—our families, our jobs, racism and liberalism in America, health matters, sports, people we trusted, people we distrusted, and risqué jokes. Conversation about religion wasn't taboo, but it wasn't something we talked about. We liked each other too much to engage in discussions about differences between the denominations of our preference. Jack was a member of the Catholic Church. I am a Protestant.

An editorial dated August 19, 2001, in the Durham *Herald-Sun* observed that: "It was as Durham County Manager from 1985 to 1991 that Mr. Bond did some of his best work. He was an early advocate of downtown revitalization. He pushed through bond issues that led to improvements at the Durham Arts Council building, the Carolina Theatre and the Hayti Heritage Center. He also is credited with helping the downtown Community Shelter for HOPE."

The memorial service for John Percy "Jack" Bond was held at Duke University Chapel on August 21, 2001. His family gave me the honor of presiding at the service. I believe the following excerpts from the reflections by Sharon Goode-Laisure, longtime friend of Jack and Carol, captured her sentiments and the sentiments of others who spoke at the service:

> *Jack was every bit as much a teacher as he was a leader. . . . He was as proud of his protégés as he was of his children, and he didn't hesitate to peep*

over those glasses and tell you what you needed to hear, when you didn't nail something as you should have. . . . He seemed to enjoy writing but I guess one could expect that from an English major. . . . He was a master strategist with public policy issues. . . . It is simply incredible to me the number of people across the country who owe their professional development to crossing paths with Jack Bond.

Tributes and salutations were given by Alpha Phi Alpha fraternity and Sigma Pi Phi fraternity. An organization in which Jack's wife Carol is a member, the Links, Inc., also saluted him. Rev. Brendan R. Horan, S.J., was officiate for the funeral liturgy.

Two months after the memorial service at Duke Chapel, I attended the memorial service and inurnment for Jack at Arlington National Cemetery. The service was attended by approximately forty relatives and friends.

Orville Powell was city manager of Durham at the same time that Jack Bond was Durham county manager. Orville is now a clinical associate professor in the School of Public and Environmental Affairs at Indiana University, and he is author of *City Management: Keys to Success*. The book is dedicated "in memory of John P. Bond III, who served his country with dignity and honor, being awarded the bronze star medal for meritorious service in Vietnam and later distinguishing himself as both a city and a county manager."

I suspect that a number of persons who read this vignette will wonder if Orville Powell is an African American. He is not. Some may even wonder if one of them reported to the other on an organizational chart. That was not true either. The city and county governments in Durham are coequals. The city manager of Durham is responsible to a council of seven members including the mayor. (When Powell was city manager, the city council was made up of thirteen members.) The county manager is responsible to a board of commissioners that has five members. Perhaps the two governing bodies will merge someday, a move long advocated by some citizens, lay and professional.

Since the first Jack Bond memorial golf tournament, Jack's widow, Carol, has served as honorary co-chair. I have played in the tournament for three years. Several others who were among Jack's closest friends in Durham have participated in each of the five years that the tournament has been held: Willie L. Covington, Durham County register of deeds; Wendell Davis, deputy Durham County manager; Michael Palmer, director, community affairs, office of public affairs and government relations, Duke University; and George K. Quick, Durham County finance director.

Understandably, another Sigma Pi Phi Fraternity member, Lowell Siler, chose not to absent himself from Durham to play golf, having been installed as county attorney just three days prior to the 2009 tournament. Both Lowell Siler and Michael J. Palmer came to Durham County government when Jack Bond was manager, and they regarded him as their mentor and friend.

[42]

In Memory of Jimmy Hayes—
Classmate, Actor, Friend

RAPHAEL THOMPSON, a retired member of the School of Business
faculty at North Carolina Central University, served unofficially as
coordinator of reunion activities for our college class of 1948. (My wife,
Ozie, served with him prior to her illness.) I sent the letter below to Raphael after I attended classmate, and fraternity brother, Jimmy Hayes's memorial service.

January 9, 2002

Dear Raphael,

I have just returned from Jimmy Hayes's funeral in Carthage. While I
am not one who attends a funeral each time I read an obituary in the local
paper, I never pondered whether I would attend this one, fate—especially
the weather—permitting. It was a good decision. I rode down and back
with three of Jimmy's relatives. The day was beautiful and the camaraderie
good. You should know that your presence was missed, and I know that
you would have been with us were it not for your nasty cold.

Everything went well at the funeral service . . . until . . . Well, as I told
you recently, I have taken upon myself the challenge of writing my memoir
and I am enjoying it very much. (No target date and no commitment to
finish, or for that matter, to write at all.) We arrived at the church some
forty minutes before the service began. I went with my traveling companions to the Hayes family house, across the street from the church. After
greeting the family, I returned to the church. With time on my hands, I
took out my pad and began writing notes for future reference in memoir
writing. My friends saw what I was doing and so did Jimmy's sister, Har-

riet, who also lives in Durham. They began to whisper, evidently wondering what I was writing about. I later learned that Harriet said I was writing a statement on behalf of our class to be read during the funeral service. The others agreed it must be so.

When the service began, the mortician tapped on my shoulder and asked if I were "Dr. Baker." I pointed to Donald Baker, driver of the car in which I rode. The mortician then went to Donald (he was sitting with the family) and tapped his shoulder. When I saw Donald turn and say something while pointing to me, I knew I was in trouble. The mortician returned to me and asked if I knew I was to make a statement during the service. "Not yet," I replied in consternation. Sarah Bell-Lucas was sitting next to me and overheard the conversation. In her inimitable, authoritative fashion, Sarah whispered, "You *gotta* do it." I agreed to do it.

It seemed only seconds later—although I know it was longer—that the minister was saying, "We will now have a statement from Dr. Walter Brown.

I walked to the front of the church and, without a single written note, opened my mouth. I guess God took over from there. It was as if I had rehearsed it. People were gracious in their praise.

Basically, what I said was that the pin on my lapel was given to me on the occasion of the fiftieth anniversary of the North Carolina College at Durham, Class of 1948, and that Jimmy Hayes was my classmate. Jimmy loved the class. Jimmy loved his classmates. He loved NCC. On the occasion of the class's forty-fifth reunion, Jimmy was given the floor at our reception. It was at that time that he both mesmerized and entertained us with what I was to learn later was his signature feature: "Touch Hands with Those Who Stay." I said that I did not learn until his death that Jimmy was *not* born and reared in New York. But, upon reflection, it was evident that he had assimilated positive aspects of New York, where he performed in Broadway productions, of Carthage, and of the John Hall Presbyterian Church, and that the result was a nobleman, a prince, a jewel. I said it was my privilege to represent the NCC class of 1948 and indeed the entire NCCU family in thanking Jimmy's family and the members and friends of John Hall Presbyterian Church for giving Jimmy to us for some fifty-five-plus years. I thanked them, said "God bless all of you," and returned to my seat.

Dinner was served to family and friends after the service. I ate and enjoyed every morsel on my mounded plate: chicken—fried, baked, and in dumplings—baked ham, green beans, collard greens, macaroni and cheese, black-eyed peas, okra, potato salad, candied yams, stuffing plus gravy, rolls, sweet potato pie, coconut cake, chocolate cake, lemon meringue pie, pound cake, coffee, and fruit drinks. After leveling the mound before my dessert, I knew then that I would neither miss nor be late for my aerobics classes the next week.

I hope to see you soon, and I sincerely hope that you are feeling better.

Fraternally,

Walter

[43]

Jim Blue, Predictably Special in All Seasons

I MET DR. JAMES Blue on the campus of North Carolina Central University in the early 1970s, but our friendship began after my family and I relocated to Durham in 1980. A mutual interest in fishing brought Jim and me together. An outing in his boat at Jordan Lake is one of my most memorable experiences.

Jim Blue was born on November 6, 1930, the fourth of five children, in Carthage, North Carolina, in Moore County, sixty miles east of Raleigh. His first role model was his father, James F. Blue Sr., a kind and gentle man who worked as a planer in a wood-finishing mill his entire life. Jim said his mother, Barbara Leslie Blue, was a saintly woman and community matriarch. She died in 2003 just weeks before her ninety-ninth birthday.

Jim's schooling began in Carthage's Pinckney High School, a union school—that is, a school with grades one through eleven. One of four "colored" high schools in the county, Pinckney was named for a former principal who was also a minister. Jim remembers the school as an archetypal symbol of separate and unequal education for Blacks, poorly equipped and continually in need of repairs. He said the school's only redeeming quality was that it was close enough for him to be able to go home for a hot lunch during recess.

As he was too young to enter school legally that first year, Jim repeated the first grade and received no credit for his first year of attendance. His sixth birthday came three weeks after the October 15th cutoff date for first-graders. When he was in the eleventh grade, the state Department of Public Instruction made twelve grades a requirement. He said it took him thirteen years to finish high school. He also said this became a pattern of deferred or extended requirements throughout his educational career.

James F. Blue. *(Courtesy of James E. Shepard Memorial Library University Archives and Records, North Carolina Central University, Durham, North Carolina)*

Jim Blue placed great value on the extended-family concept, and he was often reminiscent about related occurrences—births, graduations, weddings, christenings, funerals, and holidays—that triggered gatherings by relatives and community members.

When he was a child, his family kept a tab at the community grocery store, a place where men hung out and talked about an endless range of subjects. He remembered that men also hung out at the barbershop, a place where he was forbidden to go. Jim conceded that the barbershop wasn't the only off-limits place for him, but he explored other places anyway.

He knew the location of his uncle's whiskey hideouts and bootleg whiskey houses, the most famous of which was Miss Lucy James's, where knife fights and shootings took place, most often on Saturday nights. "Denizens named Dirty Red, Big Goon, Five Cents, and Clietus Skinner ruled there," he told me. His friend Tom lived in that area, and Jim said he often visited Tom without the consent or knowledge of his parents. Tom made a career of military service. He died in Maryland in the early 1990s.

Throughout elementary school, Jim suffered severe asthma attacks. Yet he scored high on both teacher-made and standardized tests. In high school, he was an excellent student-athlete despite continuing problems with asthma. He attained honors as a student leader and was co-captain of the basketball team, first quarterback on the football team, a bus driver, and a member of the glee club. He said his adoration for a girlfriend kept him from attaining top scholastic honors at graduation, "but two conference championships and making the conference's all-star team somewhat compensated."

Jim graduated from high school in 1949 and entered Johnson C. Smith University on a basketball scholarship. Located in Charlotte, North Carolina, Johnson C. Smith is a historically Black, Presbyterian-affiliated school. He spoke forthrightly, saying, "The rigors of study, training, and part-time work proved to be too much for an asthmatic, lovesick athlete." He returned home and sought employment after being turned down for the military draft because of his history of asthma.

In September 1950, following seasonal work as a waiter at the Holly Inn Hotel in Pinehurst, North Carolina, Jim went north to find employment. For the next seven years, he worked in Atlantic City, New York City, and Long Island, New York, in various jobs including busboy, truck driver, parking attendant, waiter, and handyman. He said that the succession of dead-end, unfulfilling jobs and a new girlfriend named Addie Wall made change inevitable.

Jim and Addie married February 16, 1957. He described their marriage as "a wonderful journey that spanned forty-four years." Jim's hobbies included jogging, locksmithing, fishing, and providing neighbors with roses from the garden that he and Addie enjoyed. He said the high points of his forty-four-year journey with Addie were the adoption of their two children, Regina Miriam and James III. Regina is now the mother of two children, and James adopted two children from South Africa.

When Addie insisted that Jim resume his formal education, he showed his appreciation and new resolve by enrolling at another historically Black college, North Carolina Agricultural and Technical College in Greensboro (now North Carolina A&T State University). He became active in the sit-in demonstrations at the Woolworth's store in Greensboro that sparked other protests leading to passage of the Public Accommodations Law. He was unsuccessful in his bid to become student government president at North Carolina A&T, but he found a measure of solace when a charismatic and popular schoolmate with leadership skills and a talent for turning a phrase—a schoolmate by the name of Jesse Jackson—was subsequently elected to that office. Jim and fellow students continued to be civil-rights activists.

Jim graduated summa cum laude from A&T in 1961 and won a Danforth Foundation grant to study at the predominantly White University of North Carolina at Chapel Hill (UNC–Chapel Hill). In 1962 he received the master's degree in education. After a year teaching physical education at a junior high school in Greensboro, he was employed as an assistant professor in the department of physical education at North Carolina Central University (NCCU). At the same time, he enrolled in the doctoral program at UNC–Chapel Hill, and in 1972 he received the PH.D. in higher education from that institution. At NCCU he later served as dean of students and vice chancellor for student affairs. He retired as a member of the university's physical education faculty in 1995.

Following retirement, Jim became more active in his church, Covenant Presbyterian Church in Durham. It was an extension of his childhood participation in the church of his family, John Hall Presbyterian Church in Carthage. He recalled that when he was five or six years old, he assisted his father in cleaning the sanctuary, firing the boiler, and cleaning the church grounds.

"I literally walked in my dad's footsteps after a light snowfall on the way to start a fire before church service, actually having to jump from one footprint to the next," Jim told me. He became an elder at John Hall when he was twenty-six years old, an unusually young age for such an honor at any church. He maintained membership at this church until the early 1980s, when he and Addie transferred their membership to Covenant.

Addie's death in September 1998, coincident with the illness of my wife Ozie, fortified our friendship. We leaned on each other in camaraderie and commiseration by phone and e-mail, and over breakfasts at Briggs's, Elmo's, or Le Coco's restaurants, often without advance planning. It was during these times that I gained insights about Jim that helped me understand what a remarkable person he was and how he got to be that way.

When my daughter Jackie and I awoke on the morning of December 5, 2002, we were unpleasantly surprised to find that our house had neither heat nor lights, a happenstance, we thought. It turned out that residents on our street were among the 1.5 million people in North Carolina without electrical power because of an ice storm. We decided to stay put, hoping for a short-time inconvenience. The situation was not as grave for daughter Jennifer, whose apartment had power. She was providing refuge for several of her co-workers at Monumental Life Insurance Company, then located in downtown Durham.

For seven consecutive days, North Carolinians endured what the media described as a natural disaster, the result of a statewide ice storm. On the first of the seven mornings, I called Jim Blue to compare notes. To my surprise, he and the other residents in his neighborhood had power. True to his nature, he invited Jackie and me to leave our cold house and come to his place. He already had a guest who who had been iced out of her home about ten minutes away, Barbara S. Darden, the lady who would become Mrs. James Blue the following February 8.

Jim said that he had "never thought of marrying again" after Addie's death until he fell in love with Barbara, whom he met at Covenant Presbyterian Church. "When I met Barbara, I felt that we would complement each other well," he told me. He added, "She is bright, affable and attractive." He said further that after taking her on a date with his ninety-seven year old mother, he asked Barbara to marry him. Their marriage vows were spoken at Covenant in 2002. Jim, tall and long-limbed, and Barbara, of average height with a single braid hanging to the small of her back, made a striking couple.

Jim's happiness in his marriage to Barbara left fewer opportunities for our breakfast meetings at our favorite haunts, although we kept in touch by phone and e-mail. Some of his e-mail jokes were simply hilarious. I also was hosted with lunch at their new home.

After roughly two years in their marriage, Jim began to fight with a number of serious health issues—problems affecting his vision and ultimately the dreaded diseases of leukemia and lymphoma. When I visited him at Duke Hospital, it was evident to me that he was still characteristically optimistic and determined. Indeed, he was discharged after a time with a report that his cancer was in remission. It turned out that the remission was short-lived and he was released to go home with hospice care. Barbara was at his side through it all. On April 4, 2009, she phoned to tell me that her dear husband, my special friend, had died. As has happened with far too many, cancer had overtaken his once-strong body.

The marriage of James S. Blue and Barbara Sellers Blue was fulfilling for themselves and beneficial to others, particularly Durham's Covenant Presbyterian Church, where they served unselfishly in music and several different auxiliaries. When this vignette was written, Barbara S. Blue was still a stalwart in the church's services to its members.

[44]

Gentleman without Portfolio: Louis Weathers

I KNEW Louis Weathers as an unlettered man married to a lettered woman. He was a handyman and part-time tailor at the Washington Duke Hotel haberdashery in Durham, North Carolina. His tailoring was limited to basic clothing alterations, a skill acquired on the job under the watchful eye of Jethro Dawson, a much older man who retired nearly two years after Louis was hired. Weathers's wife, Laura, was a registered nurse who had risen to supervisory level at Lincoln Hospital, the medical center for Durham's Black citizens.

Louis and I met at a dance sponsored by the graduate chapter of Kappa Alpha Psi fraternity at Durham's Algonquin club. He was as dapper as anyone I had ever seen, live or in pictures. A one-button, gray, double-breasted suit draped his muscular frame. A white-on-white shirt formed the background for his tie in a soft pink fabric. The tie matched a large handkerchief in his pocket. French cuffs extended just the right length beyond the coat sleeves. And his plain-toed patent-leather shoes glimmered with a spit shine.

I was taking a breather at the bar after consecutive dances of the latest dance craze, called the twist. Chubby Checker made popular both the dance and a song with the same name in 1960. Louis was standing at the bar; I greeted him. "Beautiful suit!" I said. "I know you didn't buy a suit like that in Durham."

"You better b'lieve I didn't get it here, "he said. "You must know something, my man. I mean you talk like you 'preciate good threads and all. What's yo name?"

"Walter Brown. I'm going to take my wife this Bloody Mary. How about walking over with me?"

As we walked, Louis introduced himself. "Glad to meet you, my man. Louis Weathers. Some cats call me Chi 'cause I was in Chicago before I come here."

"Baby, this is Louis Weathers," I told Ozie. She greeted Louis with a smile and handshake before relieving me of her drink.

During intermission, Louis introduced me to his wife, Laura. She was older than he by at least ten years, or appeared to be. Her heavy makeup and aquamarine dress with sequins on the bodice did not make her attractive. After brief pleasantries, Laura Weathers left immediately for small-talk circles in other parts of the ballroom.

I danced another dance, this time the two-step with Ozie. Louis found his way over to the bandstand. I've noticed that some men spend much of their time at the bandstand when they are neither good dancers nor comfortable in conversation. I walked over to him.

"Great band," I said. "And that vocalist is something else. I could listen to her all night."

"Yeah, but that band ain't from here," said Louis. "From up the road somewhere, I bet. D.C. or Baltimore. I've seen a lot of bands play like that in hot spots before I come here." I listened, which seemed to be exactly what Louis Weathers wanted—and needed.

Over the course of a year, Ozie and I saw Louis at three or four socials. The pattern repeated itself. His interactions with others were brief. He seemed especially ill at ease when he and Laura were in small-group conversations. It appeared, however, that Ozie and I had the key to what Louis's psyche called for: the feeling that he was just as important as anyone else, if not more so.

In the spirit of Jess B. Semple, the matchless plain talker of Langston Hughes's creative genius, Louis was hard on Durham's middle-class Blacks. In his estimation, they flaunted pretentious lifestyles. I heard it over and over again. "These cats ain't hittin' on nothing, man. All of 'em wearing jive clothes they bought in this town. Me, I goes up to New York and Philly, places like that to get my threads. Goes up there two or three times a year to get my stuff soon's it comes in style. And that's least two years before it gets here. See this suit I wearing? It ain't even got here yet." Louis paused, then added matter-of-factly: "'Course, when this gets here, I'll be wearing something else."

Louis said I should let him make some threads for me. "You got a P.H. degree, man, but that ain't enough. You need to look the part. Hell, if I had your degrees and my shit, this town couldn't hold me no longer'n I put gas in my car." Another pause. Another footnote: "If you want to know something: I'm thinking about splitting from Durham myself."

Nearly eight years passed before I saw Louis Weathers again. He was a bellhop at the Lowes Hotel at L'Enfant Plaza in southwest Washington, D.C. I was with Lewin and Associates, a consulting firm with offices in the same complex as the hotel. Louis graciously accepted my invitation for dinner at home with Ozie and me. That evening, I was wearing a sport coat he had made for me in Durham. A lady friend accompanied Louis. I didn't get her last name; Louis simply introduced her as Pearl. She was in her forties, reserved and attractive. She was also demonstrably in love with Louis.

He was as refreshing and wily as when I last had seen him. Pearl had a felicitous smile that suggested she had heard the spiel before: "Look, Doc, I got the concession for the shoeshine stand at the bus station downtown. I works part time at a tailor shop on Seventh Street plus hopping bells at the hotel where I saw you. I tried my best to get my old lady to leave Durham. I said to her: 'I'm tired of us running around with a lot of pr'tending people.' Then I said, 'If you come with me, I'll have you living like these damn people pretend to live.' But naw, she wants to stay there and be buried in Beechwood." Again, the characteristic pause and footnote: "They ain't gonna bury me in Beechwood. Gon' bury me in Arlington or some damn where." Louis gurgled when he said, "Arlington."

In the fall of 1980, seven years after that memorable evening with Louis and his friend, Ozie and I returned to Durham. I would miss the occasional chats with him in the square and restaurants at L'Enfant Plaza. He was a villager who lent credence to the view that any friendship can be fulfilling where there is good chemistry and honest interactions irrespective of perceived social class. Louis's former "old lady" died in Durham in 1996. I hope she found her niche there despite Louis's characterization of people in Durham, North Carolina. And I ain't just pr'tending.

[45]

Calligraphy: A Positive Addiction

I N 1994, twenty-eight years after the Armentrouts and Browns became family friends in Silver Spring, Maryland, Ozie and I attended the White House ceremony where President Bill Clinton awarded the Presidential Medal of Freedom to widely acclaimed historian John Hope Franklin.

During the reception following the awards ceremony, Professor Franklin's son, John Whittington Franklin, asked me what I felt was a rhetorical question: Would I like to visit the White House calligraphy studio? The next thing I knew, "Whit" and I were exchanging pleasantries with Ann Stock, the White House social secretary. He told Ann that I was a master calligrapher and asked if she could arrange a visit. Ann said she'd be glad to take me and asked if I was ready to go then. I was ready except that I needed a moment to ask Ozie if she'd like to go as well. A resounding "yes."

Ushers and security guards nodded dutifully as we passed them down a flight of stairs, along the hallway, and into the area where four calligraphers were lettering on a variety of documents. Miss Stock introduced Ozie and me to them and indicated that I was a calligrapher. They seemed pleased to meet a fellow scribe. We then met the fifth staff person, who was sitting at a station apart from the others, working at a computer. The incredulity of it all, I thought: a computer in the palace scriptorium! He was making entries on a spreadsheet.

My credentials as a lettering artist appeared to have been established when I said that my interest in calligraphy was sparked by a calligrapher friend, Russell Armentrout. A calligrapher I surmised to be advanced in age said that Russell had retired the previous year and that they sorely missed him. The others smiled and nodded in agreement.

Russell and Hope Armentrout were one of the first families with whom we developed close ties when Ozie, the girls, and I moved to Silver Spring, Maryland. They were members of Woodside United Methodist Church when we joined the church. Their daughters, Gail and Amy, were our daughters' schoolmates at Woodside Elementary School. The girls became inseparable.

Russell saw that I was enthralled with what I regarded as exemplars of calligraphic letter forms and suggested that I watch for announcements of beginning calligraphy classes. At the time, travel demands in connection with my work at VISTA (Volunteers in Service to America) prevented me from taking a class. But beginning in 1968, when I was with the U.S. Department of Labor and traveling much less, I took my first calligraphy course at Montgomery County Community College in Rockville, Maryland. Englishwoman Ann Pope was the instructor. When on travel thereafter, I practiced writing letter forms in hotel rooms. I was hooked.

Nearly a year later, I took workshops on Roman Bookhands and Gothicized Italic under Shelia Waters, sometimes referred to as the dean of Washington-area calligraphers. Whether it was Shelia's reputation or the influence of the Washington Calligraphy Guild, almost every calligrapher of international prominence sooner or later taught a class or conducted workshops in metropolitan Washington.

I was never a flag-waver for covered-dish dinners, but luck smiled on me at the church dinner where I met Patsy Crouch. It was at that dinner that I also learned of Patsy's interest in calligraphy. I would later learn from Shelia Waters that she regarded Patsy as one of her most gifted disciples. Like the Russell Armentrouts, Patsy and her husband, Bill, were also members of Woodside United Methodist Church.

Patsy Crouch became my tutor. As a member of the area's inner circle of accomplished calligraphers, Patsy was assured advance registration in calligraphy classes sponsored by the Calligraphers' Guild. Invariably, she interceded on my behalf, and in time she entered some of my work in local exhibits, even when I felt the work was not quite good enough. I became a member of the guild and maintained the membership in it for a couple of years after my family and I moved back to North Carolina.

In addition to Patsy, five other leading calligraphers made their mark on me in a variety of classes:

- Mimi Armstrong, under whom I studied Heraldry at the Smithsonian Institution. She also introduced me to the incomparable *Book of*

Kells. Twenty-five years later, I saw the original *Kells* at Trinity College in Dublin, Ireland.
-   Maury Nemoy, a graphic designer for television, motion pictures, and record companies, who helped me gain an appreciation for expressionistic calligraphy as an art form.
-   Ieuan (pronounced ya'on) Rees, who gave illustrated lectures on the formation of letters in medieval manuscripts. Even Ieuan's free-hand demonstration letters on the blackboard were awe-inspiring.
-   Julian Waters, a book designer at the Smithsonian Institution and the son of Shelia Waters, who conducted a workshop I took on Black Letter Capitals. The workshop focused on Old English letters, referred to as Gothic or Fraktur.
-   Robert "Bob" Williams, a book designer for the University of Chicago Press, who conducted a workshop on Illuminated Manuscripts. Bob showed a vast knowledge of the evolution of the Roman alphabet and was gifted in helping students understand how historical developments influenced the changing character of letter styles. I will probably never know whether I was the only workshop participant who did not know until he entered the hall that Bob was an African American.

Records of the First International Assembly of Lettering Artists (1981) show that I was the only North Carolinian to attend that conference. The Assembly was held at St. John's College in Collegeville, Minnesota. Foremost among the guest artists was the British calligrapher Donald Jackson, a scribe to Her Majesty's Crown Office in the House of Lords. Through the years, I have aptly referred to this one-week experience as "glorious." Other international conferences have been held at least biennially, but we who attended the first international conference have received special recognition at subsequent conferences. I have proudly worn this badge of honor.

My interest in calligraphy did not wane when I returned to North Carolina. Indeed, my interest increased, as evidenced by some of the activities I've engaged in over the years:

-   Membership in the Carolina Lettering Arts Society and one of its subsidiaries, the Triangle Calligraphers' Guild.
-   Teaching calligraphy classes for the art departments of Durham Technical Community College and North Carolina Central University.

- Conducting workshops for the Durham Arts Council and to inmates at the Federal Correctional Institution at Butner, North Carolina.
- Participating in a two-week workshop at Colby College in Waterville, Maine, sponsored by the Calligraphy in Maine Guild. The guest artist was Peter Halliday of Staffordshire, England. He later became president of the London-based Society of Scribes and Illuminators.
- Conducting a study of characteristics of calligraphic societies in the United States, funded in part by a grant from the North Carolina Central University faculty research committee. The study appeared in the May-June 1984 issue of the *Journal of Calligraphic Arts*.

In calligraphy classes that I taught for the North Carolina Central University art department, I frequently used illustrations of manuscript exemplars from the British Museum Library, the Victoria and Albert Museum, and other libraries in the British Isles. My interest in such historic works became so keen that I became determined to see originals firsthand, in the British Isles.

John Sharpe, then curator of rare books for the Perkins Library at Duke University, favored me with letters of introduction to curators at the British Museum Library and the Victoria and the Albert Museum, both in London. Further, he solicited their cooperation in permitting me to review selected manuscripts. My reception at each of the libraries evidenced that Sharpe was highly regarded not only by his peers at Duke University but by those beyond the shores of North America as well.

I basked in every step of my 1985 sojourn:

- J. P. Hudson, head of large collections at the British Library Department of Manuscripts, arranged for me to have a guided tour of the museum after I examined a magnificent collection of ninth- and fifteenth-century manuscripts, many of them illuminated.
- At the Victoria and Albert Museum, I was assigned a desk and given a pair of vacuum-packed hygienic gloves with which to handle the manuscripts. I selected the manuscripts from the museum's catalog. A clerk delivered documents to me for two days, one document at a time. An entry in my journal reads, "I caught myself breathing aloud unashamedly as I looked at wine lists, poetry, prayer books, and floral designs on vellum and parchment, some with decorative illuminated letters."
- Having seen an exhibition of the beautiful *Lindisfarne Gospels* at

the British Museum Library, I decided to visit the Cathedral at the University of Durham, where the cathedral treasury included the enshrined body of Saint Cuthbert, Bishop of Lindisfarne. Many of Saint Cuthbert's relics are also housed at the Cathedral.

– Lydia Lindsey, then an assistant professor of history at North Carolina Central University, was doing research in connection with her doctoral dissertation in European history. She knew her way around London and neighboring cities and helped to guide me to places that I should logically visit.

I confess that an additional incentive for going to Durham, England, was that I wanted to visit the place in Great Britain for which I presumed my hometown was named. I went to Durham and was captivated by the city, the cathedral, the castle, and the university. At the cathedral's treasury, I was awed by the splendor of chalices, jewelry, textiles, and religious documents, including a four-volume Bible with stamped leather bindings that was given to the monks of Durham by Hugh of Le Puiset, a twelfth-century Bishop of Durham.

During the BritRail ride en route to Burton-on-Trent, England, I took stock of the remarkable chain of experiences and persons who had influenced my interest in the calligraphic arts. I honored the names of Russell Armentrout, friend and White House calligrapher; Ann Pope, my first calligraphy teacher; Patsy Crouch, my tutor; and the other accomplished calligraphers under whom I had studied. I thought of Lana Henderson, chair of the art department at North Carolina Central University, where I had been privileged to teach calligraphy as one of the lettering arts; and of Duke University Curator John Sharpe, whose introductory letters on my behalf I appreciated beyond measure.

But more than this, I reflected on the courses I took in History of Education before the Renaissance and History of Education since the Renaissance at New York University in 1949. Neither during nor since the time I took the courses have I been able to explain why I chose to write a term paper on "The Influence of Monasticism and Monastic Education in the Evolution of the Modern Roman Alphabet." It was not among the topics suggested by Professor William Brickman. But even at that time, I had a special interest in the history of lettering and, with Professor Brickman's concurrence, I wrote a paper that I remembered thirty-six years later while touring the British Isles.

*fascination
+ love for
other cultures*

I was glad to see Peter Halliday again. Upon my arrival at the hotel in London, there was a letter from him welcoming me to England and an invitation to visit him and his family at their home in Burton-on-Trent. I accepted Peter's invitation with heartfelt thanks. He, his wife Deanna, and their three children could not have been more gracious. I cannot recall what made us notice the coincidence that the Halliday and Brown families belonged to the same Protestant denomination and that our respective churches had the same first name, "Trinity."

I told Peter about my itinerary up to that point and my scheduled visits to Manchester, Bath, Edinburgh, and Dublin before returning to America. He marveled that I was visiting historic places in the British Isles that he had never visited. I was not taken aback, however, having met many Americans who had never visited historic places in their own states or cities.

In Manchester, I visited the Rylands Library, where I spent most of my time viewing the Arabic collection, described in the orientation literature as documents with many superb examples of calligraphy. I was in total agreement. When I saw the Coptic collection of theological, liturgical, and historical manuscripts, I wished that I were multilingual, with proficiency in Arabic, Latin, and Greek. I was told that the Arabic collection covered roughly 1,000 years.

I reasoned that if a climber could spend as much as two weeks ascending a mountain, I could certainly spend less than a day in travel to see the *Book of Kells*. The boat ride from Holyhead, England, across the Irish Seas to and from Dublin took three and a half hours each way. Never before had I examined an admit card with such scrutiny as the card admitting me to the Long Room of Trinity College Library. The lettering was in half-uncial, the letter style used by the Irish scribes who in about 800 A.D. transcribed the celebrated book telling the lives of Matthew, Mark, Luke, and John.

The *Book of Kells* was open to an ornamented page of spectacular beauty and encased in glass on a waist-high table. Viewers moved in single file to see the precious document. Enchantment and reverence were reflected in their countenances. I identified with them.

In Scotland, the High Kirk has stood as the city church of Edinburgh for more than a thousand years. I reveled in seeing the cathedral's manuscripts, some of which had been its property since the Middle Ages.

Superlatives are in order in describing the contemporary calligraphy at the Crafts Study Centre of Holbourne Museum in Bath, England: bril-

Author and other calligraphers from the Research Triangle area of Durham. I was then teaching calligraphy for NCCU's Art Department and was a serious student of the evolution of the modern Roman alphabet. The dapper gentleman in the second row, center, is Dr. John Sharpe, Curator of Rare Books at Duke University's Perkins Library.

liant, exquisite, stunning, inspiring. The artists whose work I noted in my journal were Dorothy Mahoney, Dorothy Hutton, Irene Wellington, Irene Base, and Ann Hechle.

I met Ann Hechle in 1981, when she was a guest artist at the Calligraphy Connection in Collegeville, Minnesota. Her artistic talent was evident in one of the Centre's works, titled "The Creation." It was inspired by two passages from the opening stanzas of the Book of Genesis and St. John's

For everything
there is a season,
and a time for
every matter
under heaven.
...a time:
to be
born, and a time
to die;
...plant and pluck up
a time what has
to been planted
...to kill
and to heal;
to break down
and to build up;
to weep &
to laugh;
to mourn
and to dance;
...CAST AWAY STONES and
GATHER STONES TOGETHER;
...embrace & refrain
from embracing;
...seek and lose;
keep & cast
rend and away;
sew
...keep silence, & speak;
...love
and hate; and a time
for war and
a time '99
for peace.
Ecclesiastes 3.

A poem from, THIS ROAD SINCE FREEDOM by C. Eric Lincoln.
Done in calligraphy with Mr Lincoln's permission by Walter M. Brown

Poem by C. Eric Lincoln in calligraphy.

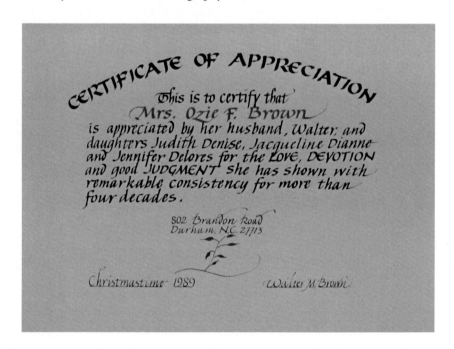

CERTIFICATE OF APPRECIATION

This is to certify that
Mrs. Ozie F. Brown
is appreciated by her husband, Walter, and
daughters Judith Denise, Jacqueline Dianne
and Jennifer Delores for the LOVE, DEVOTION
and good JUDGMENT she has shown with
remarkable consistency for more than
four decades.

802 Brandon Road
Durham, N.C. 27713

Christmastime 1989   Walter M. Brown

where there is hatred, let me sow love,
where there is injury, pardon,
where there is doubt, faith,
where there is despair, hope,
where there is darkness, light,
where there is sadness, joy.

Lord, make me an instrument of thy peace.
O divine Master, grant that I not try to be comforted, but to comfort,
not try to be understood, but to understand;
not try to be loved, but to love,
for it is in giving that we receive,
in forgiving that we are forgiven,
and in dying that we are born
to eternal life.

1998

Francis of Assisi
1182-1226

calligraphy
-walter m. brown

abcdefghijklmnopqrstuvwxyz

calligraphy   '97
walter m brown

32
Alexander
Calder

FRIENDSHIP

Oh the comfort, the inexpressible comfort, of feeling safe with a person; having neither to weigh thoughts nor measure words, but to pour them all out just as they are, chaff and grain together, knowing that a faithful hand will take and sift them, keep what is worth keeping, and then, with the breath of kindness, blow the rest away.

Calligraphy: Walter M. Brown · 1985

George Eliot

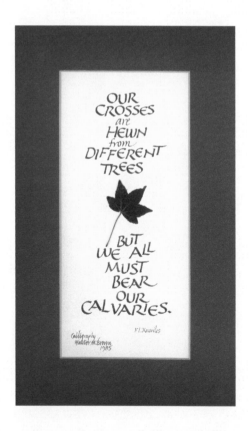

OUR CROSSES are HEWN from DIFFERENT TREES

BUT WE ALL MUST BEAR OUR CALVARIES.

F.L. Knowles

Calligraphy
Walter M. Brown
1985

Let those
love now
who never
loved before;
And
those
who
always
loved,
now love
even more.

Thomas Parnell
c1700,
translated from
Pervigilium Veneris
c200

Calligraphy Walter U. Brown
1999

CERTIFICATE OF FAMILY MEMBERSHIP

This is to certify that

_____ is a descendant of CHARLES ATKINS and MARY TRICE ATKINS whose offspring were Martha Atkins Patterson, Sarah Atkins Couch, Richard Atkins, Retta Atkins Atkins, Thomas 'Tommy' Atkins, Ora Atkins Tate, Lizzie Atkins Jones, Robert 'Bob' Atkins, James 'Bud' Atkins, Sophronia Atkins Strayhorne, and Harriett Atkins Holloway.

This declaration was made to me by a knowledgeable descendant.

Dianne P. Pledger
Executive Director
Hayti Heritage Center• Durham, NC

Of all the creatures that
creep,
   swim, or fly,
   . Peopling the earth,
the waters
         and the sky,
From Rome to Iceland,
Paris to Japan,
   I really think,
the greatest fool
      is man.

The Art of Poetry

NICHOLAS BOILEAU DESPREAUX 1636~1711

WALTER BROWN-2000

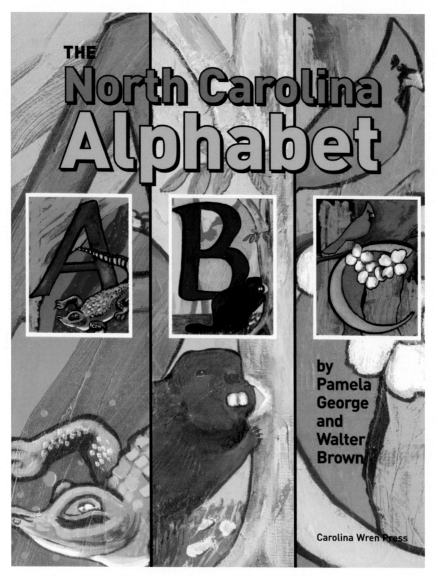

An illustrated children's book, a collaboration with artist Pamela George.

Roman alphabet as letter art.

A TASTE
OF TRINITY

2007

175th Anniversary

Gospel, both of which begin with "In the beginning . . ." Of this work and a poem in calligraphy by David Gasocyne, my journal entry read, "I stood transfixed as I looked at these works on vellum, in raised and burnished gold leaf, powdered gold, water color, and stick ink."

Perhaps the exclamation point to my career in calligraphy was made in my article, "So You've Taken a Calligraphy Course," which appeared in the *Calligraphy Idea Exchange* (Spring 1987). In it I make the point that "the essence of an artist's style is the amalgam of purposeful study and practice together with cumulative life experiences."

Except for accomplished calligraphers, few persons appreciate the investments in time, study, and money it takes to become an accomplished calligrapher. Since I retired in 1992, I have had almost no interest in the craft as a source of retirement income. Accomplished calligraphers are fortunate if they have an outlet for their talents as letter artists with greeting-card manufacturers, publishing firms, schools and colleges, and yes, as White House calligraphers. Otherwise, the monetary rewards are rarely commensurate with the levels of effort.

My satisfaction comes mainly from making cards and notes for the sick or bereaved; congratulatory messages to friends who have achieved milestones such as birthdays, anniversaries, advancements in education and other endeavors; and for persons whom I appreciate simply for who they are.

Another source of satisfaction is interaction and study with fellow calligraphers in the Triangle Calligraphers' Guild. Its members live mainly in the Raleigh-Durham–Chapel Hill area, and in other nearby cities in North Carolina. The Guild meets monthly and sponsors periodic workshops and conferences not only for its members but also for all members of its parent organization, the Carolina Lettering Arts Society.

In the years of my retirement, two experiences in calligraphy have given me extreme gratification. The first was an open-ended stint as resident calligrapher at the Hayti Heritage Center in Durham. Subsequently, I was collaborative artist in the publication of a children's book, *The North Carolina Alphabet,* published in 2006 by Carolina Wren Press. The progenitor and principal of this collaboration was Triangle-area artist Pamela George. "Pam" was among the first persons I met when I returned to the Department of Education at North Carolina Central University after my fifteen-year hiatus. As professors at NCCU, we worked on research projects of mu-

Author Pamela George signing a copy of *The North Carolina Alphabet* for four-year-old Seirra Holmes at the Regulator Bookshop in Durham. *(Brown family papers)*

tual interest and often compared notes on teaching methodology. She also showed a greater appreciation than most in my pastime as a calligrapher, although her talent as a visual artist was manifest more in later years than during our full-time responsibilities in teaching and administration.

In retirement, Pamela George continues to demonstrate that she is a highly purposeful and talented individual. I was attending one of her exhibitions when she extended to me an invitation to join her as a letter artist of a book designed to simultaneously teach children the (Roman) alphabet and familiarize them with things natural to the state of North Carolina. Pam led and I followed as we responded to media requests for information about the book and the artists. We appeared together for book signings and at an appreciable number of schools and libraries in the state, and highly magnified replications of *The Alphabet* have hung prominently for long times at the main public libraries in Durham and Greensboro.

I was already a student of calligraphy when in 1976 psychologist William Glasser said that people can become addicted to behavior that leads to a rewarding and fulfilling life. Among the activities Glasser listed were running, aerobics, bike riding, walking, mountain climbing, weight training, and meditating. I believe that had Glasser known any calligraphers, beginners or accomplished, he would have added calligraphy as a form of addictive behavior. I believe also that the extent of my addiction to this letter art form is an indicator of the degree to which it helps to make life more meaningful for me than it might be otherwise.

[46]

Church since the Cradle

WHEN I WAS a boy at West Durham Baptist Church, Mr. Al Borland sometimes broke out just before the benediction, singing, "I want to be ready to walk in Jerusalem just like John." The congregation followed his lead. Most did anyway. I seethed mainly because Mr. Al always did it just at the time we were supposed to go home—or wherever our worshipers went after Sunday morning services.

I didn't know who *John* was, when or why he walked in Jerusalem, or what he did to get ready for his walk. Not until sixty years later did I learn that the scriptural basis for this African American spiritual is Revelation 21:2. Perhaps Mr. Al could have told me, if I had been brazen enough to ask.

I relish my memories of West Durham Baptist Church. I loved the people of this compassionate and benevolent membership who earned their living as maids, janitors, chauffeurs, tobacco-factory hands, porters, laborers, masons, mechanics, teachers, clerks, and neighborhood grocers. My parents lived next door to the church during my earliest years. Rev. Thomas Carr Graham had been the church's minister since 1921, six years before I was born.

Much of what I admired about West Durham were the ways in which it reflected Reverend Graham's dignified demeanor. He was educated in the public schools of Iredell County, North Carolina, and at Shaw University in Raleigh. Shaw awarded him an honorary doctor of divinity degree in recognition of his commitment to the total welfare of his membership and his visionary leadership of the community.

Until I became enamored of college vespers services, Sunday worship services at West Durham Baptist were the sum and substance of my for-

West Durham Baptist Church family in the 1940s. *(Brown family papers)*

mal worshiping experience. But by the time I returned to Durham with my wife, Ozie, and a daughter who was less than a year old, we had worshiped together at Union Baptist Church in Hartford, Connecticut; St. Mark AME and Abyssinian Baptist in New York's Harlem; and St. James Presbyterian in Greensboro, North Carolina. We were eager for a change in worship experiences, and I doubt that anyone at West Durham Baptist Church was surprised when we left the church in 1953. Yet the members could not have been warmer and more gracious to us through the years. My mother maintained active membership at the church until she died.

There were times that Ozie and I wished we could take a plane to New York to attend Harlem's St. Mark Church on Sundays. Its services featured a sage and eloquent minister in the person of the Reverend Sweeny and a choir whose singing would have made attending the church a special experience even if there had not been additional incentives. It was at St. Mark where we learned that some church choirs had paid soloists. In this instance, at least one soloist was Nathaniel Dickerson, the African American singer with the Mariners on the Arthur Godfrey radio variety show.

Ozie and I had pretty much given up on formal ties to a church when Douglas Moore came to Durham as minister of Asbury Temple Methodist Church. The church was then on Lawson Street in the southern part of the city, a stone's throw from North Carolina College at Durham, where Doug had been our schoolmate. A native of Hickory, North Carolina, Doug earned a master's degree from Boston University School of Theology, where he was a classmate of Dr. Martin Luther King Jr. He also attended the University of Grenoble in France.

It was impossible not to like and respect Doug Moore. He, along with several other young Black citizens of Durham, conducted a sit-in at the

Royal Ice Cream parlor on Roxboro Road in the northern section of Durham. This turned out to be the first such sit-in in America, followed soon thereafter by a sit-in by students from North Carolina Agricultural and Technical College (now North Carolina A&T State University) at the Woolworth's store in Greensboro, North Carolina. The Greensboro sit-in is widely regarded as the nation's first sit-in to protest racial discrimination in public accommodations. Most African-Americans in Durham over the age of sixty, and an appreciable number of historians, know better.

Doug Moore told Ozie and me that our former choir director at North Carolina College, Miss Ruth Gillum, was the volunteer choir director of music at his church. We decided immediately that he could count on two more volunteers. For the next several weeks we enjoyed rehearsals but with no intention to sing at the Sunday services.

It didn't require agonizing deliberations to realize the unfairness of re-hearsing with the choir of ten or twelve voices and not singing with them at their church services. When we sang as volunteers at the Sunday services, we found we had much in common with Asbury's members. Some, like the Norman Johnson and Ross Townes families, were already our friends. Others were easy to like from the time we met them. And so, in response to an altar call on a date I can't recall, I squeezed Ozie's hand as we walked together to Rev. Douglas E. Moore and declared our intent to become members of Asbury Temple Methodist Church. Our twelve years of membership at this small Black church of sixty or so members were gratifying and fulfilling. Our daughters Jackie and Jennifer were born during that time span.

I preceded other members of my family in our move to Maryland in 1965. Our youngest child, Jennifer, was born prematurely two weeks before I left Durham, and I was preoccupied with her health. People in the Valley subdivision of Montgomery Hills in Silver Spring, Maryland, were downright effusive in welcoming us as the first Black family in the neighborhood. I was to learn a day or two after unpacking some of our bags that a sensible—and evidently compassionate—resident with prior knowledge of our anticipated arrival had made an appeal to fellow neighbors to receive us without incident.

We had been in the promised land for little more than a week when we were visited by a former North Carolinian who said, "You are to be congratulated, Walt. Nice house. Nice car. Good job. You're in a county where the education level and per capita income are among the highest in

Left to right: Helen Jones, Rev. Frederick Terry, and Mama. *(Courtesy of Ms. Winifred McQueen)*

the nation. Your children will attend good schools. It can't get any better than this."

Roughly a month later, however, by which time another African American family had moved into the neighborhood, a Confederate flag appeared in the window of the house directly across the street from us. Two teenage boys, one of whom lived there, threw cherry bombs in our yard. Police came in response to my call, made notes, and thanked us for calling, but I never knew if they followed up.

As it turned out, the man of the house with the Confederate flag was a pathetic figure. He came over and introduced himself one afternoon when I was working in the yard. In the course of exchanging pleasantries and moments of ad-libbing, I asked about his hobbies and pastimes. His answer was quick and unequivocal: "Drinking liquor." Our unceremonious acquaintanceship ended soon thereafter. The family moved out of the Valley long before we did.

I never shared the cherry bomb and flag incidents with the flattering friend who had commented, "It doesn't get any better than this." Maybe I was trying to assuage guilt feelings. After all, I had heard more than once that Blacks who lived in the Maryland suburbs instead of the District of Columbia were turncoats. On the other hand, I was on travel a lot and I often awoke before dawn, wondering about the safety of my family.

PROTESTS AGAINST racial segregation and discrimination were raging throughout the country. The war in Vietnam was haunting concerned citizens everywhere. The declaration that "it can't get better than this" had an increasingly hollow ring. I began to visit churches, a different one each week or so, including the Woodside United Methodist Church in Silver Spring. Then Ozie and I visited Woodside together. We signed the attendance book, and in a nothing-to-lose frame of mind, checked the column headed, "Desire a call."

The following evening, two men from Woodside Church visited our home. We engaged in conversation that ended with their invitation to join the church, an invitation we agreed to think about seriously. But when they had gone, Ozie and I reasoned that the men had not realized that they were about to visit a Black family. We also reasoned that they were in a bind and were obliged to do what their mission required—extend to us an invitation to church membership.

On the next evening, we were visited by the church's senior minister, Dr. William Hall. He could not have been more explicit. "We are about to move into a new church facility," he said. "We also want to move into a new era of discipleship, and we would love to have your family and our family as one." He then added, "If you join, some of our members may leave as a kind of backlash, but in the larger scheme of things, that will be a small price to pay." On August 21, 1966, Ozie, Judy, and I joined Woodside Methodist Church. Jackie and Jennifer joined in 1974 and 1978 respectively.

In our judgment, Dr. William Hall had few peers as a preacher. He was assigned as a district superintendent in the Baltimore Conference the year after we joined and was followed by three other outstanding senior ministers before we returned to North Carolina in 1980: Rev. Marion Michael, Dr. Lewis Ransom, and Dr. Warren Ebinger.

A stressful chapter in our lives opened when Dr. Ralph Stiller, our children's pediatrician, informed us that there was a hole in Jennifer's heart the size of a fifty-cent piece. She was too young and too frail for surgery without the risk of serious complications or worse. She would have to wait until she was old enough and strong enough for surgery. Jennifer was four and a half years old when she had heart surgery at the Washington's Children's Hospital. Reverend Michael was then Woodside's minister. It was the longest day of our lives, a day that might have seemed longer except for the support of family, Woodside's members, and other friends. I can't possibly recount the times, none of which were at special events, that I looked at Jennifer and marveled at how well she was faring.

Ozie enjoyed membership in the United Methodist Women. The weekly Wonderful Wednesday evening fellowship hours were made to order for bonding with other families as well as with our own family. A group of us went camping at Camp Harmon in West Virginia. At first, Ozie preferred to sleep in our station wagon instead of our family tent. Being a good example for the kids was the persuasive plea.

After a fellow worshiper overheard me singing ("lustily," as John Wesley pleaded), I was invited by Dr. J. Edward Moyer, Woodside's minister of music, to join the chancel choir. Under Dr. Moyer's direction, we sang in the annual choir festivals at Constitution Hall. There was hardly a dry eye in the hall when another African American in our choir, Dorothy Horton, sang the solo lines to *He Touched Me*.

The night of April 4, 1968, was fateful. More than a hundred cities nationwide went up in flames following the assassination of Dr. Martin Luther King Jr. With heavy hearts, Ozie and I joined others at Woodside on the morning after the rioting in prayer for our country.

On September 18, 1974, Ozie and I celebrated our twenty-fifth wedding anniversary in Woodside's sanctuary and fellowship hall. Reverend Mike's successor, Dr. Lewis Ransom, his wife, Sally, and about a hundred guests helped to make the occasion a cherished event.

Six years later, Ozie and I agreed that accepting a professorship at our alma mater would be an appropriate chapter to end my career. Leaving Woodside was one of the things we regretted most. After commiserating with us, Dr. Ebinger referred us to his friend, Dr. Robert Young, chaplain of the Chapel at Duke University, for counsel. Ozie and I had a good conversation with Chaplain Young, who told us that the church in Durham most like Woodside was Trinity United Methodist Church. After visiting Trinity and several other churches, Ozie and I agreed that Trinity's Sunday-morning services were in fact most like Woodside's services.

Not long after our second or third visit to Trinity, I was experiencing excruciating leg pain. X-rays showed that the source was a herniated spinal disc. Ozie called Trinity and left word for Pastor Belton Joyner that I was a patient at Durham Regional Hospital and asked that I be remembered in prayer. The next morning, Belton (as he preferred to be called) paid me a visit and prayed with me, and we had conversation that included a brief discussion of possible membership for my family.

On the afternoon of the same day, another patient at Durham Regional visited me. She was well-advanced in age, and after giving her name, told me that she was a member of Trinity United Methodist Church. "Reverend Joyner told me that you and your family may join Trinity Church," she said. I told her that the subject had also been discussed with my family and that we were considering joining. "Well, I certainly hope so," she replied.

That did it! I had never seen Mabel Barnhart before, but neither had I seen a more gracious manner nor discerned a more sincere comment. When Ozie and the girls visited that evening, we all but sealed an agreement to join the church. I remembered, and my mother confirmed, that Trinity Methodist Church was one of the buildings that her father—my grandfather—had helped to build in the late 1920s. A stonemason by trade, he died in 1960. My brother William and I have laughed more than once in imagining that granddaddy Walter Tate would characteristically exclaim "name o' God" if he learned that my family joined a predominantly White church that he had helped to build a half-century before.

Yet I also have an affinity for Unitarianism that dates back to my attendance at the First Unitarian Church in Boston in the summer of 1961. For over a year, between the pastorates of Belton Joyner and Gray Southern at Trinity, I attended the Eno River Unitarian Fellowship in Durham. I might have stayed, but I simply wasn't turned on by the music. Besides, Ozie stayed at Trinity, and I never became reconciled to us in regular attendance at separate churches.

Sometimes I feel that Daddy Tate is smiling, having seen Trinity United Methodist church become increasingly diverse in ethnicity and leadership, Ozie and me singing in the chancel choir, Jacqueline serving on the task force that conducted a study on envisioning Trinity's future, Ozie in a circle of the United Methodist Women, and Jennifer as a member of the handbell choir. I know he smiled when I was serving on the church's board of trustees during the pastorate of Gray Southern and as a delegate to the annual conference of the United Methodist Church during the pastorate of Susan Pate Greenwood.

Our fiftieth wedding anniversary was a grand affair at Trinity. I can almost hear Mama's papa saying, "name o' God."

[47]

You Will Love My Brother Will

WHEN I represented our family in a salute to my brother Will at his retirement celebration in 1992, I said that he was the greatest man I knew. That was even before his first appointment to the University of North Carolina Board of Governors in 1995.

One story that I shared at Will's retirement celebration recalls his commencement exercises at Hillside High School in 1945. Just before the diplomas were given out, Principal William McElrath asked the audience to hold applause until all members of the class received their diplomas. The exercises proceeded. Diplomas were awarded, hands were shaken, and signs of exuberance abounded.

When Will stepped forward to receive his diploma, Mr. McElrath went to the microphone. The principal said he realized that he had asked the audience to hold their applause, but he also realized that Will was a student who would long be remembered for his career at Hillside and deserved a special salute. A sustained ovation followed. McElrath did not say what contributions he had in mind, but it probably had something to do with Will's performance as major of the school patrol organization and president of the Hi-Y Club. Both groups helped to maintain order in the school corridors and playgrounds and helped keep the building and playgrounds clean.

I have bulging files of newspaper articles and editorials, awards programs, and copies of citations about Will. Some mention that his work history includes shoeshine boy, graveyard digger, and cook. He attended Durham's Lyon Park Elementary School, as did Benjamin Ruffin, who in 2002 completed his term as chairman of the UNC Board of Governors. Without question, the odds are against two African American men from

Durham's West End or any place similarly situated being members of this board, certainly not at the same time.

In high school, Will worked part time at Rowland and Mitchell Tailors in downtown Durham, an experience that factored into his decision to earn diplomas in tailoring at North Carolina Agricultural and Technical College in Greensboro, North Carolina (now North Carolina A&T State University), and the American Gentlemen School of Designing in New York City. He still saves money by doing his own clothing alterations.

Will lived with me in an apartment in New York City when he attended the American Gentlemen School of Designing. I was working as a night-shift keypunch operator at the Federal Reserve Bank of New York. He did most of the cooking, and with a smile said I was extravagant because I wanted to eat at restaurants sometimes. On weekends, he worked as a waiter at White Turkey Farms in Danbury, Connecticut.

When tailoring became a crowded field with the influx of veterans after World War II, Will returned to school. He earned a BS degree in chemistry at North Carolina Central University (1954); the master's degree in school administration at Columbia University (1961); and a certificate in school administration at the University of North Carolina at Chapel Hill (1968). His wife, Jennie Deveaux Brown, a classmate at North Carolina A&T College, worked as a bookkeeper at Durham's Lincoln Hospital. In 1984, Shaw University awarded Will an honorary degree, doctor of humane letters, and in 2003 he was awarded an honorary degree by Fayetteville State University.

WILL'S PROFESSIONAL career spanned forty-one years, beginning as a chemistry teacher in Summerville, South Carolina and at E.E. Smith High School in Fayetteville, North Carolina. After his second year of teaching in Summerville, he was offered the position of principal there, but he declined because he preferred to teach. Later, he was principal at three public schools in Fayetteville before being promoted to associate superintendent of Cumberland County Schools.

On April 1, 1992, an editorial in the Fayetteville *Observer-Times* noted in part:

> [His] persuasive, aggressively reformative insight into the complexity of
> the problems he faced was, together with unflagging endurance and opti-
> mism, one of the central qualities that allowed him to play an important

and successful role in shepherding the Fayetteville City Schools out of the era of segregation into the era of integration.

Speaking then as a principal, he challenged the students to be the best they could be, obviously persuading more than he lost. He also withstood criticism from both sides of the racial divide, without losing his bearing.

Just as his career did not end when the era of segregation passed, his public service was not confined to his calling as an educator. Some years ago, when the Cumberland County Board of Commissioners took it in its head to privatize and perhaps to sell Cape Fear Valley Medical Center, Dr. Brown was chairman of the hospital board of trustees. He stood firmly in the way of that effort to dispose of a fundamental public asset, not alone, but arguing with unflagging courage to the board that sets the budget of the public schools that employ him that it was making a serious mistake. This was the same man who at a critical time stood up before the Fayetteville City Council to push for and help win a worthwhile downtown revitalization effort.

On Sunday, October 11, 1994, the Cumberland County School System dedicated its new year-round elementary school in Will's honor. Later, on December 17, a complimentary editorial appeared in the Durham *Herald-Sun* headlined "South toward Home":

> *Like other cities, Durham has lost a fair number of its best and brightest to other places. Eli Evans is one of them. So is William T. Brown.*
>
> *William T. Brown? If you lived in Fayetteville, you'd know who Bill Brown is. He went there in the mid-50s, fresh from earning his degree at N.C. Central University. Brown was a good teacher. He was also a good administrator, so good that he worked his way up to the No. 2 position in the schools.*
>
> *Fayetteville's school system has gone through merger, too. Brown devoted a great deal of his time and energy to keeping things on an even keel. Even so, he found spare hours to tutor at-risk students to help them pass the state competency test.*
>
> *In October, Cumberland County named its first year-round school for William T. Brown. He may not be well known these days in his hometown, but Brown is no less deserving of honor for what he has accomplished in his adopted county. In more ways than one was Cumberland's gain our loss.*

A week later, on December 24, my letter of appreciation appeared in the *Herald-Sun*. In it I said the letter was "not only for myself but on behalf of our family, Will's former contemporaries in the West End community, his schoolmates at Durham's defunct Lyon Park Elementary School, Hillside High School, North Carolina Central University and his peers in public education throughout the state."

Will was appointed to the Board of Governors of the University of North Carolina System in March 1995. He was nominated by state senator C. R. Edwards. On March 30, the Fayetteville *Observer-Times* ran an editorial headed "Policymaker Brown." It noted that Will joined another citizen of Fayetteville, H. D. Reaves, in representing Cumberland County on the board, and added: "Named by the state Senate, Brown is eminently qualified to wear the mantle of educational leadership at this highest level. . . . The Board of Governors especially needs a Will Brown. He brings practical experience in education combined with a clear vision of how the public schools and the higher education system must work together for North Carolina's young people."

Will would have been a central figure wherever he cast his lot, whether it was Washington, D.C., Atlanta, Georgia, or Butte, Montana. E. E. Miller, former and revered principal of Fayetteville's E.E. Smith High School, used to delight in telling how Will was recommended to him. Mr. Miller said that he went to the career placement bureau at North Carolina College at Durham, looking for a recommendation for a science teacher at his school. At that time I was the director of the placement bureau.

In those days, given the comparatively small size of student enrollment and of graduating classes in particular, college placement officers were asked to do more than transmit résumés of job seekers. They were asked for their personal recommendations of possible candidates. Mr. Miller said that he wondered who I could have been talking about when I prefaced my recommendation with comments to the effect that I had known the individual all of his life and would recommend him irrespective of his relationship to me. And having said that, I recommended my brother, William Thomas Brown.

In 2000, the Donning Company published *Our Century,* a compilation of fifty-two weekly articles that appeared in the Fayetteville *Observer's* 1999 "Sunday Conversations" department. Editor Charles Broadwell noted that "the stories are a testimonial, not only to the strength, courage and perseverance of these citizens, but to the legacy of mankind as a whole."

Under Fayetteville's school desegregation plan, White students entered

E.E. Smith for the first time in 1971. It was also Will's first year as Smith's principal, having succeeded his mentor, Mr. Miller. I am greatly impressed with the article that appeared in *Our Century*, a portion of which is included below, describing some of the attributes of Will's character and personality that have contributed to his success and have garnered the admiration of those who know him:

Curious White people started paying visits as he got adjusted to his new job at Smith.

"I remember that summer I could not do my paperwork because of people visiting the school to see if the roof was there, to see if the water came from Filter Plant Drive and all, and I was dealing with them just like I would be dealing with my mother, although I knew that I was going to have to work late nights because we had to get the school ready to open."

A group of concerned Whites, most of whom he knew, stopped by.

"They wanted to talk with me and I said, 'OK, what is it that I can help you with?' This is July, but it turns out I needed my overcoat. They started that snow job. 'Now, we know you; you know we don't have anything against you.' I said oh, lord, here it comes. 'You're a fine fellow.' I knew the infamous b-u-t was coming; I knew it was coming. All of this fine stuff, all of these accolades. 'But there's one problem that we have with our children coming to school here.' And I said, 'What's that?' 'You have a'—by that time we were being called Black—'you have a Black principal and a Black assistant principal.'

"I said, 'Is that a problem?' 'Well, we think so. Our children will not have anybody to relate to.'"...

"But then I had to say to those people [visiting the school] . . . 'Oh, I hear you'—notice I didn't say 'understand you'—'but let's think. Anthropologically speaking, the last time I saw John Sasser [the principal at Terry Sanford High School], he appeared to be a White man. . . . The last time I saw Perry Warren [Sasser's assistant], he appeared to be White. The last time I saw Jack McGinley, principal at Reid Ross, he appeared to be White. The last time I saw Don Landreth [McGinley's assistant], he appeared to be White. Now, if two people of the same race are a detriment to the administrative operation of those schools, you all tell me what you did over there.'"

"Case closed."

Having read about Will up to this point, you might see him as a bearded figure in a robe and sandals, or as a flaming activist in an Afro hair style and his arm raised and fist balled. You might see anger in his countenance and imagine that nothing evokes laughter from him. You'd be dead wrong. His hair, now white, is cut closely as it was when Mama was our barber. He has a wonderful sense of humor and frequently uses it to make his point when discussing issues of the day. He dresses smartly and at five feet eight keeps his weight at about 175 pounds.

My accolades to Will have highlighted his career accomplishments. But in my heart, he is the greatest because of what he overcame to become a giant in education and humanitarianism.

I am two years older than Will. When our parents divorced, I was four years old and Will was two. We were never abused physically or verbally by our parents, but our father was partial toward me. Even in my adolescent years he was always giving me things—clothes mainly, expensive clothes. His clothiers became my clothiers. Mama didn't try to stop him, and I was too naive and self-centered to insist that our father divide his favors equitably.

I didn't flaunt my privileged status. As I saw it, the more Daddy Matthew Brown gave to me, the more Mama and my stepfather, William Horton, had to give to Will, Leonders, and Charles. Amazing, to be sure, but I never had a fight or a heated argument with any of my three brothers. In high school, Will began to evidence outstanding qualities in scholarship, leadership, and his personality. It was about that time that our father began to behave like a man toward him. Will was deferential toward Daddy right up to his death in 1981.

Daddy's obituary included as survivors his wife, Eleanor M. Brown; daughters E. Maccene Brown and Delphine Brown; and three sons, Thelbert J. Brown, Walter M. Brown, and William T. Brown. Will and I were his only children by our mother. Our families lived on Fayetteville Street in Durham, three houses from each other. Daddy and his family from his second marriage were members of West Durham Baptist Church, the same church where Mama was a member until her death in 1992.

There is a particularly gratifying note about me in *Our Century*: "To this day, Will Brown refers to himself simply and proudly as Mama's second son. And her first son, by the way, is his personal hero, Dr. Walter M. Brown, retired dean of the school of education at N.C. Central University."

Will's handwritten note on the inside cover of my gift book of *Our Century* reads,

"Dear Walter, From the beginning, God knew that I would NEED A QUALITY SUPPORT SYSTEM throughout my LIFE. Accordingly, through Mama, God gave me YOU, THE WORLD'S GREATEST BROTHER. Thank you for being all God intended you to be relative to Mama's Second Son. With love, Will." I have never received a more heartwarming and humbling compliment.

WILL'S WIFE, Jennie, retired in early 1992 as a bookkeeper at the American Red Cross at Fort Bragg. "Sunset" for her was September 7, 2008.

Will's son, Julian, was executive director of the Carolinas Minority Suppliers Development Councils until he became physically unable to continue in that capacity. He now lives with Will and is a full-time volunteer at Fayetteville's E.E. Smith School, where he works with its parent facilitator in continual linkages between the school and the community. His motivation comes in part from adhering to the adage that "it takes a village to raise a child."

[48]

You Will Love Ozie, Too

Wᴇɴ ɪ'ᴍ alone, whether walking, driving through the countryside, working in the flower and vegetable gardens, or setting the table for my next meal, I see Ozie in a collage with ever-changing configurations. She made a lovely dress look good, one she bought ostensibly to make herself look good.

I hear and see her on my mother's lawn, running and calling, "Daddy, Daddy, Judy can walk," announcing and celebrating a major milestone for our first child.

Jeanne Lucas, prior to her days as a North Carolina senator, liked to tell that their pinochle club members teased Ozie when she insisted on checking with me before making any commitment for a change in meeting dates or to engage in any activity other than playing pinochle at members' homes.

Charles Nicholson, North Carolina Central University emeritus professor of education, twice told me with candor about the dynamics of an office party in celebration of one faculty member's birthday in the Department of Biology. Charles, who was a party guest, observed that at one point there was small talk about making certain kinds of changes in lifestyle with changes in age. A change that evoked considerable babble and laughter was changes in domestic partners. Ozie was detached and uninterested in the subject, Charles said, and he said to her, "Everybody is talking about getting a new mate. Aren't you going to get one, too?" She said to him, "I was married to Walter M. Brown, I am Mrs. Walter M. Brown now, and I will be Mrs. Walter M. Brown when I die."

For our fifteenth wedding anniversary, I selected an oil painting at a gallery in Washington, D.C., at least two months before the anniversary

Walter, Ozie, and the JDB girls: Jennifer Delores, Jacqueline Dianne,
and Judith Denise. *(Brown family papers)*

date, and I frequently went over to look at it in the interim. I knew Ozie
liked surprises, and this was to be a biggie. It also factored into making a
happy anniversary.

Basically, the kitchen was Ozie's territory where she was in control and
where she passed on her homemaking skills to our daughters. A rule of
meal preparation was that each food group and color should be represented for dinner meals, and it is one that Judy, Jennifer, and especially
Jacqueline continue to follow. Once in a while over the years I ventured
into Ozie's kitchen and surprised her with my culinary skills. One of my
favorite breakfasts was sautéed salmon and eggs, with grits, hot biscuits,
and coffee. I prepared this dish, and I have fond memories of Ozie dancing
to the table.

After buying a house in Maryland, and while I was waiting for Ozie and
the girls to join me, I selected the master bedroom furniture and had it in
place when they arrived. I have always suspected that Ozie felt the furniture was too large for the size of our bedroom, but she never voiced any
criticism, and we rejoiced in having a beautiful and well-crafted bedroom
suit.

A. J. Howard Clement,
Ozie, and Maynard
Jackson, former mayor of
Atlanta, Georgia. *(Brown
family papers)*

One of my fondest and most lasting memories of family life with Ozie and the girls was how much and how frequently we laughed together. They loved to hear me tell jokes, especially when I mimicked or was animated, and Ozie appealed to me to tell the same jokes when we had guests. When the guests were gone, we laughed at the fallout. Simply put, Ozie loved the girls, our daughters, the JDB girls: Judith Denise, Jacqueline Dianne, and Jennifer Delores. We liked to read to them and do reenactments as called for. We all laughed.

Whenever I made a speech, reading, prayer, or rendered any kind of performance in public, Ozie would have me believe she had never seen a better performance. I was just as laudatory in my praise when she took Jackie and Jennifer as toddlers by train to visit Judy in the Hull House Art and Music camp near Chicago, Illinois. She rented a car, drove to the camp with buildings designed by famed architect Frank Lloyd Wright, and enjoyed selected camp activities before returning to Maryland.

In the wake of Ozie's death, such are the memories and images that move in and out and around in my mind, for as one of my all-time favorite lyricists and ballad singers, O. C. Smith would characterize the manifestations of Ozie's love: "If that's not loving me, God didn't make little green apples, and it don't rain in Indianapolis in the summertime."

O. C. Smith also sang a ballad with lyrics by Bobby Goldsboro—lyrics that could not express more appropriately my feelings of missing Ozie's presence: "It was in the early spring, when flowers bloom and robins sing, she went away. And I'd love to be with you tonight, if only I could."

[49]

Twilight

IT MAY have been denial by Ozie, my misunderstanding, or a combination of both, but it is possible that Ozie showed signs of dementia long before I recognized them. For instance, she was rated "outstanding" by her supervisor, Dr. Walter Pattillo, in "office management," but only "very good" in "typing correspondence, reports and other documents related to instruction and department operations." And when I visited her office from time to time, I saw that she was using the electric typewriter instead of a word processor, as the secretary in my office was using. Everybody associated with Ozie loved and respected her, employees and students alike, but there was no discernible effort by Pattillo to keep her from retiring after her sixty-fifth birthday in 1991.

Early in 1993, I made plans for us to take a vacation about which Ozie was pleased and I was excited, a tour of the Canadian Rockies sponsored by Phi Delta Kappa Education Society. We took the trip in the summer of 1993, and in terms of the Rockies' beauty and our accommodations, it was as enthralling as I could have imagined. I remember, however, that Ozie became extremely agitated when she was asked for identification at the US-Canada customs office. Tour costs included gratuities for every service, including hotel accommodations and meals. Ozie asked repeatedly about the cost of meals and whether I was going to tip the wait staff. But she enjoyed interactions with our tourist companions and seemed to love the total experience—except for the scene at the customs office.

Back home, we resumed the good life of retirement despite behavioral indicators that I attributed to—or maybe dismissed as—absentmindedness, fatigue, or premature aging: asking the same question over and again, misplacing things in inexplicable ways. But the indicators began

Walter and Ozie on group tour of the Canadian Rockies. *(Brown family papers)*

to defy rationality, such as putting prepared foods in dresser drawers and clothes closets, dressing in business attire for cookouts or picnics, putting on pedal pushers and tennis shoes to attend a choral music recital (I know someone for whom such attire is normal, but not Ozie), and getting flustered when a computerized telephone message did not engage in conversation with her. Another sign of her illness appeared when the headlights of our car automatically turned on when the engine was started and stayed on while the engine was running. Whenever she was a passenger in our car during the day, she always asked, "Why do all those cars have their lights on?" She was referring to oncoming motorists. She never took issue with an answer and never asked an additional question about the lights, but she never stopped asking the same question. Once, when she was at our carport door and I was backing out of the driveway, she hailed me to say that my lights were on. I simply smiled and thanked her as if I had turned them on unintentionally.

I sensed that Ozie knew that all was not right with the world when she agreed without hesitation to go with me to see a doctor "who might help us with what seems to be a problem." After the diagnosis by staff of the Duke University Geriatrics Center, I was told that she had a vascular disease of the brain. When I asked the team if they thought I had overreacted in making the appointment, one member replied, "Definitely not." The others expressed agreement, virtually in unison.

Ozie was in tears when we reached the car. "What is wrong with me, Daddy?" she asked. I said there was nothing that we couldn't handle, and I reasoned that she was upset by the kinds of questions asked by the medical team, which included a psychometrician, a clinical psychologist, and a psychiatric social worker.

I read everything I could get my hands on. I attended support groups for families, loved ones, and caregivers of dementia patients at the Ridge Road Baptist Church in Raleigh, North Carolina, and I occasionally attended the support group sessions at Duke Hospital in Durham. I also compared notes with my friend, John Hope Franklin, who had lost his wife, Aurelia, when she had the disease.

By this time, our daughters and I had arranged to have Ozie's mother, whom we called Mimi, moved from an assisted living center in Hartford, Connecticut, to a nursing home in Wheaton, Maryland. We drove up to see Mimi about every two months. Ozie would forget the visits within one day and ask when we intended to visit her mother. I was caregiver and guardian for my wife and my mother-in-law at the same time.

Ozie's mother was ninety-four when she died on August 6, 2001. I wrote her obituary, which appeared in the Durham *Herald-Sun* on August 8, 2001. It read in part:

> *A native of Americus, Georgia, Mrs. Alexander moved to Hartford, Connecticut, in the early 1940s. Until her retirement in 1982, she was owner and principal operator of Thelma's Beauty Salon in Hartford. She was predeceased by her husband, John I. Alexander.*
>
> *In many ways, Mrs. Alexander typified the dauntless Black Americans who migrated from the American South to the urban north, seeking better opportunities for themselves and their children. Her only child, Ozie Foster Brown, graduated from North Carolina College in Durham.*

Rev. Susan Pate Greenwood officiated at the graveside rites for Ozie's mother in Durham's Beechwood Cemetery, which were attended by granddaughters Jacqueline and Jennifer Brown, and family friends William P. Malone and John Hope Franklin, in addition to myself. Before Ozie became ill, she made all necessary arrangements for her mother's body to be properly prepared upon her death and for the body to be transferred to Durham for burial. When I mentioned her mother's death to Ozie, she did not respond—not even with body language. I never heard her mention her mother's name again.

In 1992, when I retired as dean of the School of Education at NCCU, my colleagues in the School gave me a surprise dinner party that included an opportunity for participants to make a contribution to a scholarship to be established in my name. It was the kind of grand occasion that one still remembers in 2009 as if it were held yesterday. Charles Alcorn and Pamela George were principals in planning the event which was held incidentally at the Washington Duke Inn & Golf Club.

The retirement party at Washington Duke

Several years later, I arranged for the scholarship account to be converted to the Walter M. and Ozie F. Brown Fund for Students in Distress. In 2008 a benefactor in Wilmington, North Carolina informed NCCU that she would make a financial gift to the university only to be added to its special fund for students in distress. When the university's Office of Institutional Advancement searched its files, it discovered that the only fund it had for students in distress was the fund I had designated/converted for that cause. The gift was received and added to the Fund. It is at least one additional resource for students whose goals can be reached because someone cared.

[50]

Evening Star

SEPTEMBER 18, 1999, marked the fiftieth anniversary of our wedding. Our daughters, Judith, Jacqueline, and Jennifer, asked how I intended to celebrate the occasion. I was wondering if it should be *celebrated* at all. How does a couple celebrate a wedding anniversary when five years earlier one of them was diagnosed with dementia?

The daughters were in full accord: There would be an anniversary celebration even if they had to plan it themselves. There didn't have to be a ceremony or anything like renewing vows, just a reception with a few friends. Yet I knew that I would take on much of the responsibility for planning and paying for such a celebration if I acquiesced.

By late summer 1999, I was engaged in anniversary planning full throttle. Invitations would be designed and sent out. "The girls" would be the signatories. The ceremony would be held September 18, 1999, at one o'clock in the afternoon at our church, Trinity United Methodist Church in downtown Durham, North Carolina. No gifts from our guests.

It took place as planned. Ozie, the girls, and I had prayer with our pastor, Rev. Susan Pate Greenwood, in her office before going to the fellowship hall, where the guests were already enjoying themselves. Longtime friend Janice Nicholson welcomed the guests on behalf of the church and told of an experience in 1984 when she, Ozie, and about ten other adults chaperoned students from Durham's Brogden Middle School on a European tour that included visits to Germany, Switzerland, London, and Paris. The trip was led by Rita Thorpe Tyson and her mother, Vivian Branch Thorpe, with whom I had been a student at Hillside High School in the 1940s. Six additional Trinity members and North Carolina Central University professor Octavia Knight rounded out the contingent of chaperones.

Other anniversary program participants were harpist Winifred Starks Garrett and vocalist Elizabeth Linnartz. There were tributes by Ozie's former pinochle club member, North Carolina senator Jeanne Lucas; former co-worker Dorothy Campbell; my golfing buddy, Stewart Fulbright; and family friend, history professor John Hope Franklin. Our daughter Judith and my brother Will gave salutations from the family. Before the repast, I thanked the program participants and guests for coming.

Perhaps the most emotional feature of the afternoon came at the end of the program, when Ozie's sorority sisters formed a circle around her seat and sang the Delta Sigma Theta hymn. I could tell that Ozie was pleased but confused. (When the presiding participant asked our daughters to stand, Ozie stood with them.) On balance, however, our fiftieth anniversary celebration was a beautiful chapter. Everyone who had any involvement made it so. In retrospect, our daughters were right in insisting that our fiftieth anniversary was a cause for celebration.

I don't relive the experience of moving Ozie from our home to a residential care center any more than I have to. She was admitted to Spring Arbor of Durham, an assisted living center, in mid-March 2000. But there are times when the sun shines right through the rain, like it did on September 18, 2001. In a letter to our daughters the next day, I shared the bittersweet experience as follows:

I had a wonderful visit with Mommy yesterday. I called the Director of Spring Arbor, Barbara Rauch, and told her that it was our fifty-second wedding anniversary date. I asked permission to join Mommy for lunch, whereupon Barbara extended a congratulatory note and a gracious invitation. That was shortly after 11:00 A.M. When I arrived at Spring Arbor about an hour later, an attendant directed me to the center's lovely Sun Room. Upon entering the room, I was surprised to see a table set for two with linen cloth, flowers, and a picture of Mommy and me in formal wear. "September Song" was being played on a CD player.

I managed to hold back all but one tear as I thanked Barbara, two attendants, and the chef who had come to the room by that time. Barbara asked that I wait while she went for Mommy. In very short time, Barbara and another attendant escorted Mommy to the Sun Room, where I was standing. The staff had dressed Mommy stylishly and made her up so she was absolutely beautiful. Barbara was teary when she gave me Mommy's hand, saying, "Here is your bride."

The foodservice director, a brother in dreadlocks, oversized jeans, and ankle-high boots, extended a hand to me and smiled as he said, "Fifty-two years is a looooong time, boss man. Y'all just sit down and relax, and I'll be right back with your food." Salads were already on the table. Our entrée was baked chicken, turnip greens, macaroni and cheese, pinto beans, cornbread, and iced tea.

I continue to be amazed at how quickly the staff created a perfect setting for our celebration. They left us alone for our fine hour. During the meal, I said words and phrases, trying to bring back old memories. And would you believe it! I said an open-ended sentence: "Before we married, you were working at Travelers _____." Without hesitating, she completed the sentence with "Insurance Company." She smiled and even called the names of some classmates and friends: "Johnnie Mae Pittman, Pauline and Norman."

I closed the letter with love.

The next year, Ozie began to wander from the Spring Arbor campus, an act that would be possible grounds for a liability suit in case of an accident. She had also become combative. Her psychiatrist, Dr. Schmader, confirmed what the center staff and I had observed: Ozie's dementia had advanced to Alzheimer's disease. Spring Arbor did not have a facility to care for Alzheimer's patients, and I had to find a new place for her. Besides, I was told, she needed to be in a facility where she would be in confinement. Talk about a heart-wrenching revelation!

On October 2, 2002, Ozie was admitted to the Alzheimer's facility of the Brian Center on Fayetteville Road in Durham—behind a gate that could only be opened by attendants who knew the code. The center was less than ten minutes from our home. I asked to be given the code, and my request was honored. I visited frequently, but some visits were very short, as when I saw that she was in deep slumber while other patients were participating in structured activities led by the staff. Unfortunately, the road ahead would be even more stressful, with the kinds of experiences known to caregivers throughout the land.

[51]

Crossing the Bar

THE FATEFUL call from the Brian Center of Health and Rehabilitation in Yanceyville, North Carolina, came on May 27, 2008. A Brian lady said she was "deeply sorry" in saying that "Mrs. Brown passed peacefully during the night." She had volunteered to make the call, she said, because Ozie had been like a mother to her. I changed the focus of our conversation for a moment and said it was easy to understand her fondness for my wife because Ozie was passionate about individuals she really liked. I also wondered how often such calls were made from nursing homes with roughly 140 patients. The Cremation Society people would be in touch with me very soon, she told me. Then I heard a faint sob as she wished the best for me and the rest of my family. I wished for her the same.

One of my most painful recollections as a caregiver was a letter from the Brian Center in Durham, North Carolina, dated March 26, 2006. It was a notice of "regret" to inform me that their "secured unit for dementia patients would be closed, effective June 30, 2006." An apparent attempt at placation was a statement that the Center's social-services staff would be available to discuss "alternative placement for your loved ones." My house was a little less than four miles from the Brian Center in Durham. Yanceyville, the location of the center recommended to me by a staff member who seemed genuinely concerned, was forty miles away.

I later had reason to recall the lyrics of a hymn by William Cowper: "God moves in mysterious ways." From the beginning, when my daughters and I visited the center in Yanceyville, we were favorably impressed with the facility and the staff, and we were quite willing to make the trade-off in distance between the two locations. Ozie's condition declined steadily

The author and his daughters following Ozie's memorial service at Trinity United Methodist Church in Durham, North Carolina. *(Brown family papers, photograph by Carol Bond))*

at both places, but I am convinced that it would have been so anywhere, regardless of circumstance or our means.

When the news of Ozie's death was reported to our pastoral team at Trinity United Methodist Church, the church's senior pastor, Duke Lackey, and the assistant pastor, Olive Joyner, responded immediately. They visited our home that same evening, extended condolences, and assisted in planning a Service of Remembrance for Ozie. And they appeared to suffer me gladly in my biases.

I believe I can be justifiably pleased with at least two observations in Ozie's obituary, which appeared in the Durham *Herald-Sun*: "Ozie Brown was a lady of quiet dignity and the epitome of cheerleader and supporter of her family." Also, "Walter once said that Ozie comes as close to being loved and admired by everyone she touches as anyone I have ever known." Without fear of contradiction, I say the service was simply beautiful; but more importantly, it was what Ozie would have wanted, from the prelude to the recessional. Neither our daughters—Judy, Jackie, and Jennifer—

nor I had imagined the service would be attended by so many persons, including former Durham neighbors and friends of over fifty years who drove from Atlanta: Ed and Carol Davis and Olga Bryant.

The service was held on the morning of May 30, 2008. Judy, Jackie, Jennifer, and I met with Duke and Olive in Duke's study. While the congregation was standing, the pastors led us as we entered the sanctuary through a side opening near the front. Actually, the beauty of Ozie's Service of Remembrance was its simplicity: Reverend Lackey's homily and Reverend Joyner's prayer; "reflections" by Janice Nicholson, John Mayfield, and daughter Judy; our church choir's rendition of John Rutter's "For the Beauty of the Earth"; the selection of "Amazing Grace" by flutist Lauren Crowell and pianist Grover McNeill; and the silent walk by the family and pastors to the church's lawn and columbarium in which Ozie's cremains were placed next to the niche reserved for mine. The service ended with a reception conducted by Trinity's United Methodist Women in the church parlor.

It was as if Ozie and I had wanted to show how, in planning her Service of Remembrance, we were influenced by Sunday afternoon vespers services in the mid-1940s at the North Carolina College for Negroes.

[52]

John Hope Franklin:
Historian, Teacher, Friend

O N FEBRUARY 10, 2009, I was called by Larry Kline, a retired Duke Divinity School professor and fellow member of Trinity United Methodist Church in Durham, North Carolina. I reasoned that something was amiss, because neither of us had ever phoned the other. Larry told me that as he was leaving a satellite area of the Duke Medical Center, he saw medics taking John Hope Franklin from that same area to an ambulance.

Larry had seen John Hope with me at least three times before this occurrence: when JH attended my and Ozie's fiftieth wedding anniversary celebration at our church on September 18, 1999; when he spoke at the Service of Reconciliation at Trinity in January 2000; and when he sat with my family at the Service of Remembrance for Ozie in May 2008.

I thanked Larry, and after a call to the hospital emergency center, I went straightaway to see John Hope. He was comatose, but I sat with him anyway, wondering what the diagnosis would be. He was admitted for ongoing care that same evening. Except for the day that I didn't drive because of hazardous weather conditions, I visited John Hope daily until he took his last breath, some six weeks later. On my way to the hospital that day, his son, John Whittington Franklin, called my cell phone with the fateful revelation: "He's gone." I was in too much of a stupor to focus on anything else John Whittington said, except that there would be a service on the eleventh of June, the date of his parents' sixty-ninth wedding anniversary.

I DO NOT presume that all of my readers have prior knowledge of John Hope Franklin's life and works, an African American born in an all-Black town, Rentiesville, Oklahoma, in 1915; a man whose scholarly attainments

John Hope Franklin in the living room of his home with the author. *(Brown family papers, Carol Bond photographer)*

as an historian are unparalleled in twentieth-century America. In too many instances I have been surprised that otherwise knowledgeable persons, African American young people in particular, know little or nothing—mostly nothing—about this remarkable man.

He was the grandson of slaves owned by Chickasaw Indians. His father was an attorney and writer who moved to Tulsa, where he established his law practice in anticipation of the family's arrival. The Tulsa race riot in 1921 delayed the family's reunion for five years, a time during which four-year-old John Hope learned to read and write as he sat at the back of the class in the one-room schoolhouse in Rentiesville, where his mother taught.

As a six-year-old boy traveling by train from Rentiesville to Checotah, Oklahoma, he and his mother were put off the train because she refused to move from a carriage designated for Whites only. As a Boy Scout trying to help a nearly blind White woman across a road, the woman told him to take his "filthy" hands off her. It is remarkable that despite these early indignities, this young man had the intelligence and strength of character to choose the path of a scholar whose intellectual gifts brought change to the American culture and educated the world about an objective history of his country.

John Hope Franklin graduated valedictorian of Tulsa's Booker T. Washington High School, and in 1931 he entered Fisk University in Nashville, Tennessee. He was a member of the school's debate team, which toured Black and White colleges. Ostensibly he looked forward to a career in law. This interest was snuffed when he was spellbound by the teaching of his history professor, Theodore Currier, and he chose history as a career for himself. He went to Macon, Mississippi, on a field trip to study the lives of Black tenant farmers, and while leaving a store where he bought ice cream, his life was threatened by group of White farmers.

At Fisk, he met his future wife, Aurelia Whittington, a student from Goldsboro, North Carolina. He graduated from Fisk in 1935 and received a PH.D. in history from Harvard University in 1941. He completed his dissertation while teaching at St. Augustine's College in Raleigh, North Carolina. The dissertation was subsequently published as *The Free Negro in North Carolina, 1709–1860*. Also in 1941, he moved twenty miles west to Durham to teach at North Carolina College for Negroes, now North Carolina Central University (NCCU). It was at North Carolina College that he did much of the writing on what would become a landmark book, *From Slavery to Freedom* (1947). From North Carolina College he moved to Howard University in Washington, D.C. in 1947.

In 1956, he went from Howard to Brooklyn College as chairman of its History Department; from there to the University of Chicago as History Department chairman and John Matthews Manly professor in 1964; and to Duke University as James B. Duke professor of history and later as professor of legal history (1982). On one occasion after another, he was recognized for service on national commissions and delegations, including the National Council on the Humanities and the twenty-first General Conference of UNESCO. He was also recognized as Pitt professor of American history and institutions at Cambridge University, consultant on American education in the Soviet Union, Fulbright professor in Australia, and lecturer on American history in the People's Republic of China.

To those achievements he added an amazing number of publications, including *From Slavery to Freedom*, which has become his most successful book, selling three million copies. Numbered among other recognitions were his assistance to Thurgood Marshall and the NAACP Legal Defense

Fund in preparing to successfully argue *Brown v. Board of Education*, and his past presidency of Phi Beta Kappa, the Organization of American Historians, the American Historical Association, and the Southern Historical Association. The Jefferson Lecturer (1976), the Presidential Medal of Freedom (1995), the John W. Kluge Prize in the Human Sciences (2006) are indicative of the esteem in which he is held by members of the academy, as are hundreds of organizations that brought honor to themselves in bestowing honors on him.

Within twenty-four hours of his death, there was an outpouring of media reports throughout the world on John Hope Franklin—his life and accomplishments of ninety-four years. In some instances—probably not as much as professor Franklin would have wanted—the life of his late wife and supporter, Aurelia Whittington Franklin, was noted.

The June 12 headline in the Durham *Herald-Sun* newspaper read, "Thousands Celebrate the Franklins, Bill Clinton among Those Honoring Renowned Historian and Wife." With my friend Carol Sawyer Bond and my daughters, Jacqueline and Jennifer, I attended the memorial service at the famed chapel of Duke University. At the invitation of John Hope's son, John Whittington Franklin, and daughter-in-law, Karen Roberts Franklin, we attended the memorial luncheon at the Washington Duke Inn and Golf Club.

M Y REMINISCENCES of John Hope Franklin begin with how I met him in 1944 when Mrs. Christine Davis, a reference librarian at North Carolina College recommended for my reading Charles Wesley's *History of Alpha Phi Alpha Fraternity*. The *History* was in its fourth printing, having first been published in 1929. I learned that the fraternity was founded at Cornell University in 1906 as the nation's first intercollegiate Greek letter fraternity for African Americans.

Mrs. Davis had learned that the fraternity's chapter membership at NCC was down to one student, Samuel Hill—popular around campus as "Kid"—a premedical student from Asheboro, North Carolina. "Kid" had a military draft deferment, and I was too young to meet the draft-age eligibility requirements. I could not have been more favorably impressed than when I learned about the "Alpha men" on the NCC faculty, among them Alfonso Elder, mathematics; William Robinson, physics; Albert Turner,

Chancellor Charlie Nelms. *(Courtesy of James E. Shepard Memorial Library University Archives and Records, North Carolina Central University, Durham, North Carolina)*

law; James Taylor, educational psychology; and John Hope Franklin, history. They were regarded by their peers and students alike as scholarly gentlemen and outstanding teachers. Elder later became president of NCC (1948–1963). Other Alpha men who served as president or chancellor of the institution were: Albert N. Whiting (1967–1963), Tyronza R. Richmond (1986–1992), and Julius L. Chambers (1993–2001). In 2009–2010, the academic year of the university's centennial celebration, Charlie Nelms was serving as its chancellor. Nelms was appointed university chancellor in August 2007.

Mrs. Davis added that Franklin was adviser to the fraternity's chapter at NCC, Gamma Beta, and she "strongly" recommended that I take at least one course under him.

Little did I realize that the spring quarter of my sophomore year at NCC, the quarter of my eighteenth birthday, would be a veritable launching pad. I took one of Dr. Franklin's courses—History 333, American History 1865–1943. I applied for membership in Alpha Phi Alpha fraternity, and fate decreed that John Hope Franklin, "Kid" Hill, and whoever else decided that I was worthy of membership in the fraternity. Against this backdrop, I was a one-man line in my initiation. From that time on, I have striven to exemplify the fraternity's characterization as an organization guided by aims of "manly deeds, scholarship, and love for all mankind."

The following September, I was drafted into military service. Within in months, I was assigned to the U.S. Army's Occupation Forces in Europe, but not before a White cab driver refused to take me from the train station in Columbia, South Carolina, to Fort Jackson, South Carolina, apologizing; "They ain't my rules, they the boss's rules." I had been in my European unit but a few months when the U.S. government offered the options of reenlistment for three years—initially—with a monetary bonus, or an early honorable discharge. I chose to divorce from my military uncle, partly because I didn't want to be drafted in the first place, but mainly because I was dreaming daily about returning to school.

I was driven by my view that, while I may not have been serious enough about scholarship, having entered college soon after my sixteenth birthday, I damned sure would be serious about scholarship from that time on. I was discharged in November 1946, and I reenrolled at North Carolina College when the winter quarter began in December. One of my academic excursions on this new horizon was a course in journalism under Charles A Ray, the faculty member who was then John Hope Franklin's best friend. This was followed by a string of courses under another of his close friends, the esteemed sociologist Joseph S. Himes.

In 1920, Alpha Phi Alpha fraternity launched the national Go to High School, Go to College educational campaign with participating local-chapter activities that included African American history programs, motivational speeches, and career orientation programs at elementary and secondary schools. Twenty-eight years later (1948) at North Carolina College, the Gamma Beta and Beta Theta Lambda chapters—undergraduate and graduate respectively—sponsored a week-long Annual Education and Citizenship Observance Program. This observance included a Sunday afternoon vespers service, a debate on whether a civil-rights bill would work effectively in the South, a radio interview of students from participating high schools, an oratorical contest, and a college-sponsored reception for high school students. On the same theme and on my birthday, April 9, I was the chapel program speaker at Durham's Hillside High School, the school from which I had graduated five years earlier.

Alpha Phi Alpha fraternity launched another national citizenship campaign during the 1930s, A Voteless People is a Hopeless People. In his commentary on the implementation of this campaign, Charles Wesley wrote: "All over the country significant activities were conducted. There were public meetings, public forums, oratorical contests, popularity contests, discussions of jury service, the ballot and representation in state and national affairs." When I read about this campaign, I was persuaded that joining the ranks of this fraternity would add meaning to my life in citizenship and in service. In my family, voting has not been debatable, but a given. As for myself, I equate the failure to vote with a death wish.

My mother would probably say it was divine intervention; some would call it serendipity or just plain luck. I don't claim to know, but John Hope

Franklin and I marveled that from other sojourns, we moved back to Durham, North Carolina, in the same year, 1980.

We bonded through our interest in fishing, good chemistry between ourselves and our families, and our membership in Sigma Pi Phi fraternity, the other fraternity for which John Hope was my sponsor, along with Charles Ray.

At John Hope's invitation, my family was hosted by his family for dinner each Thanksgiving and Christmas. Through the years "family" included: Aurelia; John "Whit" and Karen; Aurelia's mother, whom we called "Grandmother"; JH's foster son, Bouna Ndiaye; and JH's longtime secretary at the University of Chicago, Margaret Fitzsimmons. Exceptions were when the Franklins observed holidays in Maryland.

John Whittington Franklin and Bouna Ndiaye became friends when they met in Senegal, West Africa, before Bouna came to the United States to attend college. When Bouna enrolled at NCCU, where he was an honor student, the Franklins gave him a home with them. The friendship that Bouna and I developed when he was one of my calligraphy students is ongoing. Bouna was often amused when John Hope and I bantered in games of verbal one-upsmanship. Even Ozie surprised JH when he brought his brand-new Lexus for us to see, and Ozie playfully said the Lexus "would make a good fishing car." In our family, we usually designated our older car as the "fishing car." More than once JH jovially shared this humor on social occasions.

I have a vivid recollection of the experience that let me know what it was like having John Hope Franklin as an associate in the academy. At Duke University in 1990, he chaired the selection panel for college juniors to receive research study grants as seniors at their respective institutions. The grants were sponsored by the Dana Foundation Program on Preparing Minorities for Academic Careers. John Hope appointed Gena Rae McNeil, then chair of the Department of History at Howard University and one of his doctoral students at the University of Chicago; Wesley Elliott, professor of chemistry at Fisk University, and me, then dean of the School of Education at NCCU, to serve with him on the panel.

After the first round of deliberations, I noticed that John Hope was strangely quiet and seemingly hesitant about moving on. We had carefully examined the applicants' résumés, academic transcripts, the essays in which they described their scholarly interests and activities, and recommendations from faculty members at their respective institutions. But JH was concerned about a particular entry in each applicant's file, namely, the qualifications of persons designated to serve as their faculty mentors. There was a turning point in our work, and an experience that helped me appreciate why my friend excelled in so many endeavors: he focused on key variables that others either glossed over or did not see at all.

Ozie and I glowed with pride in 1995 when we were privileged to attend the White House ceremony at which President Bill Clinton awarded John Hope Franklin the Presidential Medal of Freedom. For a reception at the Cosmos Club in Washington, John Hope permitted us to invite friends from Silver Spring, Maryland, Voyce and Katie Whitley. On the evening after the award, Ozie and I were John Hope's guests at a dinner hosted by the Vernon Jordans at their home. I will always remember that Jordan began the dinner by rising from his seat and saying, "It's a long way from Rentiesville, Oklahoma, to the White House in Washington, D.C."

On a profoundly somber note, I was fortunately at hand when John Hope called to ask me to accompany him to the nursing home where his beloved Aurelia had just died with the cursed Alzheimer's disease. Friends have commented on my good fortune in having John Hope's support when my beloved Ozie died with the same illness.

A 2000 highlight for me was the book signing for John Hope at the Special Occasions Bookstore in Winston-Salem, North Carolina. The celebrated writer and poet Maya Angelou was among the patrons who came to purchase books with his autograph. I was delighted when Miss Angelou invited us to lunch at her home, and more so when John Hope accepted the invitation. It was a joyous occasion—unanticipated and greatly appreciated—with a gracious hostess.

I smile in writing that being with John Hope in his familiar haunts—restaurants, selected marketplaces, bookstores, public forums—was like ambulating with a rock star at his or her own show. For instance, I overheard a Durham resident thank John Hope for making Durham his home as well. The wait staff at local restaurants when taking his order virtually filled in the blanks, saying "no salt" before he could tell them. Moreover, people of every station asked to stand with him before a camera—a request he never even seemed inclined to deny.

In 2005, I was privileged to travel with John Hope Franklin on a promotion tour sponsored by the publisher of his autobiography, *Mirror to America*. We began at the Free Library of Philadelphia (Pennsylvania), where a staff member favored me with a tour of the Library's collection

of manuscripts and handmade books
illuminated with gold and precious
jewels—an unanticipated lesson in medieval calligraphy. It was followed with
readings and signings at the Library of
Congress, on the *Diane Rehm Show*,
and at the Politics and Prose bookstore, all in Washington, D.C.; at the
Auburn Avenue Research Library, on
Good Day Atlanta (WAGA-TV) and the
Paula Gordon Show (WGUN-AM), and at
the Jimmy Carter Presidential Library
in Atlanta, Georgia; at Fisk University in Nashville, Tennessee; at Texas
Southern University in Houston; at
the Oriental Institute, Breasted Hall at
the University of Chicago; at the Miami Book Fair International at Miami
Dade Community College, Miami,

John Hope Franklin celebrating the
ninety-fourth anniversary of his birth.
(Courtesy of Carol S. Bond)

Florida; on the *Tavis Smiley Show* at the Los Angeles Public Library; at A
Clean Well Lighted Place bookstore in San Francisco; at the First Con-
gregational Church in Berkeley, California; at Harvard Law School, Cambridge, Massachusetts; at the Cincinnati (Ohio) Museum; and at Barnes
& Noble bookstore in New York City.

Another memory that brings pleasure and which emphasized his pride
in his ancestry and the importance of family friends and history is the first
time John Hope and I fished at a pond that I'd been given special permission to use. I introduced him to the groundskeeper, saying, "This is my
friend, John Hope Franklin." The groundskeeper extended his hand, saying, "John Franklin, glad to meet you." Immediately, and with emphasis,
JH replied, "John *Hope* Franklin," whereupon the man obliged, this time
with a slight stress on "Hope." On a different day and at a different fishing site, when we were weaving our way through a stubbornly resistant
thicket, John Hope said we were "Lewis and Clark on a transcontinental
journey."

At a dinner with Loren Schweninger, JH's coauthor of *Runaway Slaves*,
Loren said the meals he most enjoyed were hosted by John Hope at Durham's restaurants, such as Parizäde, Nana's, the Washington Duke Inn,

2009 photo of the Beta Theta Lambda Chapter, Alpha Phi Alpha Fraternity, Inc. *Seated, left to right:* Walter Brown, Ron Patterson, Carl Pickney, Eric Heath, Al Richardson, and Donald Lowrance. *Standing, left to right:* Roger McDougal, Robert Cox, Baldwin Gammage, Leonardo William, Oliver Hodge, Rodney Shepard, Harvey Farrell, Al Herring, Christopher Pickett, Edward Clemmons, Roy Charles, Samuel Vaughan, a visiting Alpha brother, Donald Barringer, and James Schooler Jr. *(Brown family papers, Gerald Tharrington photographer)*

and Four Square. I knew whereof Loren spoke, but I felt that fate was kinder to me because he and his wife, Pat, lived in Greensboro, fifty miles away, and I was privileged to have impromptu meals with my friend, John Hope, more often and on no special occasions. But most of the time, John Hope and I broke bread at more pedestrian restaurants, and enjoyed them immensely. The chemistry between us was manifested as we enjoyed conversation and visits over good food. Sometimes, as when we were at a country store buying bait for fishing, we yielded to cravings for pork skins and peanut candy bars. The "food" did not always have to be *haute cuisine*.

An example of the chemistry between our families was John Hope's response to an appeal by our daughter Judy on behalf of her colleagues at Georgetown Day School where she was a fifth-grade social-studies teacher. Judy invited John Hope to speak at the Ben Cooper Memorial Lecture, held at the Washington (D.C.) Hebrew Congregation School, and she had the honor of introducing John Hope as speaker on the occasion.

Still another example of our family chemistry was the way that John Hope Franklin befriended my daughter Jacqueline when she was having problems of depression and self-esteem. At times Jackie cared for John Hope's orchids when he was on travel. But, worth a thousand times more, he attended Jackie's commencement and sat with our family at Durham Technical Community College, just as if she were his daughter. His caring ways figured prominently in Jackie's recovery. John Hope and my daughter Jennifer also had a special bond. He teased her about her "taking charge" of every event where family was involved, and she pampered him whether or not it was needed. Both loved it. "Dr. Franklin" was a term of endearment for my daughters.

John Hope was also hospitalized about two years before the emergency of February 10, 2009. I visited him soon after I received a call from his son, who was then affectionately called "Whit." A no-visitors sign hung on his door. When I reported to the nursing station nearest John Hope's room and gave my name to the nurse on duty, she exclaimed, "Oh, so you're the best friend. Go right in to see him." I believe that exclamation gave me as much gratification as John Hope received from any of his 140 honorary degrees.

Everywhere I turn, and in much of what I do, I experience reminders of John Hope Franklin. I miss the "chap"—as he was wont to say at times.

Afterword

IN 2008, the North Carolina Central University School of Education published a magazine, *Teaching Matters,* that highlights the careers of its five education professors emeriti: Charles Alcorn, Marvin Duncan, Charles Nicholson, Barnetta White, and me. A group photograph of the honorees includes the current dean, Cecelia Steppe-Jones. Charles Alcorn's picture is an inset in the group photograph of the honorees. He died shortly before the magazine was published.

I attended the celebration of the life of Charles Levant Alcorn, held October 27, 2008, at University Presbyterian Church in Chapel Hill, North Carolina. It was a service befitting his nobility. In closing his meditation, celebrant Robert E. Dunham read a piece of prose that he said reflected "in part, at least, the kind of life Chuck lived." The piece, simply called "Wise Wishes," had been shared with Dunham by one his friends, and I humbly close my memoir with this piece as an expression of those wishes by which I try to live myself:

1. *A few friends who understand me, yet remain friends.*
2. *Work to do that has real value.*
3. *An understanding heart.*
4. *Moments of leisure.*
5. *A mind unafraid to travel, even though the trail be not blazed.*
6. *A sight of the eternal hills and the unresting sea, and of something beautiful the human hand has made.*
7. *The power to laugh.*
8. *Nothing at the expense of others.*
9. *The sense of the presence of God.*
10. *The patience to wait for the coming of these things, and the wisdom to know when they come.*

Acknowledgments

F OR ALL intents and purposes, a substantial portion of this book comprises a series of acknowledgments and quotes, for in it I have written about individuals whose lives have most significantly influenced my life, and about some institutions that have done the same. Beyond this I am heavily indebted to certain persons without whose encouragement and expertise this book would still be a mere gleam in my eye:

The staff of the Durham County Library in Durham, North Carolina, especially *Lynn Richardson* of the North Carolina Room.

R. Kelly Bryant, acclaimed old-guard archivist of documents related to the history of African Americans in Durham.

Archivists in the Durham Public Schools who provided documents for authenticating reports related to my days in elementary and senior high school.

Attorney *William A. Marsh,* who helped me in "replaying" boyhood days.

Brooklyn T. McMillon and *Andre Vann,* North Carolina Central University (NCCU) archivists whose expertise and love of their work gave me one up in much of the writing that centered on my years at NCCU.

Roger Gregory, at whose invitation I read to an appreciative audience of NCCU alumni.

Andre Stroud, a former calligraphy student whose skills were of value in preparing the final manuscript.

Floyd Hardy, NCCU director of library services, who was never too busy with administrative duties to give me direct, personal service when needed.

Deborah Hazel, who seemed to enjoy rendering service as a reference librarian as much as I enjoyed the service.

Daughter *Judith,* who critiqued first cuts of my vignettes before they were critiqued by others.

Acknowledgments

Carol Sawyer Bond, the author's friend and colleague in manuscript preparation.

William Lawrence, who assisted me in recounting key events in public education.

Classmates and instructors at the Osher Lifelong Learning Institute (OLLI, formerly the Duke Institute for Learning in Retirement), whose critiques and encouragement were continual incentives.

Lorraine Wechsler and *Susan Bauer,* teachers of the OLLI writing classes at Duke, for whom I wear a badge of honor as one of their students.

Carol Sawyer Bond, whose support was unwavering in her literary critiques and in the preparation of documents for reviews by others and for final printing.

Arthrell D. Sanders, former student and retired NCCU associate professor of English, who critiqued my manuscript as if she had a proprietary interest in the outcome.

Ronald Roddy, who came to my rescue with computer expertise more times than I can remember.